AGAINST THE NEW GODS

Borgo Press Books by BRIAN STABLEFORD

Against the New Gods, and Other Essays on Writers of Imaginative Fiction
Algebraic Fantasies and Realistic Romances: More Masters of Science Fiction
Alien Abduction: The Wiltshire Revelations
The Best of Both Worlds and Other Ambiguous Tales
Beyond the Colors of Darkness and Other Exotica
Changelings and Other Metamorphic Tales
A Clash of Symbols: The Triumph of James Blish
Complications and Other Stories
The Cosmic Perspective and Other Black Comedies
The Cure for Love and Other Tales of the Biotech Revolution
The Devil's Party: A Brief History of Satanic Abuse
The Dragon Man: A Novel of the Future
The Eleventh Hour
Firefly: A Novel of the Far Future
The Gardens of Tantalus and Other Delusions
Glorious Perversity: The Decline and Fall of Literary Decadence
Gothic Grotesques: Essays on Fantastic Literature
The Great Chain of Being and Other Tales of the Biotech Revolution
The Haunted Bookshop and Other Apparitions
Heterocosms: Science Fiction in Context and Practice
In the Flesh and Other Tales of the Biotech Revolution
The Innsmouth Heritage and Other Sequels
Jaunting on the Scoriac Tempests and Other Essays on Fantastic Literature
Kiss the Goat
The Moment of Truth: A Novel of the Future
Narrative Strategies in Science Fiction, and Other Essays on Imaginative Fiction
News of the Black Feast and Other Random Reviews
An Oasis of Horror: Decadent Tales and Contes Cruels
Opening Minds: Essays on Fantastic Literature
Outside the Human Aquarium: Masters of Science Fiction, Second Edition
The Plurality of Worlds: A Sixteenth-Century Space Opera
Prelude to Eternity: A Romance of the First Time Machine
The Return of the Djinn and Other Black Melodramas
Salome and Other Decadent Fantasies
Slaves of the Death Spiders and Other Essays on Fantastic Literature
The Sociology of Science Fiction
Space, Time, and Infinity: Essays on Fantastic Literature
The Tree of Life and Other Tales of the Biotech Revolution
The World Beyond: A Sequel to S. Fowler Wright's The World Below
Yesterday's Bestsellers: A Voyage Through Literary History

AGAINST THE NEW GODS

AND OTHER ESSAYS ON WRITERS OF IMAGINATIVE FICTION

by

Brian Stableford

THE BORGO PRESS

An Imprint of Wildside Press LLC

MMIX

*I.O. Evans Studies in the Philosophy
and Criticism of Literature*
ISSN 0271-9061

Number Forty-Eight

Copyright © 1983, 1999, 2002, 2003, 2009 by Brian Stableford

All rights reserved.
No part of this book may be reproduced in any form without the expressed written consent of the publisher.

www.wildsidebooks.com

FIRST EDITION

CONTENTS

Acknowledgments 7
Against the New Gods: The Speculative Fiction of S. Fowler
   Wright 9
David Brin 91
Jonathan Carroll 106
Samuel R. Delany 115
Joe Haldeman 127
Robert Irwin 138
Graham Joyce 146
Michael Shea 153

Bibliography 161
Index 172
About the Author 186

ACKNOWLEDGMENTS

The long title article of this collection is a composite, stitched together from an article of the same title published in *Foundation* 29 (November 1983) and the introduction that I wrote for a new edition of *Deluge* published by Wesleyan University Press in 2003. (I could not reproduce them separately because the introduction reproduced a good deal of material from the earlier article). The article on Samuel R. Delany is also a composite, the text of the article that I wrote for the second edition of Scribner's *Supernatural Fiction Writers: Contemporary Fantasy and Horror* (2 vols., 2002), ed. Richard E. Bleiler, being supplemented by descriptions of other novels not strictly relevant to that article, abstracted from articles written for various other reference books; again, I could not reproduce the articles separately because of duplication of information and the awkward formatting of some of the material. The articles on Jonathan Carroll, Robert Irwin, Graham Joyce, and Michael Shea are from the same project as the original of the Delany article. The articles on David Brin and Joe Haldeman are from the second edition of the same publisher's companion volume on *Science Fiction Writers*, also edited by Richard E. Bleiler, published in 1999.

I am greatly indebted to the surviving members of Sydney Fowler Wright's family who helped me in my research into the life and works of the author, particularly Nigel and Margaret Fowler Wright and their son Augustine, who allowed me to see Fowler Wright's remaining typescripts and many associated materials. Nigel was kind enough to read me relevant sections of the 1933-37 diary, and also solicited biographical information and assistance in locating source-materials from other members of the family, including Mrs. Patricia Fowler Wright, Mrs. Valerie Deeson and Lady Blair-Kerr. I am also grateful for the help rendered in facilitating this research by Chris Morgan and Andy Richards. I should also like to thank David Brin, Jonathan Carroll, Robert Irwin, Graham Joyce, and Michael

Shea, who were kind enough to check the first drafts of the articles on their work and suggest corrections where necessary.

—Brian Stableford
September 2009

AGAINST THE NEW GODS

The Speculative Fiction of S. Fowler Wright

Sydney Fowler Wright belonged to the same generation as H.G. Wells, John Beresford, and William Hope Hodgson, but while these contemporaries were making their names as writers of speculative fiction in the years before the Great War, Fowler Wright was working as an accountant in Birmingham. He did not begin publishing literary works until after the war, and his early efforts were in the form of poetry. His first novel, completed in 1920, failed to find a publisher and he ultimately published it himself in 1927. It was highly praised by British reviewers, became a bestseller in America, was filmed in Hollywood and launched its author upon a new career as a prolific writer of speculative fantasies, historical novels and crime stories after his accountancy business was bankrupted. At the height of his literary fame he was nominated by the *Daily Express* as one of the ten best brains in Britain, but his career proved to be meteoric. By the time of his death in 1965 he was so completely forgotten that not a single obituary appeared. *The Times*, in fact, continued to copy his name ritualistically from year to year in their list of birthdays, until one of his sons pointed out that he had been dead for several years.

Speculative fiction accounts for only a small fraction of Fowler Wright's total output. He published fifteen novels and a collection of short stories of this kind, although two of these were potboilers published under the name "Sydney Fowler", which he attached to his many hastily-written crime stories. Scientific romance was by no means his first love, but among his published works his stories in that vein nevertheless occupy a special place. In the preface to *The Throne of Saturn*, which brought together almost all his speculative short stories, he makes the following observation:

"One who is a friend, a man of no mean literary judgment, and who has been kind to some things which I have written, recently surprised me not merely by saying he could not read a phantasy of which I was the author, but that he could not understand anyone writing such books if capable of other and (inferentially) better work.

"Was this judgment sound?

"Every work of imagination widens the frontiers of reality. It may have no objective reality, but precisely to that extent it adds to creation's sum. Men were; beyond that they built imaginations of things which were not. They may not have imagined facts; but it was a fact that they imagined things which had not been, and may never be.

"A foolish criticism of *Ivanhoe* (foolish alike whether correct or not) is that it represents a scene which has little historical basis. But it would be wiser to say that (being vivid as it is) the more it be a work of baseless imagination the more admirable it is.

"It is the contemporary habit to give first place to novels which portray men and events truly, observation rather than imagination being the inspiration. There is no need to depreciate such work, but they are only of the highest rank if it is better to crawl than to soar.

"To recognise this is not to assert that every fantastic tale is of high literary merit. It may be a sounder proposition that it is such in proportion to the verisimilitude which it attains. Beyond that, all serious works of imagination will contain a philosophy of life, and, the more they are without basis of mundane fact, the more clearly will that philosophy appear.

"For these and other reasons, having written works of imagination of many kinds, both in prose and verse, among which phantasy has not bulked prominently, I am disposed, without claiming any absolute value for such works, to place them relatively not last but first." (p. vii)

Fowler Wright's affection for speculative fiction has several bases. He took delight in the exercise of imaginative power, and liked to startle his readers with bold new ideas. He also had what he called a "philosophy of life" and an interest in developing and communicating it. His wilder fantasies are both exploratory and expository; they helped him to examine the logical consequences of his beliefs, and helped him to publicize convictions that he held strongly. He was alarmed by the prospect of technological advancement, suspicious of science, antipathetic toward machinery and dismayed by certain trends in politics and popular mores. In speculative fiction he examined these trends and displayed other worlds from which they were absent. He aspired to show, in his own phrase, "where the new gods lead", and he laid down a determined challenge to the worshippers of these new gods. On balance, though, the exploratory appears to have outweighed the expository in motivating his work; his tone is usually cool and detached, and he strives to be ingenious rather than hectoring when he attempts to be persuasive in his fiction, although he was rather more inclined to play the crusader in non-fictional tracts. He appears always to have been pessimistic about the possibility of persuading the people of England to adopt a different course, and content to offer them visions of possible worlds without urgent exhortations to choose. He usually assumes that the choice is already made, that the new gods will triumph in the short term, but that in the fullness of time it will not matter.

Writers of speculative fiction are often idiosyncratic, but Fowler Wright stands out as a highly distinctive character even in such motley company. He was never the kind of writer who could capture the sympathy of large numbers of readers; at best he could aspire to fascinate them for a while by leading them in new imaginative directions. Every work of the imagination, as he says, widens the frontiers of reality, and Fowler Wright worked on frontiers rarely visited by other writers, in order to report on strange vistas that no one else had yet glimpsed. His favorite imaginative territories were not calculated to attract millions of armchair tourists; there is nothing intoxicating or euphoric about their exoticism. For the most part, they are more closely akin to tracts of arid wilderness than lands flowing with milk and honey. It is not surprising, therefore, that his work ultimately proved to be rather esoteric, but it is no less intriguing for that.

Historians of speculative fiction have not paid overmuch attention to Fowler Wright, who has suffered the neglect common to most of those who carried on the tradition of British scientific romance between the two world wars. Such comments as have been made reflect a common sense of puzzlement about his work; it is not easy, on superficial acquaintance with his work, to figure out what he is trying to do and why. The philosophy of life to be found in his imaginative fictions is not an easy one to describe accurately, nor is it easy to sympathize with it. It would be worth making the effort merely to solve the intellectual puzzle, but it is also worthwhile to analyze his work more carefully for two other reasons. On the one hand, there is food for thought in his works that can still offer an intellectual challenge to contemporary readers; on the other hand, Fowler Wright offers an interesting case-study in the wider project of relating the content of imaginative fictions to the personalities and historical situations of their creators.

* * * * * * *

Sydney Fowler Wright was born on 6 January 1874 in the Midlands town of Smethwick. He was the son of Stephen Wright (1841-1936), an accountant, and Emily Gertrude Fowler (1843-1882). He was sent to King Edward's School in Birmingham but he left in January 1885, having completed only two terms, shortly after his eleventh birthday.

Later in life Fowler Wright offered various flippant explanations for his early removal from formal schooling, all of them excuses arising from a keenly-felt obligation to avoid mentioning the fact that his father had run into severe financial difficulties—an embarrassment that eventually caused Stephen Wright to emigrate to the USA in 1895. The same strict code of etiquette made Fowler Wright equally reluctant to mention or discuss the financial hardships that he experienced more than once in the course of his own career, although the spur provided by financial necessity was certainly a powerful force in shaping his literary work.

The main consequence of Fowler Wright's removal from school was that he had to take responsibility for his own education, and he did so with an altogether typical determination. He was exceptionally methodical as well as highly intelligent, and he applied himself assiduously to his own idiosyncratic curriculum, developing his language skills by means of the intensive study of literary texts. The central figure in his studies of his own language was Sir Walter Scott; meanwhile, he studied Italian by making his way through Dante's *Divine Comedy* and French by reading Alexandre Dumas, preferring direct engagement with literary exemplifications of the languages in question to more orthodox forms of "second-hand" learning. This was typical of his attitude to life and knowledge; he was always a determinedly independent thinker, ever-ready to form and trust his own judgments, with scant regard for common opinion.

Although the members of his immediate family were devout Baptists—his father was a lay preacher and one of his sisters became a missionary—he became a resolute freethinker.

It is worth noting here that many other significant contributors to the distinctively British genre of scientific romance born in the nineteenth century were also freethinking sons of devout fathers. Grant Allen (1848-1899), George Griffith (George Griffith-Jones, 1857-1906), Fred T. Jane (1865-1916), M. P. Shiel (1865-1947), C. J. Cutcliffe Hyne (1866-1944), J. D. Beresford (1873-1947), Cyril Ranger Gull (1874-1923) alias "Guy Thorne", William Hope Hodgson (1877-1918), and Gerald Heard (1889-1971) were all the sons of clergymen, and John Gloag (1896-1981) described his father as "painfully religious". Members of Fowler Wright's post-Darwinian generation tended to accept—although their fathers often would not—that a fundamental change had taken place in the attitude that a reasonable person had to take to the Church's mythology and network of beliefs. Much exploratory speculative fiction consists of attempts to re-conceptualize the Earth's place in the universe and humankind's place in nature—thoroughly revising the obsolete models formerly promoted by the Church—and to examine the moral and intellectual corollaries of the new perspectives thus produced.

Fowler Wright's defection from dogmatic faith did not prevent him from retaining a strong sense of moral conviction, based in a sincere admiration of Christ's principles, or from adopting a sternly ascetic lifestyle cast in a Puritanical mould. He did not smoke or eat meat, very rarely drank alcohol, and exercised with rare determination, taking a great delight in walking in the countryside. He was also a keen cyclist—a hobby he shared with H. G. Wells. During the 1890s he undertook several extensive cycling tours, including expeditions through France and Belgium.

As with several other major writers of scientific romance—J. D. Beresford and M. P. Shiel are notable examples—Fowler Wright was prepared to turn the skepticism that had distanced him from his father's faith upon the scientific "faith" that aspired to replace it. He considered that what was "proved" today might easily be "disproved" tomorrow, and thought it stupid to replace the dogmas of religion with the dogmas of contemporary science. The real truth, he felt, must lie elsewhere, waiting to be explicated in such a fashion that it would show up the deficiencies of traditional religion and contemporary science. This was, of course, a fairly common belief of the period—few people, no matter how destructive their skepticism, doubted that there was, somewhere, a perfect and appropriate faith waiting to be discovered and revealed. It was not simply writers of scientific romance who went looking for it in odd places; religious fantasists like G. K. Chesterton and the Powys brothers were embarked upon a similar quest in different imaginative territories, and so were all the new cultists determinedly re-inventing all the old heresies.

Fowler Wright was by no means alone in the powerful self-confidence that, by the exercise of his own rationality, unassisted by authority, he could find this one true faith. If anything, what distinguishes him from most of his contemporaries was the modesty with which he accepted his inability to convince others that what he had found was, in fact, the genuine article. Men like Shiel and John Cowper Powys might not have been confident of being believed as they tried to plant signposts on the way to a new revelation, but at least they were hopeful. Fowler Wright was never even that.

Although he had no formal qualifications Fowler Wright followed his father into the profession of accountancy. He married Nellie (Julia Ellen) Ashbarry in 1895; she was a well-educated woman of considerable social status, with a strong interest in literature, and the marriage must have increased his fervor for self-education as well as fostering his ambition to write. Nellie was to bear him six children before her death in 1918: Islaine (1900-1936), Gilbert (1902-1936), Esther (1905-1990), Roger (1906-1982), Alan (1907-1999), and Katherine (1908-2001). He subsequently married Truda (Anastasia Gertrude) Hancock in 1920; she was the mother of four further children: Valerie (born 1924), Yolande (1926-1995), Diana (born 1928), and Nigel (1932-1987).

Although he and Nellie had not much money to start with, Fowler Wright made a considerable success of his first career. The family lived in various rural locations in the Midlands before settling at Storrage House, Beoley, near Alvechurch, in 1910, although Nellie's poor health required her to spend the winters in the Welsh seaside town of Barmouth; she was eventually buried in Beoley. During his first marriage Fowler Wright developed a keen interest in all things natural; he kept numerous domestic animals and became an enthusiastic gardener—attempting, among other projects, to produce a green carnation.

The interests that were later to manifest themselves in Fowler Wright's literary work, and the opinions that were to be robustly dramatized therein, were crystallized while he was still working as an accountant. He became a fervent libertarian, deeply antipathetic to what he saw as a continuing erosion of individual freedom and responsibility by legislation and bureaucracy. He had a profound dislike of the police and other agents of the law, on account of their increasing intrusion into matters which ought to be none of their concern. He was a passionate believer in natural justice, and felt that the "justice" promoted by contemporary English courts was a crude perversion. His love of nature generated a determined antipathy toward technology in general and motor vehicles in particular. Having been born and grown to adulthood before internal combustion engines came into common use he always regarded them as ugly, dangerous and unnecessary invaders: murderous despoilers of a once-green-and-pleasant land.

Although he never professed any particular admiration for the works of Jean-Jacques Rousseau, Fowler Wright's own philosophy had many points in common with Rousseau's, including his antipathy to the supposedly-perverting aspects of "civilization" and his insistence that the basis of morality was a tacit social contract whose obligations must be taken very seriously. Fowler Wright was quite ready to turn the skepticism that had distanced him from his father's faith upon any and all rival faiths—including the notion, stridently challenged by Rousseau, that social and technological progress were identical or interdependent.

When the Great War broke out Fowler Wright was recruited by the War Office to help expedite the production of vital war equipment. This work required a great deal of traveling, including trips to the continent to procure equipment and to investigate the under-performance of the French arms industry; he was in Paris when the city was in danger of falling to the Germans. His work for the War Office brought him into contact with a great many prominent people, including Winston Churchill, and it did not end with the war—the economic problems with whose solutions he was assisting continued long afterwards.

The necessity of commuting regularly between the environs of Birmingham and London—and sometimes undertaking longer expeditions—meant that Fowler Wright spent a great deal of time on trains. It was probably in the course of these journeys that he eventually began writing prose fiction for his own distraction. None of the manuscripts survive, but he seems to have had difficulty finishing the projects he began—as might be expected, given the circumstances of their composition.

It is now impossible to tell how many of Fowler Wright's later works were based on partial manuscripts produced in the 1910s and early 1920s, but we can be certain that his endeavors included a sprawling text of a languorous disaster story, in which Britain was inundated by a great flood, and a vision of the far future whose inspirational debt to H. G. Wells's *The Time Machine*—the principal founding text of the British genre of scientific romance—was scrupulously acknowledged. The pattern of his publications in the early 1930s strongly suggests that Fowler Wright must have made considerable progress on at least one other Wellsian fantasy and at least one historical romance during his days as a commuter.

It seems obvious, given the presumable contents of so many of these early efforts, that Fowler Wright had formed a strong interest in scientific romance at a relatively early age. It seems, however, that he considered scientific romance more a medium of relaxation than a kind of high art. He regarded the lyric poetry he wrote in the same period as his "real" literary work. Much of that appears to have been lost too, but it was work of that kind that he first took the trouble to publish. He was entranced by Thomas Malory's *Morte d'Arthur*, which he probably read in the J. M. Dent edition of 1893, and set to work on a modernized version of his own shortly after his marriage, although he did not publish any of it until he issued *Scenes from the Morte d'Arthur* under the pseudonym Alan Seymour in 1919.

The new social connections that Fowler Wright forged before and during the war were by no means restricted to matters of business. He made contact with many other people who shared his interest in poetry, including some who shared his opinion that it was a potentially-powerful instrument of education, by means of which members of the newly-literate working class might be able to follow schemes of self-improvement similar to the one Fowler Wright had been forced to apply to himself. In June 1918, as the war was nearing its end, Fowler Wright assisted in the launch of the small press magazine *Poetry*, whose first editor was Charles John Arnell. At first Fowler Wright remained very much in the background, but he soon took on a more active role.

* * * * * * *

The first excerpt from the *Morte d'Arthur* project to appear in *Poetry* was in the January 1920 issue. "Alan Seymour" took over the editorship of the magazine in August 1920, immediately declaring an intention to make it "of increasing interest to the students, as well as to writers, of poetry". Fowler Wright had, of course, taken on the financial responsibility of maintaining *Poetry* along with the editorship, and he immediately unleashed his expertise upon the problem of its commercial viability, while scaling back his other professional activities.

Arnell had augmented the magazine's meager subscription fees by means of the still-popular device of running a series of competitions, whose entrants paid a small fee. Fowler Wright broadened the scope of this strategy considerably, introducing free competitions for schoolchildren (while offering the opportunity for schools to buy multiple copies of the magazine at a special rate) and running special competitions for the inhabitants of particular regions of England and her former colonies, thus mounting subscription drives in Australia and Canada. The Merton Press, which he established to publish *Poetry* in 1923, soon began to issue anthologies and collections of verse; many of these featured the competition-generated produce of individual counties, while others were financed by the authors according to the usual principles of subscription publishing. *Poetry* also advertised and reviewed the produce of similar small presses, notably the Swan Press, whose Leeds-based proprietor Sidney Matthewman was a friend of Fowler Wright's. Matthewman's anthologies of the work of Yorkshire poets may have given Fowler Wright the idea of publishing the Merton Press "County Series" of anthologies.

Once he became the editor of *Poetry* Fowler Wright began to appear in its pages far more frequently, although most of the work he did for it was either non-fiction or translation. After the September 1920 issue he abandoned his pseudonym because he had discovered that there was a poet publishing under the (presumably real) name of Ivan Alan Seymour. In the following months, alongside a series of essays entitled "Notes on Prosody", he serialized his translation of texts taken from Pierre Louÿs' *The Songs of Bilitis* (although he was always careful to maintain the fiction that the works in question really were by a Sapphic poet called Bilitis). In 1921 he began publication of a translation of Dante's *Divine Comedy* that was to continue sporadically throughout the magazine's lifetime. He further emphasized his eclecticism by publishing a poem "From the Sanskrit" in 1921 and "Songs from Balochistan" in 1922.

By far the most significant of the devices which Fowler Wright invented to promote *Poetry* and its educative mission arose out of the competitions that invited entries from the far-flung reaches of the British Empire. The November/December 1921 issue of the magazine announced the formation of the Empire Poetry League, whose "official organ" *Poetry* then became. One of Fowler Wright's daughters became the secretary of the organization, which established a "club room" in Belgrave Road in London. The League attracted many prominent members, and the sponsorship of the project was sufficiently generous in its early years to allow *Poetry* to adopt a larger size and more imposing format in 1923.

Many new contributors were recruited to the magazine in 1923, among whom the most famous were G. K. Chesterton (who served a term as the League's president), H. E. Bates, E. Temple Thurston, W. H. Davies, "A.E." (G. W. Russell), May Kendall, Israel Zangwill, Dorothy Una Ratcliffe and Wilfred Rowland Childe. The League hosted lectures on poetry in numerous venues, and held annual meetings at Fowler Wright's new home, a fine house called Oaklands situated in what was then the village of Handsworth (it has since been swallowed up by Birmingham's urban sprawl). The involvement in the League of the ballet dancer Ninette de Valois—who performed at Oaklands in the course of the 1926 meeting—prompted a widening of its concerns, and a corresponding change in the magazine's title to *Poetry and the Play*.

The June 1923 issue of Poetry featured two poems by Olaf Stapledon, which helped to revitalize the literary endeavor that the author in question had virtually abandoned after having a small volume of his poems privately printed in 1914. Stapledon, who became a friend of Fowler Wright's, remained a more frequent and more regular contributor than most of those recruited during the Empire Poetry League's first flush of enthusiasm. Other writers featured in the magazine in the late 1920s who went on to produce notable works of imaginative fiction included John Metcalfe, Moray Dalton and Alfred Gordon Bennett, but we can only speculate as to whether Fowler Wright's example played any part in their inspiration. He was scrupulous in maintaining the tight focus of the periodical, and never reviewed any prose works or published any articles touching on the potential of prose fiction as a visionary medium. When he decided to publish a work of prose fiction himself—*The Amphibians: A Romance of 500,000 Years Hence*—he paid for Matthewman's Swan Press to print the first edition in September 1925.

It seems likely that the first edition of *The Amphibians* was intended for private circulation only and that the print run was very small; Sam Moskowitz quotes a figure in an article on Fowler Wright collected in *Strange Horizons* (1976) that is certainly wrong. Fowler Wright did, however, use the Merton Press to produce a larger edition for public sale in March 1926. The novel was the first part of his epic of the far future; it is probable that he had offered it, unsuccessfully, to commercial publishers, and that *Deluge* had also begun collecting rejection slips by this time.

Fowler Wright had also used the Merton Press to reprint *Scenes from the Morte d'Arthur* and several works from *Poetry*. The *Song of Songs and Other Poems* (1925) included a "reconstruction" of a hypothetical original version of the Biblical *Song of Solomon*, the poems previously collected in *Some Songs of Bilitis* and "Songs of Balochistan". The first volume of an anthology series called *Voices on the Wind* featured a good deal of his own work, and he also issued a slim volume featuring *The Ballad of Elaine* (1926), a further excerpt from the *Morte d'Arthur* (although the version of the poem that appears in the full text is somewhat different). The Merton Press published nothing more after 1926, probably because it was overburdened with debt, but Fowler Wright immediately founded another company, Fowler Wright Ltd., which took over the "County Series" of anthologies (after two volumes had been issued under the Empire Poetry League imprint) and its companion series, "From Overseas".

In 1927 Fowler Wright Ltd. issued another novel, *Deluge*, derived from an even earlier manuscript. Fowler Wright subsequently used the imprint to issue *de luxe* editions of his translation of *The Inferno* (1928) and *The Riding of Lancelot* (1929), although he employed a utilitarian paperback format for his polemical essay entitled *Police and Public* (1929)—which was announced as the first of a series although no others appeared. He was declared bankrupt late in 1928 or early in 1929 and was forced to sell Oaklands, so he had to rethink not merely his strategy as a writer and publisher, but his entire lifestyle. Having already changed direction once in life, when he had married Truda and "retired" from full-time accountancy in order to have more time for the promotion of culture, he was now compelled by circumstance to change direction again—at the age of fifty-five—more sharply than before.

The financial and personal misfortunes that Fowler Wright's family suffered in the late 1920s eventually formed the basis of one of his novels, *Seven Thousand in Israel* (1931), but their precise details are carefully obscured by the process of fictionalization and it would be hazardous to infer too much from an analysis of that text. The blame for the ruination of the novel's hero, John Oakley, is laid squarely at the door of the Excess Profits Duty: a tax introduced by the government to counter wartime "profiteering". Although its collection was deferred so as not to affect economic activity, E.P.D. eventually bankrupted many businesses that had made a vital contribution to the war effort. Its effects on Fowler Wright were magnified by the fact that he had accepted directorships in some of the businesses that he had recruited to provide equipment during the war, all of which were bankrupted when the government finally decided to call in the tax bill and punish all the companies that had helped Britain win the war, condemning most of them to summary execution. E.P.D. was not the only contributor to Fowler Wright's misfortunes, but it was certainly the most oppressive, and its effects undoubtedly encouraged his exceedingly low opinion of political systems and the working of artificial "justice".

Having failed to maintain the impetus it built up in the early 1920s, the Empire Poetry League petered out the 1930s (although its Jamaican branch survived, in the care of J. E. Clare Macfarlane, until the end of the 1950s). It must have cost Fowler Wright far more money than it had ever generated for the upkeep of *Poetry and the Play* but he continued to edit the magazine until its last issue in Summer 1931. Fowler Wright did not, however, follow John Oakley's example by expiring under the burden of his tribulations. He was rescued from the threat of financial ruination by the amazing success of the only work of prose fiction to have been issued by Fowler Wright Ltd., which had subsequently taken on a remarkable life of its own. Before considering the substance of that work and its remarkable career, however, it is appropriate to make a close examination of his first-published scientific romance.

The Amphibians and *The World Below*

The main body of the story told in *The Amphibians: A Romance of 500,000 Years Hence* is set in a future so remote that man has disappeared from the Earth, to be replaced by other intelligent species, including the gentle telepathic Amphibians and the giant troglodytic Dwellers. A third, rather more primitive race is that of the loathsome Killers. The novel's narrator—who is not named by the narrative voice, though one of the other characters addresses him as "George"—is asked by a scientist to take part in an experiment. The scientist has a machine that will transmit objects into the future, and although he has successfully transmitted and recovered several inanimate objects his two previous experiments with human subjects have failed: the men have not returned, although one did re-appear briefly to gather some equipment before setting out again.

The narrator, who needs money badly—although we are not told why—agrees to investigate their fate in return for a fee to be paid to someone named Clara, who is presumably his fiancée, although this is not explicitly stated. In general, Fowler Wright's work tends to be parsimonious with the prefatory material that brackets the strange adventures of his characters, and is often infuriatingly uninformative about them.

The narrator of *The Amphibians* finds himself on the edge of a great plain, near a great wall alongside which runs an opalescent pathway. There are caves in the wall, and tunnels leading into the depths of the world. Everything is apparently artificial, even the outlay of the giant plants on the plain. He is sheltering in a cave when he sees a humanoid creature, apparently female, running along the path. His emergence from hiding is so startling that she stumbles from the pathway and is seized by an apparently-carnivorous plant. He destroys the plant but cannot save its victim, who communicates with him telepathically and plants in his mind a compulsion to carry through some unspecified mission.

The narrator is briefly captured by a giant yellow-skinned humanoid, but escapes. Hurt and fearful, he is eventually found by other creatures like the one killed by the plant. These approach in a column, "singing" with their thoughts, and recover from him a message implanted in his mind by their dead companion. This relates to one of their kind who has been imprisoned. These are the Amphibians, inhabitants of islets off the coast of the island continent where they are now standing. This continent is controlled by the Dwellers, from one of whom the narrator has recently escaped. The Dwellers have retired underground and have sealed off the boundaries of their territory against some unspecified menace, and have made a treaty with the Amphibians in order to supplement their food supplies. This treaty has now been breached by the Amphibians coming inland; thanks to the narrator the breach can no longer be kept secret.

The imprisoned Amphibian is being kept by the ferocious, mountain-dwelling Killers, who are saving her for one of their periodic carnivorous feasts; the troop has come to rescue her, and the narrator is bound to join in with them. He is commissioned to plan an assault, by means of which the trapped Amphibian will hopefully be rescued, because he is more able than they to contemplate and carry out such aggressive intentions. In company with one Amphibian, he breaks into the Killers' arsenal and destroys it, using "the Forbidden Thing" (fire), eventually managing to accomplish the task which he has been set.

From the moment that the narrator meets the first Amphibian he is made to feel ugly and pitiable by comparison with "her"—the Amphibians are actually hermaphrodites, but the narrator elects to use the feminine pronoun in referring to them. His subsequent dealings with them serve only to intensify these feelings of self-doubt. The Amphibians are beautiful, gentle and high-minded, and find the narrator almost intolerably loathsome. At first, they are too polite to be more than mildly critical, even when he tells them about the world from which he has come, but such is the intimacy which develops between him and his special companion that eventually he is able to penetrate this veil: "And then—for one incautious instant—she let me see her mind, and my attentions." (*The World Below*, Collins edition p. 116-17)

Partly, of course, this repulsion is occasioned by the fact that the foot the Amphibian is touching is injured, but the simile nevertheless remains: the narrator is to her what one of the monstrous Killers is to himself. In a later passage, he tells her that life in his own world is by no means wild and free, as the life of the Amphibians is, but that the vast majority must toil in desperate conditions. This is her reaction:

> "I think there are two ways of life which are good. There is the higher way, which is ours, in which all are united; and there is the lower way, of the shark or the shell-fish, of freedom and violence, which only greater violence can destroy, and which nothing can bring into slavery. But the vision which you give me is of a state which is lower than either of these, of blind servitudes and oppressions, to which you yield without willingness.
>
> "The more you tell me, the more easily do I understand the sudden violences and crafts of your mind, and the disorders through which you think. But has there been none who has pointed out to you either the road of freedom or the road of concord? Are you content with a social state as uncontrolled as the bodies in which you live so briefly? Have you no lawmakers whom you can reverence, and whom you can obey with serenity?" (p. 127)

This last remark, however, merely opens the way into one of Fowler Wright's commentaries on the dreadful state of law-making in the twentieth century, explaining how the mass-production of laws has got completely out of hand. Given this, it is perhaps slightly surprising that the climactic scene of *The Amphibians* should actually be a trial, in which judgment must be passed on a group of bat-winged creatures resembling Gustave Doré's representations of Dante's devils.

The creatures in question are specimens of a race that once held dominion over the Earth, and were preserved by the Dwellers for purposes of research until they were handed over to the Killers for disposal. When the narrator and his companion rescue the trapped Amphibian they must decide whether or not to release these creatures as well, and therefore agree to hear again the evidence of their character which persuaded the Dwellers to condemn them to death. The bat-wings' crime is that they have condemned to death one of their own kind for stealing food. The Dwellers have judged that any people who establish a society where it is possible for some to be without food while others have more than enough are irredeemably corrupt. The narrator eventually confirms this judgment.

After this strange digression the story comes abruptly to a halt, but not to an end. In a final scene, the Dwellers and the Amphibians apparently reach a new agreement, but its import is not made clear and the last line of the book is content to promise a new adventure for the two protagonists. A sequel was obviously planned, and there is evidence to indicate that Fowler Wright intended *The Amphibians*, at this point, to be the first part of a trilogy.

The Amphibians is a remarkable work in several ways. In a brief preface to the second edition Fowler Wright noted that some commentators had suggested that it was influenced by Wells's *The Time Machine* and that its social philosophy was borrowed from Butler's *Erewhon*. Actually, it is only the basic literary device that is borrowed from Wells—the debt is acknowledged in the text—and the resemblance between Butler's philosophy and Fowler Wright's is very superficial. Fowler Wright's response to the criticism states that he had not read *Erewhon*. *The Amphibians* is, in fact, a work of striking originality in almost every respect, which shows considerable external influence only in the fraction of its imagery that derives from Dante's *Inferno*—but in its discussion of the nature of sin and the ethics of punishment, Fowler Wright and Dante are, inevitably, poles apart.

The novel is so harsh in the judgment that it passes on human nature and society that it might be held to rank as one of the most bitterly misanthropic of futuristic fantasies, but the adjective "misanthropic" does need to be qualified. It is not that the author detests his fellow men, *en masse* or individually, but rather that his distaste arises from a clinically detached contemplation of the human condition. He is quite calm and resigned in alleging that, from an objective viewpoint, one can find a great deal in the human condition to deplore and also a great deal to pity. Some other works of speculative fiction written between the wars are equally harsh in their judgments, but tend to add a note of hysteria or a note of vituperation; Fowler Wright was not given to such fierceness of feeling, and tended to maintain a casual laconism in his misanthropic observations. In general, writers employing the imaginary device of looking at humankind through hypothetical alien eyes are distinctly ungenerous in reporting their findings. Few people, reflecting on their own physical and moral weaknesses, can resist entirely the temptations of contempt. It was not men who were free from sin who invented Hell. The fascination of the Inferno is partly due to its instrumental value in controlling our capacity for evil, and self-control often involves an element of self-blackmail. Fowler Wright is unusually honest in reporting this state of affairs

The Amphibians is certainly a disturbing book, if one takes its allegations about the human condition seriously. It is alleged more than once in the text that there is a human soul, which suffers by virtue of its imprisonment in such a vile body. As the second quotation reproduced above clearly indicates, Fowler Wright sees man as a half-and-half creature, trapped between two contrasted ways of being, which are represented in purer forms in the text by the Amphibians and the Killers. The former enjoy a physical condition that is appropriate to their spiritual possibilities; the latter, being more strictly rational than humans, are free to indulge the vicious appetites built into their physical being in a way that conscience-afflicted humans are not.

What is particularly harsh and unusual about this argument is that it posits an ideal state of being that humans, virtually by definition, can never reach. This is why the readers who detected traces of Erewhonian Utopianism in *The Amphibians* were quite mistaken. Like Samuel Butler, Fowler Wright is skeptical about technology, and in favor of a "more natural" way of life, but the supernatural fellowship that the Amphibians have is not something that humans can acquire. Even if humans were fortunate enough to become telepathic (as they do, for instance, in Fowler Wright's last speculative novel, *Spiders' War*) they would still have innate tendencies toward evil built into their physical constitution.

The most important thing to note about the ideal state of being that the Amphibians enjoy is that it is an internal state of being. It does not depend at all upon their living in a placid, bountiful and comfortable environment. Their world resembles the Inferno far more than it does the Garden of Eden, but this works in their favor rather than against them. It is his insistence on this point, rather than any other item in his philosophy of life, that sets Fowler Wright apart from the other exponents of scientific romance. His reverence for nature was in no way based on the misapprehension (common among modern ecological mystics) that nature is harmonious. His notion of the ideal state of being is, in fact, based on the opposite presumption: that it is struggle and strife which are natural, and that the ideal state of being must be accommodated to that reality.

Given this, it is not surprising that Fowler Wright is pessimistic on behalf of the human race. He is pessimistic, too, on behalf of the technically-capable Dwellers and the idealized Amphibians—the text makes it clear that, although the Amphibians and the Dwellers are quite conscious of the self-destructive tendencies of intelligence, they will probably not find a way to preserve their world. This was to become even clearer when he published a version of the sequel that he had promised, although that was issued in very different circumstances, and was not cast in the form that it had originally been intended to take.

* * * * * * *

In the second part of *The World Below* the time traveler and his Amphibian companion go into the subterranean world of the Dwellers. The early chapters simply describe further stages in their phantasmagoric odyssey, each one featuring a strange and dangerous encounter. They soon emerge, however, into an enormous room where they find an artificial organism impressed with telepathic recordings: a "living book". The narrator, not without difficulty, contrives to read passages from this book, including some references to the two men he is looking for. One, it is ominously said, has been "scraped by the Vivisection Department" and the other "transferred to the Experimental Section". The companions also learn more about the new treaty made between the Amphibians and the Dwellers, relating to an impending war against the insectile "Antipodeans".

While seeking further information, the narrator and the Amphibian discover a library of living books, and pass through corridors on whose walls are projected visual images. They learn something of the history of the Dwellers, and something of the progress of the war, but all of this is fragmentary and disjointed. When they are eventually discovered by the Dwellers, the two protagonists are parted, and the narrator continues his search alone. By this time the story is being told in an almost perfunctory manner, in brief and terse chapters, as if the author simply wanted to be done with the book as quickly as possible—as he presumably did, given that he was accumulating material for publication as quickly as he could.

In a brief scene set in a laboratory, the narrator sees the Dwellers tending their war-wounded, and learns that, even in this Hellish underworld, love continues to be an important and vital force in the lives of those who live there. The narrator is imprisoned, and encounters in his captivity the only previous human time-traveler who is still alive. Alas, the man is quite mad, and does not know his friend, although he is oddly blissful in his insane innocence.

The Amphibians eventually persuade the Dwellers to release the narrator from his captivity, and it is in the company of the "Seekers of Wisdom" that he lives out his year in the far future before returning to his own time. The Seekers of Wisdom are Dwellers, and are not so different from men as the Amphibians, but the narrator still finds them contemptuous when he describes the world from which he has come for their benefit. He has to concur in many of their judgments, as he tells them a story of which he is ashamed. He finally returns to his own world a changed man, physically as well as intellectually.

Perhaps incredibly, when the narrator is asked in the epilogue whether he would be prepared to undertake another journey to the world he has visited, he says that he would—but only if Clara would go with him. He thinks that she will (and if she is cut from the same cloth as other Fowler Wright heroines, indeed she might, astonishing as this might seem.)

Taken as a whole, the composite work that became *The World Below* is exceedingly harsh in the judgment which it passes on human nature and society, but it is not atypical of its period—a similar disgust for contemporary humankind is detectable in many other scientific romances published between the wars. Similarly strident expressions of that disgust can be found in *The Seventh Bowl* (1930) by "Miles" (better known as Neil Bell), *Last Men in London* (1932) and *Odd John* (1934) by Olaf Stapledon, and the final chapter of *This Was Ivor Trent* (1935) by Claude Houghton. None of these writers detested his fellow men, but when each one attempted a clinically detached contemplation of the human condition, he found much to deplore, as well as much to pity.

It was already a common strategy for imaginative writers to look at humankind through hypothetical alien eyes and report ungenerously on their findings—H. G. Wells had employed an angel for this purpose in *The Wonderful Visit* (1895), while Grant Allen had used a time-traveling anthropologist in *The British Barbarians* (1895)—but literally alien viewpoints became increasingly common as time went by, and it was not until British scientific romance was on its last legs that any evidence appeared of a significant amelioration of this harshness. The eponymous alien in Eden Phillpotts' *Saurus* (1938) is only a little gentler in his judgment of humankind's failings than the Amphibians or the Dwellers, but when another alien population makes similar remarks in the same author's *Address Unknown* (1949) the humans eventually take umbrage, perhaps as a reflection of the greater sense of triumph with which the English emerged from the Second World War.

The ideal state of being that the Amphibians enjoy is an internal state of being rather than a mode of political organization—it is an ahistorical "eupsychia" rather than a presently-achievable "eutopia" or a futuristic "euchronia". It is, perhaps, this casual insistence on the necessity of aiming for eupsychian rather than eutopian or euchronian goals that set Fowler Wright most obviously apart from the other exponents of scientific romance. He was flatly opposed to the "utopia of comforts" to which H. G. Wells and other fellow-travelers of the Fabian Society seemed to be looking forward, and intent of creating, but he was also opposed to the Arcadian images that were often set up in opposition to it, in such novels as Richard Jefferies' *After London; or, Wild England* (1885) and W. H. Hudson's *A Crystal Age* (1887). Fowler Wright was against Hell as well as against Heaven, but was perfectly clear in his belief that Hell was the better choice, and eventually wrote the short story "Choice" to make the case explicit. His reverence for the natural world is based on the presumption that struggle and strife are not merely inevitable by desirable, and that an ideal state of being must be accommodated to that reality, in perpetuity.

It seems obvious that Fowler Wright had difficulty in sustaining his creative energy while producing the materials that were eventually improvised into *The World Below*, and it is not particularly surprising that what was initially planned as a trilogy became a curtly-concluded pair, in which much material in the later chapters is presented as if it were taken straight from the author's notes rather than being properly transmuted into narrative. Fowler Wright always made up his plots as he went along, and thus worked in continual hazard of running out of inspiration. Many of his subsequent works became similarly unbalanced or shapeless as they changed direction and lost impetus, but *The World Below* suffered more than any other from this unfortunate effect.

It is possible that the writing of the original story that eventually formed the basis of *The World Below* had a kind of cathartic effect upon its author, and that the expression of the sentiments contained in its argument constituted a partial exorcism of its nightmarish perspectives. In that case, the novel itself might be reckoned a kind of purgatory. Even though Fowler Wright never returned to the particular imaginary world of the Amphibians and the Dwellers, he was to build many more that incorporated the same essential features, and if the loss of impetus of the project including his first-published novel was the result of a kind of catharsis, it was a purely temporary release.

Deluge and *Dawn*

Like *The Amphibians*, *Deluge* was a section edited out of a much longer and never-completed manuscript, which Fowler Wright had produced in the years following the end of the Great War; he always referred to *Deluge* as his "first novel", so it was presumably written before the text from which *The Amphibians* was extracted.

The story told in *Deluge* begins with a casual account of a series of earth tremors, which profoundly alter the contours of the planet's surface, flooding much of the existing land and elevating new land from beneath the sea. Almost all of the civilized world is inundated, but, as chance would have it, a few areas of England are elevated to the point where the hilltops are still above water. The Cotswolds thus become a tiny chain of islands. The storm that accompanies the tremors kills a great many people even in those areas that remain above water, and those who survive find themselves uncomfortably born out of the womb of civilization:

> "It was not only that they were physically ill-adapted for life on the earth's surface, but the minds of most of them were empty of the most elementary knowledge of their physical environment.
>
> "Released in a day from the most elaborate system of mutual slavery that the world has known, they were unused to the exercise of mental initiative, or to independent action. They were accustomed to settle every issue of life, not by the application of any basic rules, or instinctive preferences, or by the exercise of reason, but under the blind guidance of their specialized fellow-men, or by assiduous imitation of the procedure of those around them. The great majority of them were engaged in repetition work which had not originated in their own minds, and made no call upon them for analysis, decision, or judgment.
>
> "Their perceptions were blinded by physical deficiency. They were incapable of clear thought, or of decisive action.

"They were at a further disadvantage, which was not less serious because of a less obvious kind.

"They had been restrained from many evil (and some admirable) courses, not by experience of their probable consequences, nor by observation, nor tradition, but by laws which exacted utterly illogical penalties. When the fear of these penalties was removed, they reacted variously to instincts undisciplined except by a restraint which no longer operated.

"It had been a natural correlative of such conditions that where there had been no law to coerce them they (or at least many among them) had lacked the self-control needed for the dignity or even the decencies of physical existence, and had developed communally concealed habits which would have appalled the instincts of any cleanly beast. The bodies of many of them were rotten from the contagious horrors of the degradation in which they had lived, and the deluge did no more than hasten them to a swifter and more seemly end than they would otherwise have experienced." (Fowler Wright edition, p. 5-6)

There is a reference later in this prologue to the Biblical parable of the flood, which men might have taken more seriously, but, in spite of this reference, Fowler Wright's deluge is no divine judgment on human wickedness; it is an accident of happenstance, which might result in a cleansing of the Earth and a rebirth of mankind, but which might just as easily not. As the quotation suggests, the narrative of the novel is a painstaking account of the adventures of people who mostly fail dismally to cope with the circumstances of disaster.

As with many disaster stories, there is a kind of social Darwinism underlying the assumptions implicit in the extrapolation of the basic premise, but in Fowler Wright's case this is complicated by his slightly eccentric views on medical science. He was of the opinion that healthy people did not need doctors, save perhaps on rare occasions where some treatment might be necessary for an accidental injury, and felt that people who lived an appropriate life would be sufficiently robust to resist the ravages of disease. Thus, in his view, the "unfit" individuals, who will perish even if the disaster leaves them alive initially, are not unfit because of any faulty genetic heritage, but rather because civilized life has weakened them fatally.

Deluge is mainly the story of Martin Webster, who flees from his house, along with his wife Helen and their two small children, when the storm destroys it. Helen is injured and he has to leave her with the children in order to seek help, but when the flood comes they are separated and neither can be sure that the other has survived. The third major character in the story is Claire Arlington, who finds a temporary refuge on an island with two men, but decides to seek her fortune elsewhere when they fall to casting lots for her. Eventually Claire and Martin meet, and begin to gather together the necessities of life, building a cache of goods inside a railway tunnel while they live in a hut beside the track. They are discovered by a gang of men under the leadership of the brutal giant Bellamy, and must fight for their lives—a fight that climaxes with a bloody siege of the tunnel.

Meanwhile, Helen and her babies are taken in by Tom Aldworth, a decent man who is one of the leading figures in a struggling community. After establishing some basic moral principles, the community has already had to expel two groups of dissidents: Bellamy's gang and a more organized troop led by Jerry Cooper. A war is brewing between Aldworth's community and Cooper's men, with Bellamy also a threat.

While trying to remove the lesser threat first, Aldworth lifts the siege of the railway tunnel and frees Martin and Claire. They then take important roles in the community and play a vital part in repelling Cooper's first attack on their settlement. Martin finds himself on the horns of a dilemma, however, by virtue of the fact that he has now made oaths of loyalty and fidelity to two women, and seemingly must give one up (most of the fighting has been caused by a drastic shortage of women in the post-disaster world). In the end, though, he persuades the community to accept that the decision of the women must be binding, and they choose to share him. Helen's acceptance of Claire provides the closing lines of the story.

It is important to the understanding of this ending, and much else in Fowler Wright's works to remember that his notion of sexual relationships is, first and foremost, that they constitute a contract between free individuals. His view of sexuality is in some ways an odd one, and he reacted strongly against the account of sexual development propounded by Sigmund Freud. In *Deluge* he is careful to include a scathing description of one of the degenerate members of Bellamy's gang, which makes clear his opinion that the implication of man's possession of "animal instincts" is very different from what is commonly supposed:

> "He was obsessed by a debased sexuality, such as is stimulated by the excitements and restraints of

an unhealthy civilization, and which Freud appears to have supposed, very foolishly, to be the common curse of humanity.

"An urban population, knowing nothing of animals, has quaintly given the name of 'animalism' to this lowest of human vices, but it has no affinity to the loyalty of a rat to his doe, or the tenderness of a wolf for his mate. It is, in fact, the vice which, among all the outrages by which humanity has defied the laws of its Creator to its own undoing, is most alien from anything existing among the wild creatures which men have left unmurdered, nor has it any approximate parallel among those that they have brought into servitude and association." (p. 168)

The ramifications of this argument through his works of fiction are complicated, but several puzzling features of Fowler Wright's novels can be explained by extrapolation of it. The reference in the above quotation to the Creator and His laws is one of several to be found in *Deluge*, but none of these really reflects any orthodox religiosity. In fact, Fowler Wright does not see civilized man's betrayal of his Creator as an opposition to the divine will, but rather as a reckless squandering of providence. The references are not to a personalized Creator but rather to the natural world, which, by means of evolutionary processes, was indeed the creator of mankind. Fowler Wright's horror at the squandering of nature's providence was coupled with an unbreakable faith in the bounteousness of that providence—hence his conviction that there could be no merit in the argument that births must be restricted in order to conserve resources.

* * * * * * *

The Fowler Wright edition of *Deluge* consisted of a thousand copies; it sold well for a self-published book, although copies were still being advertised for sale in the Summer 1930 issue of *Poetry and the Play*. That it was so widely reviewed was partly due to the fact that Fowler Wright had made so many friends in the literary world via the Empire Poetry League. The reviews were mostly complimentary, but the book probably would not have been reprinted, and Fowler Wright's career as a writer of fiction might well have died with it, had it not been for the huge success of the edition published in the USA in 1928 by the Cosmopolitan Book Corporation—

part of William Randolph Hearst's publishing empire, and an affiliate of the famous magazine.

When Stephen Wright had emigrated to the USA he had taken Sydney's younger siblings with him; one of his brothers, Victor, was working on the fringes of the movie industry in 1927. Victor brought *Deluge* to the attention of Hollywood, and it was in anticipation of a film version that Cosmopolitan promoted the book very extravagantly. Their press releases boasted that it was the first book ever to be produced in a first American edition of 100,000 copies, although one reviewer pointed out that Sinclair Lewis's *Elmer Gantry* (1927) had got there first; in any case, the figure was inflated by the inclusion of the copies printed for the "Book of the Month Club", of which it was an early selection (for March 1928). Subsequent claims that Deluge had sold 70,000 copies on the day of publication might also have been exaggerated, but these figures soon began to be advertised in England, where they were quoted by no less an authority than Arnold Bennett as evidence of the moribund narrow-mindedness of the British publishers who had left it to be published by its author. Harrap eventually produced a commercial edition in 1930, which was reprinted in cheaper formats in 1931 and 1932, and the novel was serialized by the *Sunday Express* in June-July 1931.

Deluge may seem to modern readers to be an unlikely bestseller, but it slotted readily enough into a subgenre that was already well-established in American popular fiction, and it carried forward—albeit accidentally—a trend laid down by some of the most successful writers active in the pulp magazines. Conventional disaster stories that represent the catastrophic destruction of civilization as a terrible tragedy, like Jack London's *The Scarlet Plague* (1912; book 1915), had been overtaken in the pulp medium by deeply ambivalent romances that took considerable delight in imagining the apparatus of civilization swept away. The heroes of this kind of fiction, liberated from the shackles of complex social organization, are free to tame the wilderness all over again, reveling in the challenge of imposing their own order on a worsening environmental and social chaos, rather than merely having to come to terms with an order already forged by centuries of history.

The Second Deluge (1911) by Garrett P. Serviss, a trilogy of pulp serials begun with *Darkness and Dawn* (1912) by George Allan England, and *Draught of Eternity* (1918) by Victor Rousseau were among the vanguard of this new kind of disaster story, but the ideological apparatus these novels applied to the post-disaster scenario was even more extravagantly developed by Edgar Rice Burroughs in numerous pulp novels, including his accounts of the adventures of Tarzan, the archetype of a new kind of "noble savage". The appeal of this kind of fiction in America was peculiarly nostalgic, drawing upon the same emotional wellsprings as the booming Western genre. The taming of the wilderness and the heroism of frontier life had become central myths of American history, and there were many readers willing to imagine that the destruction of civilization would not be an entirely bad thing. It was not simply that the opportunity to start again from scratch might enable the rebuilders of civilization to avoid many mistakes made by their predecessors, but that there was an essential virtue and joy in the hard-fought battle against natural adversity that had been lost as soon as the job was complete.

Deluge thus had the advantage, in America, of refining an ideological formula that had already become familiar in pulp fiction, without itself being an item of pulp fiction. The literary style of pulp romance was too often crude, and the quality of its intellectual discourse too often sadly lacking, to recommend its products to sophisticated readers. Fowler Wright, on the other hand, wrote elegantly—poetically, when he was in the mood, but always with commendable clarity—and he set out arguments that were as cogent as they were earnest.

It would be unjust to assert that George Allan England and Edgar Rice Burroughs were not serious in what they wrote, but their works were enmired by pulp convention and pulp cliché, and hobbled by the insistence of their editors on relentlessly hectic action. Fowler Wright, on the other hand, was free to reach his own conclusions at his own pace, and he was thus able to build a bridge between two literary audiences that liked to consider themselves quite distinct. This was probably a key factor in recommending his work for filming. The fact that the novel had some highly original and determinedly idiosyncratic features, in addition to this ready-made appeal, was all to the good. There is a sense in which *Deluge* brought together and fused the tragic and romantic strands of the disaster story, maintaining an attitude of uncompromisingly brutal realism that is nevertheless continually and cleverly subverted by the triumphs of the heroic characters.

* * * * * * *

The literary context in which *Deluge* appeared in the United Kingdom was quite different from that in the USA. Although a significant paradigm example of a benign disaster, whose destruction of civilization is seen as a consummation devoutly to be wished, had been provided by Richard Jefferies in *After London* (1885), and M. P. Shiel's *The Purple Cloud* (1901), is distinctly ambivalent about the prospect of human near-extinction, the subsequent development of British futuristic fiction had followed a path very different from that laid down in the American pulp magazines.

Fowler Wright had reached adulthood just as the fledgling genre of scientific romance took off and enjoyed a brief period of fashionability, but that fashionability had begun to wane even before the Great War broke out. The war's bitter legacy created a climate of thought that was distinctly hostile to futuristic fiction, because that kind of fiction had been one of the chief vehicles of the mythology that a world war would be "the war to end war": a means of saving and securing the British Empire. By 1918 the hollowness of the slogans employed by the war's promoters had become blindingly obvious, and the mood of such futuristic speculation as remained had undergone a dramatic bouleversement. The post-war decade was a time when disenchantment ran rife in Britain, and every thinking person became anxious about the nature and values of the civilization that millions of men had died to protect. The most obvious expression of this disenchantment was in attitudes to the prospect of further wars, but its scope was broader and deeper; it is very evident in one other notable disaster story of the early 1920s, *Nordenholt's Million* (1923) by J. J. Connington.

Winston Churchill, whom Fowler Wright had met in the course of his war work, and with whom he had corresponded, summed up the prevailing attitude to the possibility of a second "world war" in an article published in *Nash's Pall Mall Magazine* in 1924, entitled "Shall We Commit Suicide?":

> "All that happened in the four years of the Great War," Churchill wrote, "was only a prelude to what was preparing for the fifth year. The campaign of the year 1919 would have witnessed an immense accession to the power of destruction. Had the Germans retained the moral to make good their retreat to the Rhine, they would have been assaulted in the summer of 1919 with forces and methods incomparably more prodigious than any yet employed. Thousands of aeroplanes would have shattered their cities. Scores of thousands of cannon would have blasted their front.... Poison gases of incredible malignity...would have stifled all resistance and paralysed all life on the hostile front subjected to attack....

"Certain sombre facts emerge solid, inexorable, like the shapes of mountains from drifting mist. It is established that henceforward whole populations will take part in war, all doing their utmost, all subjected to the fury of the enemy. It is established that nations who believe that their life is at stake will not be restrained from using any means to secure their existence. It is probable—nay, certain—that among the means which will next time be at their disposal will be agencies and processes of destruction wholesale, unlimited, and, perhaps, uncontrollable." (quoted in *Janus, or the Conquest of War* by William McDougall, p. 23-24.)

Futuristic speculation in the Britain of the 1920s was dominated by this idea: the notion that weapons of war were already available which, if and when they were unleashed, would almost certainly result in the destruction of civilization. This was the subject-matter of such novels as Edward Shanks's *People of the Ruins* (1920), Cicely Hamilton's *Theodore Savage* (1922), P. Anderson Graham's *The Collapse of Homo Sapiens* (1923) and Shaw Desmond's *Ragnarok* (1926). It was also the specter haunting many of the contributions to the "Today & Tomorrow" series of pamphlets issued by Kegan Paul, Trench & Trübner between 1924 and 1930, including *Callinicus; a Defence of Chemical Warfare* (1925) by J. B. S. Haldane, *Janus; or the Conquest of War* (1925) by William MacDougall, and *Artifex; or, the Future of Craftsmanship* (1926) by John Gloag. The last-named title painstakingly addressed the question of whether men living in a society whose division of labor was as advanced as ours could possibly possess the skills necessary to supply their needs in the wake of a catastrophe, or the means to re-learn and re-apply them; its author came inexorably to the conclusion that they would not. This was a notion that Gloag—a friend of Olaf Stapledon and an admirer of Fowler Wright—was later to develop in several scientific romances of his own. It is also one of the theses extrapolated in *Deluge*, exemplified by the passage from the Prelude quoted above.

Where Fowler Wright differed from the majority of his contemporaries was in his refusal to see the exposure of these limitations merely as a tragedy waiting to happen. His argument is that, if this is a bad state to be in, then a disaster that would show us the error of our ways would be a useful educative experience. It is significant that his deluge is neither a self-inflicted tragedy (like the wars in the other novels cited above) nor the judgment of an angry deity (like the Biblical event from which the title is derived). It is simply the sort of thing that must be expected to happen now and again in the history of a world—and which, whenever it does, will provide a crucial test of a species' fitness to survive. Civilization and technology, by insulating people from natural challenges and dividing the knowledge and skills necessary for survival into specialisms, has rendered humankind terrible vulnerable—but all is not yet lost while some of us remain capable of surviving a catastrophe. As the passage quoted above illustrates, the argument about the loss of knowledge and skills is supplemented with another, which argues that it is paralleled by a similar loss of moral independence. Individual responsibility has been largely displaced by the quasi-mechanical regulation of law, so the sudden removal of the instrumentality of law enforcement would liberate all kinds of antisocial impulses.

Many of Fowler Wright's readers would, of course, have taken it for granted that, without the forces of law and order in place, brute force would rule supreme, but Fowler Wright differed from most of them in holding that it was over-reliance on social regulation that had created dependence upon the law. He believed that in a libertarian society, which placed more emphasis on individual responsibility than on legal coercion, society would be inured against the destructive effects of catastrophe because people would be better able to come together again and work together for the benefit of all. *Deluge* argues that, in this respect too, all is not yet lost. There are some still among us—like Martin and Helen Webster, Tom Aldworth and Claire Arlington—who are capable of independent moral action, and of such strict obedience to the implicit social contract that is fundamental to all human society that they will abide by its dictates, even when those dictates come into frank conflict with the norms and laws of the civilization in which they have grown up. That is, of course, the significance of the novel's eventual conclusion.

These twin theses are the cornerstones—with the heavier emphasis on the second—of almost all Fowler Wright's speculative fiction, which extrapolates them in several different ways. They were, in his view, both important and urgent, and it is entirely understandable that they should seem so to a man of his particular time and experience. He had not been a combatant in the Great War, but, as an accountant, he had had to deal with the businesses of men who were called up, many of whom never returned; he had certainly seen its tragic consequences. He and Nellie, as literate local gentry, had to read aloud much of the correspondence that passed between their poorer neighbors and the men at the front, most of whom never returned. His work for the War Office had given him a better insight than the great majority of his contemporaries into the way the war was organized—or, for the most part, disorganized—and the probable ways in which any future catastrophe would be mishandled by bureaucratic process and managerial ineptitude.

Deluge is not as peculiar a response to this experiential legacy as some of its critics tried to make out; it is certainly less hysterical, and more carefully-reasoned, than many of the future war novels produced in the same period. Even so, there is a certain propriety in the fact that the larger whole from which it was extracted was, and was to remain, incomplete.

* * * * * * *

Much of the remaining text of the manuscript from which Deluge was extracted was gathered into a "sequel", *Dawn*, which was announced for future publication on the dust-wrapper of the Fowler Wright Ltd. edition but was not issued under that imprint. Cosmopolitan published it in the USA in 1929—having issued another Fowler Wright novel, *The Island of Captain Sparrow* (1928), in the interim—but it did not appear in the UK until 1930, when Harrap issued it immediately after their new edition of *Deluge*.

Dawn is a much more substantial work than the second part of *The World Below*, and suffers no such decay into disjointedness. Nevertheless, Fowler Wright obviously found some difficulties in carrying forward the story told in his first novel, ten years after he had written it down. In fact, he ended up by not carrying it forward very much. The first two-thirds of the story told in Dawn runs parallel to the events in Deluge, providing a more detailed history of the community that takes in Helen Webster, and examining the stresses and strains that lead to the expulsion of Bellamy's gang and the defection of Jerry Cooper. Even when it moves beyond straightforward recapitulation, the story does not move into new imaginative territory, but is largely content to deal with a second attempt by Cooper to take control.

The major elements in the plot that are new concern the influence upon the course of affairs in the post-disaster world of two men: Henry Butcher, a careful trader who cleverly corners the market in various highly desirable commodities by careful scavenging and artful bartering; and John Burman, a farmer who lives on an islet a little way from the large land-mass on which the community is based, and who is fiercely protective of his independence. The importance of these two men is that they represent contrasting forces in human affairs. Martin, in deciding what kind of political system to adopt for his little empire, must find a way to control the anti-social enterprise of men like Butcher without doing anything to compromise the freedom of men like Burman. The problem is never set out quite so explicitly, but this is its essence.

Despite its relative substance and solidity, *Dawn* adds considerably less to *Deluge* than the second part of *The World Below* adds to *The Amphibians*. The questions opened up in the earlier novel are neither closed nor further elaborated, and the book seems lacking in any sense of dramatic urgency. Martin, once established as a leader, proves remarkably indecisive and enervated. He vacillates over the task of trying to save what he can of the knowledge of the old world by gathering a library of useful books—he begins the process of selecting a heritage by condemning to the fire the works of "a little group of the disciples of the hoary cult of the Witch of Endor"—but we hear no more of this business of rationalization. Again, when the community faces a moral crisis because a woman dies as a result of an abortion, Martin's doubts about the correct way to handle the affair lead to his favoring what the author obviously considered to be a weak-kneed solution. Martin condemns the doctor responsible to exile, but another character exacts a harsher penalty. Something very similar happens in the climax, when Martin is disposed to treat the vanquished Cooper mercifully, but finds matters taken out of his hands by someone more decisive and less squeamish.

These episodes emphasize a certain ambivalence in Fowler Wright's writings, which was to be seen even more clearly in his later novel *Power*. He had a great many ideas about what needed to be done if the world were to be set to rights, but he also had moral qualms about the actions that might need to be taken in order to accomplish the setting right. He was, of course, basically pessimistic about the prospect of saving the world, and *Dawn* displays many of his reasons for that pessimism. It has much to say about the unpromising nature of human beings, even when those most perverted by civilization are weeded out. Less noticeably, though, it asks whether even a man of great intelligence and resolve could really devise a blueprint for a better society, and whether—even if he had such a blueprint—he could in all conscience force his prescription upon others.

Fowler Wright was a believer in freedom, and recognized well enough that freedom includes the freedom to be foolish, indolent, and wicked. He recognized, too, the need for a community to draw up some kind of social contract, which must either limit or contain foolishness, indolence and wickedness. In the final analysis, he had no confidence that people would freely and willingly enter into and honor such a contract, and thus had to conclude that some element of force would always be necessary if the well-being of a community were to be preserved. Martin's story is an account of his making this unhappy discovery, trying to cope with it as best he can, and finding only an uncertain compromise.

In one way, the conclusion of *Dawn* is happier than the end of *Deluge*. The forces menacing the community have been conclusively defeated: both Butcher and Cooper have been dealt with. In another way, though, Dawn ends more desolately than its predecessor, with no note of personal triumph. The symbolic promise of a new day offered by the title is insidiously qualified in the last line by a deadly adjective:

> "He saw the futility of all endeavour. He might rule with an old wisdom, or a new foolishness, but he would die, and his will with him, and even that which he had sown in wisdom might be brought by others to a foolish flower....
>
> "He remembered that terrible bureaucratic slavery which the waters covered, when every man had been compelled to walk the same road at the same pace as his neighbours—when he could not take pleasure, or work, for his own gain or his fellows' good, but at the licensed times; when he could not find a corner of England so remote that he could build a home to his own liking without the interference and restraint of others; when he could not teach his own child in his own way, but it must be raped from him to be patterned in the common mould....
>
> "He became aware that the wind was colder, and that the night was falling around him. 'The night cometh, when no man can work.' The words entered his mind as a warning and as an unescapable doom. What use was there in thought and anxious effort in a world in which the night was always approaching?
>
> "His influence might be good or evil, but it would pass like a shadow, like an impression in water. The water might give way very easily to the moving hand, but it would close as easily behind it, and what would be altered? And the hand was Life, the water Time. Was it not a wiser rule to accept the inevitable end, and not to exhaust its brevity with a use-

less effort? 'The night cometh, when no man can work.'

"And then the thought came that these were the words of one who had the gift of putting the deepest wisdom into a simplicity of words, and that he had used them to a directly opposite argument.

"It was because of that approaching darkness that the labour should be neither delayed nor stinted. Taking no anxious thought for the morrow, the day's work must be done as best we may, because the darkness is so certain—and so near.

"The new order of life which he was striving to build with such partial success, with such inevitable errors, might disappear tomorrow, but what he did today would have become a fact unchangeable, the significance of which was beyond his seeing.

"The night moved round the earth. It followed daylight as men are followed by the over-taking feet of death, but there was no finality in its triumph.

"For behind it followed for ever the indifferent dawn." (Harrap edition, p. 362-63)

Although this passage might well have been written after the publication of *Deluge* in 1927, it makes no conspicuous attempt to supply *Dawn* with a real sense of closure—indeed, it is noticeably less conclusive than the last paragraphs of *Deluge*. One is tempted to suspect, therefore, that the reason Fowler Wright abandoned the project in the early 1920s was that the narrative had run into the doldrums, drifting on without being able to make any significant headway towards a visible destination. Fowler Wright certainly intended to carry the series further, and probably had more material in hand, but he never got around to preparing another manuscript for publication. Presumably, the survivors would have begun exploring their new world and would have found other communities on other islands, but as to what their condition might have been we can only guess.

Whatever the reasons were for the non-continuation of the *Deluge* series, its abandonment was not entirely inappropriate; the story was, in its very essence, a beginning without an end in prospect. Other British writers of tragic disaster stories found their endings in resignation to annihilation (e.g., *People of the Ruins*) or in theories of historical cyclicity (e.g., *Theodore Savage*), while American writers of romantic back-to-nature stories found it easy enough to produce allegedly-idyllic neo-Edenic microcommunities, but none of these eventualities was consonant with the premises and rationale of *Deluge*. Fowler Wright was to try them out in other novels, with varying degrees of conviction and limited success, but *Deluge* is too honest to admit that kind of narrative convenience.

The only triumph possible to the characters in *Deluge* is that they will contrive to go on, taking one day at a time, without ever knowing what the future might hold but only hoping that their endeavors will be worthwhile. The whole point of *Deluge* is that it is not the end that is important but the means: the skills that enable human beings to survive in the world, and the social contract that provides the basis of community. Such means do not require justification by the ends to which they are devoted, because they are already virtuous in themselves—and are, indeed, the definitive underpinnings of Fowler Wright's concept of virtue.

* * * * * * *

Fowler Wright made one public comment on the matter of *Deluge*'s inconclusiveness, which might need to be taken with a slight pinch of salt but is nevertheless illuminating, and useful in casting some light on the way the novel was written. A review signed "M.J.", which appeared in *The Inquirer* on 17 November 1927 concluded with the following passage:

> "Artistically speaking, 'The Deluge' has one distinct flaw. It is stated on the jacket that the book presents a problem of the 'eternal triangle,' that is not solved till the last page is reached. But in fact it is never solved at all, and by an unworthy shift Mr. Fowler Wright has given the reader an incomplete book and referred him to the 'sequel to this book which will appear shortly'. Surely a writer of Mr. Fowler Wright's calibre need not have resorted to such essentially commercial methods—his readers would have bought his next book just the same."

Fowler Wright's response to this judgment, published on 3 December, reads as follows:

> "Your reviewer is so generous in the notice of my recent book 'Deluge' that it seems ungracious to write a word of objection, but the accusation of an

'unworthy shift' to sell the book with which it closes is so serious in itself, that I feel sure that you will allow me space for a brief reply.

"The subject being too large for one volume, I think it might be argued successfully that the book closes artistically, and at a point of sufficient climax; but that is a matter of opinion on which I would not challenge another verdict. But your reviewer supposes that I had 'fully mastered the subject before sitting down to write the book, and had, therefore, achieved complete control' of my material. I am, in fact, unable to write a book in that way. If I knew, from the first, how it would end, I should lose interest in it entirely. I wrote 'Deluge' about as fast as it developed in my own mind, and when three-quarters of it were scribbled down, my ideas as to its conclusion were scarcely more definite than those of the reader would be at the same place.

"I do not advocate this method of composition. It is the only possible one for me, and must be judged by its results. I think it may give additional vitality, both to character and incident. The disadvantages are those of free-will rather than of predestination. But it renders impossible for me to contrive the wickedness which your otherwise too-kindly reviewer attributes to me!"

Some further insights into Fowler Wright's "method of composition" were offered in an interview that one of his sons, Gilbert—who had taken on the role of his literary agent—gave to the Bristol Evening Times in 1930, which includes the following comments:

"The major portion of 'Dawn'....was presented to him [Gilbert] for typing scribbled in pencil in those little books which tradesmen favour for booking down their daily deliveries.

"Another manuscript which he typed himself while in America was delivered in paper of three different sizes.

"'Other people have to suffer for his chaotic ways,' his son complained, "and no one more than I. His novels emerge from a vast sea of confusion, though he swears he could put his hand on anything if only people wouldn't dust.'"

M.J.'s was not the only review to which Fowler Wright responded. He also took exception to a piece by Vera Brittain published in the 9 December 1927 issue of *Time & Tide*, which contrasted *Deluge* with *The War of the Worlds*, arguing that Wells

> "...has always regarded humanity as barely emerging from a barbarism to which only a few great souls rise superior, while Mr. Wright considers mankind over-civilised and forcibly expresses his objection to such human achievements as medical science, tarred roads, motor-bicycles, feminism and coal-mines. He would have us all return to what he would doubtless call the Golden Age, but which the philosopher Thomas Hobbes more graphically described as a State of Nature, in which the life of man was "solitary, poore, nasty, brutish and short."

Wright's reply, printed in the 26 December 1927 issue, reads:

> "It would not occur to me to make any comment upon a purely literary criticism, even though I might differ from its conclusions, but your reviewer has attributed opinions to myself which the book does not contain, and which I do not hold.
> "To criticise a defective garment is not to advocate nudity, and so far is 'Deluge' from advocating Thomas Hobbes's State of Nature, that it represents the reconstruction of the social order as an urgent and difficult problem, which has been quickly recognised, even by many among the survivors who have no skill to contrive it.
> "It is a minor point that the book does not contain any 'objection' to the 'achievements of medical science' such as your reviewer attributes to it, and which is really little less than a random accusation of lunacy.
> "Incidentally, 'medical science' is an expression which the book does not contain, and which I should be very unlikely to use. I might write of medical knowledge, skill, practice, or theory, but 'science' is

a cant word, used in many arbitrary, confused, or dishonest ways, and is instinctively avoided by those who value precision of thought and speech."

Brittain was as annoyed by this response as Fowler Wright had been by her review, and she took full advantage of the opportunity provided by the magazine's editor to refute the criticisms, but Fowler Wright claimed the last word in the preface that he wrote for the Harrap edition of *Deluge*.

In considering other immediate responses to *Deluge*, it is most profitable to concentrate on those which attempted to assess its place within the tradition of British scientific romance and which offer clues to its subsequent influence therein.

One reviewer of particular significance in the development of scientific romance was Edward Shanks, author of *The People of the Ruins*, who had continued to champion the genre's cause. He was delighted by Fowler Wright's success, having reviewed *Deluge* enthusiastically in the *London Mercury*; in an article he wrote for the 13 January 1932 issue of *John o'London's Weekly* on "The Fifty Best Novels Since the War" he lauded it as "much the best example since the war of the kind of book that Mr. H. G. Wells used to write", bracketing it in his discussion with Olaf Stapledon's *Last and First Men*. Shanks also wrote a long and glowing review of *Dawn* for *John o'London's Weekly*, which concluded with the observation that: "Mr. Fowler Wright has left himself plenty of room for continuation, and it will be a thousand pities, it will leave one reader at least bitterly disappointed, if he does not make use of it. I might be satisfied with two more books—but I am not sure of that."

Another sometime writer of imaginative fiction who liked the book was Clemence Dane. She commented on the affinity between *Deluge* and *After London* in her review in the women's magazine *Eve* (in which Fowler Wright was later to publish two stories), and her column also found an affinity between Fowler Wright and J. D. Beresford. Another (anonymous) review commenting on the affinity between Fowler Wright and Beresford appeared in the *Inverness Courier* on 31 July 1928; its writer referred specifically to Beresford's *A World of Women*, a disaster story originally published as *Goslings* in 1913.

Deluge made a deeper impression on Storm Jameson, who reviewed it extensively and enthusiastically in the 5 May 1928 issue of *London Calling*, likening it to Cicely Hamilton's *Theodore Savage*—a book which, she says, "haunted me for weeks". The review ends with a hypothetical question: "Whom, of all the men you know, including milkmen and furniture removers, would you choose as a husband, if you were compelled by the survivors of a new *Deluge* to make a choice?" In *The World Ends* (1937), which she published under the pseudonym William Lamb, Jameson describes the inundation of Britain by a flood so similar to that in *Deluge* that it can be assumed to be the same one, and imposes the requirement of making such a choice, albeit a far more narrow one, upon the daughter of a Yorkshire farmer—who is, so far as anyone in the novel knows, the only fertile female left in the world. The decision the girl eventually makes, albeit by default, is at least as controversial as the ending of *Deluge*, and must surely have been calculated to contrive exactly that effect.

The very numerous American reviews of *Deluge* were more obviously mixed than the English ones, and those which objected to the book did so more violently—as might be expected, given that it was a product of the Hearst organization as well as the fact that its ending could easily be considered morally suspect; Llewellyn Jones, in the *Chicago Evening Post*, headlined his review "Lots of Water and a Little Bigamy". Interestingly, robust defenses of the challenging nature of the conclusion could be found in unsigned reviews in the *Christian Science Monitor* and the *Jewish Record*. Although the writer to whom Fowler Wright was most often compared in these reviews was H. G. Wells, a few of them did observe the kinship with pulp fiction of which many of its readers would have been aware.

* * * * * * *

It might be as well, before briefly considering the influence of *Deluge* within the tradition of British scientific romance, to glance at the most succinct summary of its themes that its author wrote as non-fiction. This was a brief article entitled "Science—Destroyer of Life" which appeared in the *Daily Mirror* on 5 July 1933, having been written while he was in America observing the filming of the novel. Its conclusion is:

> "Year by year, our boasted progress becomes more and more the development of rapid motions which are about the most useless and aimless of all human activities. We may remember that the Gadarene swine experimented in the same way. Let us hope that we are doing so to a different end.
>
> "But of one thing we may be sure. Civilisations may perish, but the human race will go on.

"It is even possible that, in the Creator's sight, it might not be a final calamity if the scattered survivors of poison-powders and poison-gas should be exterminated in no distant generation by a simple and more virile race (the victims protesting in a plaintive bewilderment that they had all been sent to the best schools), and the seas be clean again from the spreading of poisonous oil, and the blackened earth be green again with a new hope, and the horrors of flat and tenement, coal smoke and repetition work fade out even from the nightmares of men—and there might be a Merry England again."

Although we may be certain of *Deluge*'s direct influence on Storm Jameson's *The World Ends*, any attempt to offer a more elaborate account of its influence on the subsequent development of British scientific romance can only be speculative—as, for that matter, is any account of the influences acting upon it. It seems highly likely that Fowler Wright read and was greatly impressed by *After London*, but we do not know that for sure.

Sam Moskowitz, a relentless pursuer of hypothetical influences, alleges in his study of Fowler Wright that *Deluge* must have prompted John Collier to write the post-catastrophe novel *Tom's a-Cold* (known in the USA as *Full Circle*). This may well be true, although Collier's novel is so very obviously influenced by *After London* that it almost qualifies as a sequel to it, and it is conceivable that Collier was merely emboldened by *Deluge*'s success to write something that he had had in mind for a long time.

Another writer whose work is very similar in spirit to that of Jefferies and Collier, who may also have been encouraged by Fowler Wright's example, was the Scottish writer J. Leslie Mitchell, who produced a nostalgic prehistoric fantasy, *Three Go Back* (1932), and a lyrical post-catastrophe novel *Gay Hunter* (1934). The second novel is strongly reminiscent of *Deluge* in several ways, not least in its use of a proto-feminist heroine. These two Mitchell novels are companion-pieces, which view the future and the past in very similar terms, as identical phases in a potentially-eternal cycle. Fowler Wright was not to make this explicit in his own work until he formulated the futuristic *Spiders' War* as a sequel to the prehistoric fantasy *Dream*, but the ideological kinship between *The Amphibians* and *Deluge* must have been obvious enough to anyone who read both books, and the pattern was repeated not merely in *Dream* but also in the climax of *The Island of Captain Sparrow*.

Even if Mitchell had not read any of these novels, John Gloag certainly had, and he went on to make very explicit use of the idea that the distant past and distant future would be indistinguishable from one another in the short stories "Pendulum" and "The Slit" (both collected in *It Makes a Nice Change*, 1938) and the novels *Sacred Edifice* (1937) and *99%* (1944). Gloag's most effective novel of the benign destruction of civilization is, however, the wonderfully ironic satire *The New Pleasure* (1933), in which a drug that restores the human species' atrophied sense of smell allows the people of England to realize that civilization, quite literally, stinks.

One relatively prolific writer of scientific romance who does not seem to have been intimately acquainted with the works of his contemporaries was Stephen Southwold, who wrote his scientific romances under the pseudonyms "Miles" and "Neil Bell". His savagely sarcastic post-catastrophe novel *The Lord of Life* (1933) has some elements in common with *Deluge*, but they are most likely the result of coincidental speculation along similar lines.

Oddly enough, one major writer of scientific romances between the wars whose outlook seems, at first glance, not to overlap Fowler Wright's to any great extent was his one-time protégé, Olaf Stapledon. Despite the lack of any very obvious connection, however, *Last and First Men* does attempt to tackle Fowler Wright's two central theses regarding the effect of technological civilization on human capability and morale. The speculative train of thought generated by those questions in Stapledon's work eventually arrived at conclusions that Fowler Wright never considered in detail, but it seems likely that the future history that Fowler Wright began to map out in *The New Gods Lead* took certain cues from *Last and First Men*, in much the same way that Stapledon had taken cues from *The World Below*. Although the dialogue between the works of the two writers is by no means tightly focused, it is certainly real.

An ambivalent attitude to the destruction of civilization was not, of course, something that Fowler Wright had invented, and the kind of success that *Deluge* had in England is a testament to the number of people who were predisposed to be sympathetic towards it. The same combination of distaste for civilization and lyrical love of the countryside can be found in numerous works that were almost certainly not influenced by its example, including T. H. White's *Gone to Ground* (1935), Frank Baker's *The Birds* (1936), and D. E. Stevenson's *The Empty World* (1936). On the other hand, *The Machine Stops* (1936) by "Wayland Smith" (Victor Bayley)—which was published by Fowler Wright's long-time editor Robert Hale, who worked with Fowler Wright at Jarrolds before founding his own company—*Three Men Make a World* (1939) by "Andrew Marvell" (Howell Davies), *A Common Enemy* (1941) by J. D. Beresford, and the title-story of *The Great Fog and Other Weird Tales* (1944) by Gerald Heard probably do qualify as its lineal descendants.

Given that Fowler Wright was virtually forgotten by the time the Second World War ended, it would be overly ambitious to search for further direct influences of *Deluge* thereafter, but it is worth noting that British fiction of this kind became more and more popular after 1945, extending through the work of John Wyndham (especially *The Kraken Wakes*, 1953) and his imitators (especially John Bowen's *After the Rain*, 1958) to the work of J. G. Ballard (especially *The Drowned World*, 1962) and Ballard's admirers (especially Christopher Priest's tales of the Dream Archipelago, first collected in *An Infinite Summer*, 1979).

All of this catastrophist fiction is marked by a profound ambivalence, which almost seems to qualify as a distinctive, if not quite definitive, element of the twentieth-century English *volksgeist*. Perhaps Fowler Wright did no more than tap into that *volksgeist* and add one more voice to its inspirational chorus—but if so, *Deluge* certainly qualifies as a key note in the unfolding cantata.

Before concluding discussion of *Deluge* it ought to be mentioned that the most curious response of all to the book came from Sir Arthur Conan Doyle, who was nearing the end of his life at the time of publication. Doyle wrote to Fowler Wright saying that he had long had it in mind to write exactly such a story, and that the only means by which Fowler Wright could have got hold of the idea was that the spirits with whom Doyle was in frequent communication had transmitted it to him. Doyle did not appear to be unduly troubled by the idea that "his" plot was lost, but was very worried by the possibility that other people had access to "his" spirits. Fowler Wright, considering the letter to be fatuous nonsense, put it aside, but temptation proved too much for his son Gilbert, who quoted the letter in a satirical piece for the *Sunday Express*. Doyle was infuriated and threatened to sue for breach of copyright if Fowler Wright would not apologize. Fowler Wright declined, thinking that no fault was his, and the case went to court, where Doyle won damages. Doyle did, however, send Fowler Wright an inscribed copy of *Pheneas Speaks* (1927), in the hope of persuading the skeptic that the original letter had been perfectly sensible. Fowler Wright was later to include malicious sideswipes at Pheneas and his disciples in several works.

* * * * * * *

The success of *Deluge* opened a new world of opportunity to Fowler Wright, which he needed desperately in order to combat the effects of his bankruptcy. He must, however, already have completed his third fantastic novel before the new phase in his career began, because it appeared very quickly in America, in time to catch the wave of publicity stirred up by *Deluge*. This was *The Island of Captain Sparrow*, and, although it was by no means as well-received as *Deluge*, it did add some momentum to the new career on which he was forced to embark. It was published in Britain by Gollancz and was eventually reprinted as an early Penguin book. The new phase in his writing began in 1929, reflected in print when Collins issued *The World Below*. Fowler Wright initially seems to have thought that he might make some money out of his own publishing endeavors—or, at least, that he ought to continue the while he still could—because he issued several books under his own imprint in 1929, including the paperback pamphlet *Police and Public*.

The last-named project revealed that, like H.G. Wells before him, Fowler Wright had ambitions to become a twentieth-century sage as well as a speculative writer, whose opinions on social matters would be respected. Other titles that he optimistically announced for future publication were "The Problems of Motor Traffic"; "The Case Against Birth Control"; "The Safeguarding of Industries"; "The Ethics of Taxation"; "The Votes of Women"; and "The Channel Tunnel". He concluded this list with "etc, etc,", but the financial viability of his private press was already under threat. He never got the chance to ride these various hobby-horses in public. *Police and Public* was contentious enough to be controversial, but soon slipped into oblivion, like the pamphlets that Arthur Conan Doyle was issuing on behalf of the spiritualist cause.

Of more significance financially was the fact that the success of *Deluge* enabled Fowler Wright to begin selling short stories to the popular magazines of the day. Not unnaturally, his early tales were all fantastic in character. One of the most important, "The Choice: an Allegory of Blood and Tears", appeared in the upmarket women's magazine *Eve* in the issue for 3 April 1929. The magazine was subsequently combined with another as *Eve and Britannia*, and Fowler Wright published another striking story there in the August 1929 issue: "P.N. 40—and Love". The latter story also appeared in the American *Red Book* magazine in the same year. *Weird Tales* also published two Fowler Wright stories in 1929: "The Rat" and "Automata". These and later stories were eventually to make up the contents of the important collection *The New Gods Lead* (1932), but the window of opportunity did not stay open for long.

As soon as Fowler Wright became dependent on his writing income he made every effort to diversify his output. In 1930, alongside *Dawn*, he published the first of his historical novels, *Elfwin*, and the first of his crime stories, *The King Against Anne Bickerton*—the latter under the Sydney Fowler pseudonym. In 1931 he published his novel of contemporary life *Seven Thousand in Israel* and the first of his prehistoric fantasies, *Dream*, as well as three more crime novels. Even if *Elfwin* and *The King Against Anne Bickerton* had been wholly or partly written before the bankruptcy, as seems likely, there can be no doubt that Fowler Wright—who was already into his late fifties by this time—was a man of astonishing energy. His subsequent productivity certainly did not help his reputation, but he cared very little about that. He was undoubtedly pleased to have an audience to hear him, but he was determined to hold his own course in deciding what to offer them. He was prepared to pander to popular taste in mass-producing crime novels, but only to make sure that he could take risks with the commercial appeal of his other books. Given this, it is not surprising that his celebrity began to fade; he had no sooner burst spectacularly upon the literary scene than he became so familiar as to begin to attract a certain contempt. While he enjoyed his brief span as a luminary, though, he seized his chance to scatter what light he could.

Unfortunately for his hopes, none of the works that he published in 1929 and 1930 won Fowler Wright anything like the kind of praise that *Deluge* had attracted. His celebrity was still sufficient in 1931 for him to be recruited to the effort of promoting a book called *Red Ike* by J. M. Denwood (known in the USA as *Under the Brutchstone*)—which appeared as a collaboration, although Fowler Wright merely edited the somewhat rough-hewn text and added an introduction—but the publisher's attempt to boost the book to bestseller status with heavy advertising did not work. 1931 was Fowler Wright's most productive year, but not one of his novels of that year was successful in commercial terms, even though *The Hanging of Constance Hillier* is one of the best of his crime stories. From then on, his career went downhill all the way, and the fact that he contrived to be so prolific in his publications over such a long period of time is a reflection of ever-increasing desperation and the necessity to make what money he could. It is against that background that the remainder of his scientific romances need to be seen and assessed.

The Island of Captain Sparrow and *Dream*

Fowler Wright claimed of both *The Amphibians* and *Deluge* that he was more interested in telling a tale than delivering a message, but was not entirely convincing in his claim. In *The Island of Captain Sparrow*, however, he is much more obviously at ease, making up his story without bothering to include too many didactic asides. The novel tells the story of Charlton Foyle, who escapes from a ship when his life is in danger to become a castaway on an unknown island. As is customary with Fowler Wright, we are told little about this hero, save that he has been traveling the world aimlessly, "avoiding the death to which a dozen doctors had doomed him, yet not gaining the health without which life is of dubious value". Despite this remark, he seems fit enough as he undertakes his strenuous adventure on the island, and it seems probable that his malaise is of a spiritual kind.

The island on which Foyle finds himself has several groups of inhabitants, the most important being the descendants of members of the crew of the pirate Andrew Sparrow, who were left to guard the island as his base when he set out on a last voyage from which he never returned. This gang is led by Sparrow's son Jacob, who is an old man by the time Foyle arrives. A more active force in the affairs of this strange group of degenerates is Jacob's bestial son Nichodemus, or "Demers". The pirates have made a treaty with the people who were already on the island when they arrived: a small relic of some ancient ante-Diluvian civilization (possibly Atlantis), which is based in the temple of Gir. Unknown to the pirates, their arrival on the island has spelled the doom of this society, for they have imported diseases to which the Atlanteans have no resistance. By the time Foyle arrives on the island, only a single priest and his immediate family remain in the temple, though the pirates do not know this.

The feral inhabitants of the island are very strange. They include a population of fierce giant birds, which are apparently under the control of the Atlanteans, and which must occasionally be placated by the pirates with gifts of food. There is also a population of non-sentient humanoids formed like the satyrs of Greek mythology, which are protected from the pirates under the terms of their treaty with the priests, save for periodic hunts, when one may be killed.

Foyle finds evidence in the caves that lead from the cliffs surrounding the island to its lush interior that he is not the first castaway to reach the island in recent years, but the fate of these other visitors remains unclear until he finds one of them—a young girl—

living naked, wild and free in the forest. She is a fugitive, keeping her existence secret from the pirates, who believe her to be dead. She and Foyle hold a long conversation in the darkness, and decide that they must escape together.

Their plan goes wrong when the girl, Marcelle, tries to steal some clothing and is captured by the pirates. Jacob Sparrow plans a wedding for his son, who is temporarily absent on a satyr-hunt, and Marcelle pretends to agree in order to avoid betraying Foyle. The ritual feast following the hunt is to be attended by the priest of Gir, and this provides the dramatic climax of the book, as Foyle comes to claim Marcelle and violence breaks out, with the great birds coming to the aid of the minority.

Curiously, this climax is described from the viewpoint of the priest, who is quite without emotion and—we are told—as "remote as a god". There is, in consequence, a cool clinicality about the description, which is very close to the tone of *The Amphibians*, and a cursory quality reminiscent of the final, synoptic chapters of the second part of *The World Below*. In the end, Foyle and Marcelle flee across the island, pursued by Demers. They have the priest's child, the last of his race, with them. Foyle kills Demers but is badly wounded, and the two take refuge in the empty temple. When they are eventually ready to attempt to escape the island again, they find that their plan has been pre-empted: the remaining pirates have taken Foyle's boat. They are the sole inheritors of the island, and Marcelle will bring Foyle into her way of life rather than vice versa. The implication is that this is the only truly happy ending that could have been devised.

The Island of Captain Sparrow is basically an escapist dream-fantasy—the story of a hard-won refuge from the world, which becomes for its inheritors a substitute Garden of Eden, at least insofar as it offers an opportunity for life to be lived naturally. The play with ambiguous characters, half-human and half-animal, relates *The Island of Captain Sparrow* to Wells's *The Island of Dr. Moreau*, but the underlying ideas are very different. Whereas Wells's Prendick is forced into a horrified retreat as the beast-men begin to revert to their animal nature, Fowler Wright expels from his island the degenerate humans whose "animality" is the residue of culture. The satyrs, although they are far from harmless, are allowed to remain because they are morally innocent, but Demers—who bears the stigmata of human satyriasis—is destroyed. In this way, the argument initially set out in *Deluge* is amplified into a curiously enigmatic parable.

It is doubtful that Fowler Wright consciously set out to write such a parable—he would surely have made the story's "message" more explicit had he actually had it in mind from the outset. Nevertheless, the implication of the dream-fantasy is not too difficult to follow. Buried beneath the surface of the adventure is the same tacit championship of nature against culture that re-appears consistently in Fowler Wright's work, at varying levels of explicitness.

At the end of *The Island of Dr. Moreau*, Prendick is driven by his experiences to become a kind of priest of science, taking comfort in the peaceful contemplation of cosmology as if it were a kind of transcendence of his own bestial heritage—his fleshiness. Fowler Wright despised this kind of retreat into objective intellectualism. His hero is lured back into a state of nature by what is effectively a glamorous nature-spirit (Marcelle is called a dryad in the chapter which introduces her), eventually to find fulfillment in freedom from the corrupting effects of civilization.

Marcelle was the prototype for a whole series of Fowler Wright heroines, although it might be argued that she is herself no more than a new version of the narrator's Amphibian companion in *The Amphibians*. She retains something of the character of Claire Arlington, being strong, capable and decisive, but she has another side to her as well as her merely human attributes. When she first speaks to Foyle she is invisible, although he has glimpsed her previously. When she last speaks to him she is again invisible, leading him into the wilderness with a tempting, mocking voice. She is similar in many respects to Rima, the heroine of W. H. Hudson's *Green Mansions*, but her robustness makes her importantly different. Fowler Wright's characterization of nature is different from Hudson's in exactly the same way: Hudson was a determined Romantic, and perhaps the first prophet of modern ecological mysticism, but Fowler Wright knew well enough that natural life is tough.

There is a sense in which *The Island of Captain Sparrow* is less pessimistic than many of the author's works, but it should be remembered that it is manifestly a dream-fantasy, and must not be reckoned too closely akin to *Deluge*, or even *The Amphibians*. Fowler Wright knew that it was only in dreams that civilized men could throw off the shackles of culture and retreat into the bosom of nature; most of his heroes must do what they can with much more severely restricted opportunities.

* * * * * * *

It is worth mentioning *en passant* that one of the Sydney Fowler potboilers that Fowler Wright published in 1931, *The Bell Street Murders*, includes a science-fictional element, presenting the story of an inventor who devises a coating which, when applied to a screen, will allow the screen to record visual impressions from its surroundings. These impressions may be recalled by a watcher at any time if the watcher can summon up a mental image of the first scene of the sequence to act as a trigger. This highly unlikely device becomes the sole "witness" to the murder of the inventor, and those trying to figure out who killed him must discover the appropriate trigger signal to make the screen divulge its information.

The Bell Street Murders is not impressive, as a crime story or as a marginal scientific romance, but Fowler Wright was obviously somewhat taken with the villain of the piece, because he later wrote two sequels featuring further adventures of the same adversary: *The Secret of the Screen* (1933) and *Who Murdered Reynard?* (1947). Neither of these has any speculative content. More importantly, *The Bell Street Murders* introduced, in a very minor role, a solicitor named Jellipot, who played a rather larger part in *The Secret of the Screen* and went on from there to much higher things. He was to feature alongside the investigating police officer, Inspector Combridge, in many other novels, quickly establishing himself as the star performer. In fact, Mr. Jellipot helped Fowler Wright to find a *via media* between his desire to write crime stories of a moderately realistic kind and his intense dislike of the police; the solicitor is permitted to provide the intelligence and acuity necessary to identify and outwit criminals, while the inspector's men do the legwork.

The two novels that Fowler Wright published under his full name in 1931 were certainly not calculated to win wide popularity. Both, on the surface at least, are remarkably arid and pessimistic. *Seven Thousand in Israel*, his only attempt at a serious contemporary novel, deals with various moral crises facing its protagonist John Oakley before and after his bankruptcy. The quasi-autobiographical story is relentlessly downbeat, curiously interrupted by occasional passages where the author talks directly to the reader about what he is doing, asking rhetorical questions about the pace of the story and wondering whether the various twists of the plot are sensible. This awkward self-consciousness left no doubt that Fowler Wright was very uneasy in the writing of the story; he seems in the reflective passages to be almost conscience-stricken about the fact that the plot proceeds so bleakly and ends so nihilistically. Like Martin Webster at the end of *Dawn*, Fowler Wright appears to have felt rather guilty about his own tendency to despair, but obviously found it just as difficult as any of his exemplary characters to pull himself out of the slough of despond.

A similar tendency to despair is a key feature of the character of Marguerite Leinster, the heroine of *Dream; or, The Simian Maid*. She, however, responds to this fatalistic depression by seeking escape in lucid dreams, which are conjured up for her by a "magician"—a scientist who can send her consciousness through time to experience other lives, who might have started out as the same individual as the Professor featured in *The Amphibians*. Marguerite has already visited Atlantis and Babylon, and now wishes to go even further back, into a genuinely primitive era.

When her wish is granted she finds herself incarnate as a tree-dwelling furry primate. She is the only one of her own species who appears in the story, but there are other races co-existing with hers of whom we see rather more. There are the "cave-people", much more human in appearance, who have more elaborate tools and a more developed language than her kind. There are also the Ogpurs, a savage and degraded race. Despite the cultural advantages enjoyed by the cave-people, the person Marguerite has become—who is called Rita—considers that her own kind are a "higher" species. The Ogpurs—a "mongrel race"—are considered the lowest of the low; they, the author suggests, must be the ancestors of modern men.

Marguerite is followed into her dream by two other people, who have tracked her to the magician's lair. One is Stephen Cranleigh, who is ambitious to marry her. The other is Cranleigh's sister Elsie, who is worried about her brother. They become the cave-people Stele and Elsyà, sent abroad from their own land in search of a mate for Stele. They are drawn into a strange collusion with Rita, eventually emerging with her into an isolated valley connected to the outer world by a dangerous cave-system. The king who rules this valley and its people lives a peculiar double life, also being king of a tribe outside the valley. His outer lands are menaced by creatures like giant rats, which are swarming across the continent, and his subjects within the valley are fomenting rebellion. There are ominous matters of family politics to be settled before the fate of the three strangers can be settled, but Elsya is married to the king's son and Stele is torn between the king's daughter and Rita.

In the end, Stele and Rita try to reach one another in the caves, but cannot, and die on opposite sides of a stone wall, able only to touch by means of a very narrow breach. This frustrating ending seems to be symbolic of something in the relationship of Stephen Cranleigh and Marguerite Leinster once they have returned to their own world. He is insistent that he will marry her, but her final response to his demand, in the line which closes the book, is distinctly ambiguous as to her feelings and her intentions.

Dream is, of course, not to be construed as an attempt to represent actual conditions of prehistory deduced from paleontological evidence. It does not belong to the tradition of H. G. Wells's "A Story of the Stone Age", J. H. Rosny the elder's *La Guerre du Feu*, and Johannes V. Jensen's *The Long Journey*. Nor is it a moral fantasy like J. Leslie Mitchell's *Three Go Back* or William Golding's *The Inheritors*, both of which use the supposed fatal confrontation between Neanderthal man and our Cro-Magnon ancestors to draw conclusions about the essential nature of modern man. *Dream* does carry certain moral implications of this kind, but they are subdued and incidental. The novel has more in common with *The Island of Captain Sparrow*, in that it is a dream-fantasy whose heroine is part human and part nature-spirit, but it also has ideative links with *The World Below*, in presenting an argument about the continuity of nature and the principles on which the natural world operates, regardless of the presence or absence of man. There is a kind of glorification of the struggle for existence—but again, not strictly in Darwinian terms.

In one way *Dream* is much more pessimistic than *The Island of Captain Sparrow*. Inside the dream, the protagonists all die. There is no haven for them there, not even in the valley isolated by cliffs and caves. It is to the real world that they must return in order to live their lives—and that will be difficult, for Marguerite at least, because there is a very vital sense in which she is not, and never can be, at home there; she simply does not belong there.

Perhaps inevitably, Fowler Wright picked up where the inconclusive ending of *Dream* left off and wrote a sequel, although circumstances forced that novel to be represented in print in a different way—thus encouraging the author, much later in life, to write a second and slightly different sequel. In this instance, it is more convenient to discuss the sequels in the chronological order of their appearance rather than grouping them together—unlike *The World Below* and *Dawn*, they were probably not extracts lifted from pre-existent works, but separate endeavors composed close to the time of their appearance.

The New Gods Lead **and** *Power*

All Fowler Wright's longer scientific romances, from *The Amphibians* to *Dream*, take the reader into worlds remote from our own, into circumstances which—one way or another—are much more primitive, where the laws of nature (as Fowler Wright saw them) hold much more obvious dominion. His shorter stories written in the same period, however, follow the opposite tack: they take the reader into worlds that are less primitive, where culture has overwhelmed nature and obliterated its rule. Although the same philosophy is clearly present, the imagery of the short stories is strikingly different from the imagery of the speculative novels.

Ten short stories are gathered together in the collection *The New Gods Lead* (1932). Seven of these are grouped together under the heading "Where the New Gods Lead" while the other three are simply headed "Also". It is not entirely clear why "Appeal" is included in the main sequence, given that it is a conspicuously trivial story, which does not bear on the same issues as the rest, but the probability is that Fowler Wright considered that the seven stories might be seen as referring to a common future history, and "Appeal" is there simply because—unlike "The Rat", which is excluded, in spite of being much more in tune ideologically with the rest of the set—it does not contradict anything in the other six.

The best of the stories in the book constitute what is perhaps the most vitriolic vision of the future ever produced; they have an imaginative savagery of tone and content that is quite unparalleled. All of Fowler Wright's preoccupations and anxieties regarding the march of progress are subjected therein to bitterly sarcastic extrapolation.

"Justice" concerns the effects of a law passed in 1966 to establish a scale of penalties for the killing of persons by careless motorists. In the interests of rationality, the penalties depend on the age of the person killed, being greater according to the expectation of life of which the victims are deprived. By this time, the continued use of birth control has resulted in a population in which very many people are old, and the fact that the law has been altered to make the killing of old people effectively free of penalty had its inevitable consequence: in 1972 there is a massacre of the ancient and enfeebled, in which hundreds of thousands perish.

"This Night", set in the year 1980, is the story of an unorthodox courtship mounted by a technocratic scientist, which takes the form of emotionless blackmail. As it happens, he fails to have his evil way, but only because of an accident of fate. The overall shape of this developing future is indicated here:

> "There had been a time, in the earlier part of the century, when the world had awakened to the fact that the advances in scientific knowledge threatened the destruction of the race—were even putting the power of that destruction into any ignorant or crimi-

nal hand which might be disposed to use it... The scientists had replied that the pursuit of knowledge could not by stayed, but that the remedy lay in restricting the circulation of that which would be dangerous in unworthy hands. Laws had been passed to this end, and in twenty years they had borne such fruit that the scientists had become a caste who were above the obligations of their fellows and beyond their laws. They had resurrected a forgotten tongue, which only the elect among them were allowed to learn, and in which their records were kept. No one had more than a vague conception of what their knowledge had become, or the power it gave them. So they ruled by a great fear." (*The Throne of Saturn*, p. 24)

"Brain" carries this fragmentary future history forward to 1990, a few months after the suppression of a rebellion when "the last traditions of barbarism had gone down". Now the technocracy is quite secure and one Professor Brisket is its President. He is planning to secure absolute power for himself, having discovered various substances that can either augment the intellectual power of the brain or instill a slave-like docility. Unfortunately, his plan misfires because over-hastiness in testing his brain stimulant leads him to overlook the fact that the augmentation of intelligence is followed by a corollary encouragement of altruism. Display of this altruism, of course, leads to his instant removal from authority—nothing could be more out of place in a technocracy.

The temporal sequence of the stories is then broken. "Appeal", set in the year 1950, is the story of a trial in which the crucial evidence is that of the murder victim, recalled by means of a spiritualist medium. "Proof" is the ironic story of the French Revolution of 1984, which leads to the setting up of a eugenic tribunal charged with sending the inefficient and the inadequate to the guillotine. The plot describes some subtle and absurd test-cases, which are invoked in order to prove the wisdom of the revolution and to decide who should be its victims.

A great leap forward in time then takes the future history into the ninety-third year of the Eugenic Era. "P.N. 40" tells the story of a rebellion by two love-struck individuals against the laws of their orderly and rational society, where marriage and childbirth are strictly regulated. The eponymous heroine is a characteristic Fowler Wright invention, decisive and daring, and it is this that allows her to formulate a plan by means of which she and 48 V.C. can escape from the doomed society in order to take their chances in a perilous chaos, in which they might or might not be able to find a safe haven.

The last of the "New Gods" sequence is "Automata", which is not so much a story as a philosophical commentary on man's use of machines, foreseeing the slow usurpation of all human activity and privilege by mechanical devices. The first section is an imaginary address delivered to a meeting of the British Association, and is straightforward exposition:

> "The humility of science will hesitate to prophesy the detailed incidence of that which may be foreseen in its inevitable outline, but it may not be a too-rash guess that the industrial workman and the domestic servant will be the first to disappear from their places in the national life. Some few may remain for generations, even for centuries. But is it reasonable to suppose that the nation will continue altruistically to support the persons and families of industrial workers who are no longer needed? For themselves there may be some generous provision to avert the euthanasia which would be the evident economic expedient for the aged horse, or the dog of which a woman has grown tired, but would it be tolerable that we should allow the propagation of their useless children?" (p. 116)

The remaining sections of the story observe the unfolding of this hypothesis. In the first, middle-aged matrons gather to drink tea and compare notes on their automatic children. The preferability of machines to men is already abundantly evident to them:

> "There is a difference between the greatest man and the simplest machine which can never be bridged, and our highest wisdom is to observe it with reverence and humility. It is not a difference in degree, but in kind. We act from confused and contradictory impulses, but they with the inevitability of universal law. In a word, we are human and they divine." (p. 120)

In the final scene, the last man in the world reviews his situation as he fails to complete the task assigned to him, and then goes quietly to his inevitable fate; to be scrapped:

> "He knew that he ought to move...he knew that the oiler would be here in a few minutes to caress and comfort the joints and bearings of his companions.... Yet he sat still, wondering...The door opened, and an automaton entered. It was one of those which still bore a vague resemblance to humanity, the pattern of the first designers not having been entirely abandoned. It was thus that the human race might leave the impress of its passing flicker of life for a million years—perhaps for ever—as a mollusc may leave its fossil imprint in the enduring rock." (p. 125)

Although the other three stories in the collection are excluded from the main group, they are not dissimilar in spirit. "The Rat" is perhaps Fowler Wright's best short story, and has been widely reprinted. It concerns the discovery of a serum of immortality by an inconspicuous country doctor, who proves its efficacy by rejuvenating an aged rat and then falls to contemplating the effects of using it on his patients. He hesitates when he realizes that he must be prepared to immortalize the evil as well as the good, the mean as well as the generous. As his pondering extends, he finds that the long-term implications of his discovery very frightening. Life will be transformed once the balancing factor of death is banished from human affairs, and it will not be transformed for the better. Even when he considers his own particular case, he realizes that there is only a limited sense in which he can restore his youth, and that the prospect of living for a thousand years has its horrific aspect as well as its attractive one. He resolves to bury his discovery, but learns to his cost that new things can be as difficult to destroy as they are to create. There is not the same sarcastic exaggeration in this story as in the stories of the main sequence, nor does the author seem quite so certain of his own moral ground. Both these things work to the advantage of the story, and it is the most eloquent of them all.

The second of the three stories outside the main group, "Rule", is a rather frivolous political satire in which a government elected on a platform of reckless promises cements its position by manipulating popular culture. The idea is an interesting one, but it is not well worked-out in the story. The third and last of the additional stories is, however, a much more important and revealing one. It is a fable that offers the most explicit expression of Fowler Wright's basic philosophical position. In the book it is called simply "The Choice", but, as previously noted, the magazine version had been subtitled "An Allegory of Blood and Tears".

A man and a woman who have suffered a great deal in their lives on Earth are reunited after death in Heaven, thanks to the mercy of God. They settle down to enjoy the rewards of virtue, but find life in Heaven to be pointless in its peacefulness—to be literally soul-destroying. They ask to return to a world fit for people to live in, and God sets squarely before them the prospect they will face:

> "Birth will be a darkness behind and death a darkness before you. You will forget all that you are or have been. You will endure the night of the womb, as your body grows from the current of another's blood, and her thoughts control you; knowing panic when she fears, and causeless joy when she pleasures. You will know the terror of birth when you are cast out with a body which is not yours, but has been made weak or strong by the passions of others. You will live through helpless years under the controls of those who may be foolish or brutal. You will be scourged by the customs of the tribe that breeds you, and enslaved by instincts that you cannot kill, though your mind may hate them. You will know remorse and shame. You will desire things which you cannot reach, or you will find your gains to be worthless. You will know pain that is more dreadful than any sorrow, and sorrow that is more dreadful than any pain. You will do evil to others, and you will suffer evil continually. At the last, you will die miserably, facing the curtain of death without assurance of immortality. For if you go you go blindly." (p. 166)

Even though they know that rebirth will part them, and that they may never meet again, the man and the woman elect to take their chances. The mere heroism of their decision gives the story a superficial appeal that actually undermines the moral message, because one has to think twice about it to realize what a remarkably harsh story it really is. As with many modern fables featuring the Divine Person—those written by T. F. Powys are perhaps the closest analogues—"The Choice" emerges from a peculiar amalgam of skepticism and belief. It is neither the ironic play of the atheist (like

Wells's "A Vision of Judgment") nor the respectful tampering with orthodoxy of a writer who still accepts, fundamentally, the God of the Churchmen (as, for instance, in *The Great Divorce* by C.S. Lewis). In its way, it is more radical than either. Its basic contention is that Christians are wrong to try to balance the sufferings of this world against the rewards of Heaven. Heaven is no proper reward at all, and its presumed peaceful constancy might better be regarded as a kind of purgatory. It is in life, if at all, that we must seek and find what rewards there are to balance out the penalties of pain and misery extracted from human beings by their nature and circumstances. This is a species of Epicureanism, but of a remarkably bleak and pessimistic kind, which echoes once again the message of the preacher Ecclesiastes.

Those who find Fowler Wright a difficult writer to come to terms with may well find "The Choice" the best key to his outlook and personality: a striking combination of an image of the world which is desolate and frightful with a determined refusal to accept despair as logical or necessary in consequence. Fowler Wright was perhaps as ready as any other writer of his generation to find not Jerusalem but Pandemonium in the process of being built in England's green and pleasant land, but he was not ready to forsake that Pandemonium to claim a fake salvation. If Hell was come to Earth, no one had to like it, but it was a man's job to live in it as best he might, and not to accept the softer spiritual options offered by the cowardly imagination.

It seems that Fowler Wright must have turned this argument upon his own predilection for escapist fantasies, because he never provided any of his later works with an idyllic ending like the one he had attached to *The Island of Captain Sparrow*. All his other dream-fantasies are stories of escape *from* Heaven rather than to it.

* * * * * * *

Fowler Wright's new imaginative novel written for publication in 1932 was *Beyond the Rim*, the first and by far the best of the three orthodox "lost race stories" that followed the example set in *The Island of Captain Sparrow*. It is the story of an expedition to the Antarctic, undertaken partly to test the proposition that the world might, after all, be flat, and partly in response to a strange tale told by one Captain Sparshott of his adventures during a previous expedition.

The group, led by soldier-of-fortune Franklin Arden and the heiress Eleanor D'Acre, eventually reach a warm valley dominated by an ancient volcano, isolated from the outside world and reachable (as usual) only via a complicated cave-system. (Freud might have had some comment to make on Fowler Wright's constant fascination with isolated mini-worlds that can only be reached via labyrinthine tunnels, but we know what Fowler Wright thought of Freud.) Living in this valley are the descendants of the survivors of the pilgrim ship *Morning Star*, which left England hoping to reach the New World some three centuries before. Several Puritan families eke out a precarious living from the land. There are God's-Truths, Trustwells, and Cloutsclads. They are led by the excellent Michael God's-Truth, but he is only one member of a council mostly composed of bigoted fools, who contend that the strangers are demons who must be destroyed.

The colony is periodically menaced by the rough-living descendants of cast-out heretics, who are known as Anabaptists, although no one can any longer remember what their actual heresy was, and the elders are still fearful of heresy. The newcomers win the support of Michael God's-Truth by testifying at the trial of his daughter Patience, who is deemed a heretic because she contends that the outer world might not have been destroyed. Arden and his companions testify that in fact it has not, but this offends the other members of the community. There is a climactic battle against the Anabaptists, and then Arden and Eleanor make a desperate bid to escape across the ice, pursued by men from the valley, who will kill them rather than allow the outer world to know of their existence.

Beyond the Rim is a pure adventure story with no overtly didactic content, and as such is oddly effective. It is one of the most conspicuously well-organized of all Fowler Wright's books, maintaining tension throughout and building to an excellent double climax. Eleanor D'Acre and Franklin Arden recapitulate yet again the peculiar relationship typical of so many Fowler Wright couples: he competent yet vacillating, distinctly lacking in some crucial element of resolve; she requiring masculine aid to compensate for physical deficiency, yet possessed of greater strength of character and determination. There is a similar imbalance between the two minor characters in the expedition—Eleanor's cousin Bunford Weldon and her secretary Gwen Collinson—which is so much to the former's disadvantage that Gwen finds a more suitable mate in Michael God's-Truth's son and elects to stay in the primitive haven under the volcano. It was, however, in Fowler Wright's next imaginative novel that he presented his most careful and detailed examination of a relationship between a man and a woman, offering a much more carefully balanced situation for consideration. That novel was *Power*, published in 1933.

Power belongs to a class of stories that became quite common in the 1930s, in which lone inventors come upon discoveries so momentous in their destructive potential as to offer an opportunity to blackmail the entire world. Examples include E. Charles Vivian's *Star Dust* (1925), C. S. Forester's *The Peacemaker* (1934), Francis Beeding's *The One Sane Man* (1934), and S. Andrew Wood's *I'll Blackmail the World* (1935). In each case, a man whose identity is at first concealed demonstrates that he has the power to devastate the world, and then begins to make his demands, which are often rather well-intentioned, usually including the abandonment of war. In such stories the protagonist's ambitions are almost always thwarted; Neil Bell's *The Lord of Life*, published in the same year as *Power*, is one of the very few in which the scientist goes ahead and destroys the world. The best story in this vein—C. S. Forester's—is both scathing and harrowing in its portrayal of a well-meaning but somewhat weak-spirited man who betrays himself to the vengeance of the mob by trying to save his fellow men from the implications of their own collective stupidity.

In setting out to write a novel of this kind, therefore, Fowler Wright was by no means the first or last in the field, and seems to have been aware of the fact that he was working within a nascent tradition. *Power* is not the only novel of the species in which the blackmailer achieves temporary success, but it is the only one that deliberately sets out to examine, carefully and painstakingly, how he might tackle the practical project of achieving political reform even within one country.

The hero of *Power* is Stanley Maitland. He is not a scientist and is not personally responsible for the discovery of the devastating force with which he threatens the world—it comes into his possession when he murders the actual inventor, to save the world from a less altruistic blackmailer than he. The book is basically his story, explaining how he proves to the people of England that he really does have the power to annihilate all life from the land, and how he is thus grudgingly granted the authority to use Parliament to exact such laws as he wishes for a period of one year. It is, however, also the story of his wife, Lady Crystal, who is shocked to the core by his betrayal of party loyalties in taking such unilateral action, and estranges herself from him—perhaps too rapidly, and with ultimately fatal consequences.

Power begins from the same ideological standpoint as *The New Gods Lead*, and the early dialogue between Maitland and the inventor Feltham explains his justification for trying to turn aside the current of history:

"I began to think, and look round, and what I saw was a great civilization drifting to destruction with no leaders at all. Of course, other civilizations have gone down before ours though we don't always know how. I suppose they've been led into the abyss.

"But the curious thing about ours is that it's not being led at all. It's just stumbling on in a blind leaderless self-slavery, and if anyone interferes to lead or guide it, it just shakes him off its back in an impatient irritated way. All the force comes from below. I entered political circles and I found that no one dreams of governing in England today. They listen with their ears to the ground.

"If any governing's done at all, it's in Whitehall, not Westminster. And you get the anomaly there that the men who govern are all controlled by the same fear,—the fear of a blind force, a system to which they are slaves, and which no-one dreams of defying.

"Democracy's got the bit in its teeth, and it dashes on like a bolting horse, boasting of its own speed, and proud of the fact that no-one can rein it in now. It hasn't the faintest idea of where it's going, or why . . .

"We are looking at a civilisation without control, and without the freedom that control gives. We are a nation of slaves, and slaves to a tyrant that we cannot kill, being beyond our reach. Our new rulers are the aggregate folly and the aggregate weakness of mankind. Comfort and cowardice are the new gods." (p. 24-5)

Later in the same dialogue Maitland pins the blame for this lack of control on the march of science, which has become not merely the handmaiden but the actual focal point of this aggregate folly and aggregate weakness. At this stage Maitland seems to see clearly enough what has to be done, but when he actually takes up the reins of power it is a different story; he quickly becomes hesitant and decays slowly towards irresolution. He raises tariff barriers to protect British industry, then lowers some of them again when some firms begin profiteering. He exiles all supporters of birth control and abortion. For one reason or another, though, his plans then grind slowly to a halt.

Partly, it is clear, his hesitancy comes from a lack of support. Although a barrier already existed between himself and his wife (because of her reluctance to have children) her defection is deeply wounding, and even though her sister Jehane, who acts as his secretary, is willing to offer the moral and emotional support that Crystal will not, both are compelled to honor the contract that he has with his wife. Partly, though, the hesitation is not really Maitland's at all, but the author's. Fowler Wright, making up his plot as he went along—as usual—was drawn away from the business of political planning, apparently intimidated by the sheer magnitude of the imaginative task he had set himself. Instead, he allowed *Power* to develop into a kind of thriller not unlike his crime stories. A group of cabinet rebels, who have refused to stay on in Maitland's administration, exploit Crystal's ambivalence to trick her into providing the means to lure Maitland from his safe refuge. He is kidnapped and removed to that clichéd imprisonment beloved of all writers of melodrama—a private lunatic asylum. There he is blackmailed in his turn, as his captors try to take control of his deadly weapon for their own benefit.

The story eventually reaches the kind of climax that is typical of thrillers of the period, dramatic enough in its eventfulness but serving only to disguise the fact that the real issues raised by the book have been conveniently forgotten. Maitland is freed from his enemies, and may presumably still act as a political force even though his weapon is no longer effective, but what he will do with his influence we are not told.

Fowler Wright had set himself a task in *Power* that he believed to be impossible. He did not think that any man really could turn aside the evil march of progress. The real implication of Maitland's speech quoted above is not that the world needs benevolent dictators, but rather that even benevolent dictators could do little to change things. The plot of the novel had to be turned aside, because there really was very little progress it could make in the direction it was initially pointed.

The Vengeance of Gwa and the Future War Trilogy

In the same year that *Power* appeared, Fowler Wright published three other novels. One was his second historical novel, *Lord's Right in Languedoc*, a romance of knightly rivalries set in the time of the crusades. The others were Sydney Fowler novels—the lighthearted *Arresting Delia* and the first of the two sequels to *The Bell Street Murders*, *The Secret of the Screen*. There was then something of a hiatus in his work, and it could be argued that he never managed to pick up the thread thereafter.

Among Fowler Wright's surviving papers there are two five-year diaries covering the years 1933-37 and 1938-42. At the beginning of the former period Fowler Wright could still be reckoned a moderately successful author; although his recent books had not sold as well as his early successes, he was still managing to publish serious work. His *Life of Sir Walter Scott* had appeared in 1932 and other projects dear to his heart must still have seemed to him to be viable. During the five years covered by the first diary, though, things changed very considerably. He began to find it more and more difficult to publish his more ambitious work, and the pattern of his publications changed markedly, moving down-market year by year. His crime stories continued to appear at the usual hasty pace, but his other works began to take on the forms of other kinds of popular thriller. He was still trying to write more ambitious books, but they were not appearing in print.

In the back of the first diary there is a list headed "Books I intend to write if I live these five years 1933-37." The list is a long one and was obviously extended at various times, although even the later titles are marked "1933 ideas"—the first ones were presumably ones he had in mind at the end of 1932. The list is headed by a historical novel about the conquistador Cortés. This was to become Fowler Wright's second major project after *The Song of Arthur*, and he was to labor on it for many years. It was never to sell, but still exists today in a near-complete typescript of 1,199 pages. The second item on the list is a "novel on Mary Stuart", but this was never done; nor was the third item, whose nature is unclear from the one-word title. Of the next half-dozen items—all, apparently, intended as more commercial endeavors—three are sequels to earlier works. *The Secret of the Screen* is one; the second—a "Sea Epic of *Deluge*"— was never written. The third, initially written down as "Sequel to *Dream*" is marked "done 1934" and "*Vengeance of Gwa*". *Vengeance of Gwa* was actually published in 1934 under the pseudonym Anthony Wingrave, and is not represented, in its published form, as a sequel to *Dream*. Given the evidence of the diary, however, it seems that it is actually a further adventure of Marguerite Leinster and her companions, from which the introduction and epilogue were removed—presumably because Harrap rejected it (their cheap edition of *Dream*, published in 1933, probably sold badly), and Thornton Butterworth, who took it, did not want to publish a sequel to a book issued by a rival.

Several other titles on the diary list did eventually materialize as books or stories, though some of them were long-delayed. Other titles marked "done 1933" are *David*, which was published in 1934, and *The Knights of Malta*, which did not appear until 1942 (as *The Siege of Malta*). The former is a novel about the Biblical king—imaginatively "restored", like *The Song of Songs* from the fragmentary account offered in the Old Testament—while the latter is a completion of a novel left unfinished by Sir Walter Scott. It seems, therefore, that, for a while, Fowler Wright turned almost exclusively to the writing and planning of historical romances, although his actual publications did not reflect that intention. Another historical novel he started at this time is marked in the diary as a "story about a witchfinder", but this ended up as a rather unsatisfactory novelette eventually published in 1946.

Apart from the sequel to *Dream*, Fowler Wright apparently planned one other speculative project in 1933; this appears in the list as *The Splendid Curse*, although a subsequent note identifies it with the future-war trilogy he wrote between 1935 and 1937. The exotic adventure story *The Screaming Lake* also appears on the first list, though he did not get around to writing it until 1936. Although this was the second of his lost race stories to see print it seems to have been completed after *The Hidden Tribe*, which was written in 1935 but not published until 1938.

The major reason for the disruption of the plans set out in the diary was that Fowler Wright spent much of 1933 in the USA, making arrangements for *Deluge* to be filmed and hawking all his other works around the studios. The diary records his various meetings. He hit the ground running, finishing his historical novel *Lord's Right in Languedoc* on 27 January, only three days before Gilbert received news of an offer from Worldwide Studios for a $5,000 option to film *Deluge*. He raced to finish *The Secret of the Screen* before the beginning of April so that he could travel to the USA. He first sailed for New York on 29 April, but did not extend that first stay greatly after signing the movie contract on 10 May; he left again on 19 May, but he was already planning to return, and only stayed in England for a matter of weeks. He set sail again on 16 June, having planned a much more elaborate itinerary.

After landing in New York for a second time on 28 June, he embarked on a hectic round of meetings with representatives of Cosmopolitan, to whom he offered *Dream*; Covici-Friede, to whom he offered *Lord's Right in Languedoc, Power*, and his as-yet-unwritten biographical novel about Cortés; and John Day, to whom he also offered *Power*. Nothing came of any of these meetings, although

Cosmopolitan agreed that he could buy back the rights to those books they had already published for $1,000. He also met with a literary agency, with a view to their selling serial rights to his works, but nothing came of that either. In July he traveled to Chicago and then to Hollywood, arriving on the 16th. Although he had written a script for *Deluge* it was not used. He watched the last scenes of the movie being shot and saw a rough cut on the 24th, at which point he immediately began asking for changes. The preview he attended on 8 August distressed him even more; he was particularly annoyed by the fact that the movie had discarded the ending of the book.

While he was in Hollywood, Fowler Wright attempted to sell film rights to various existing works, including *Power* and the stories in *The New Gods Lead*, as well as new projects, including a script for a Biblical romance *Son of David* (based on the projected novel that was to be published in the UK as *David* in 1934). *Son of David* attracted enough interest to persuade him to extend his stay in Hollywood, and he began to look for other scriptwriting work. He talked to representatives of Warner Brothers, Universal, Fox and MGM, and even met with a Disney executive at one point. He agreed to work for Warner on a script entitled *Shanghai Orchid* and for Universal on an adaptation of Robert Louis Stevenson's novella "The Suicide Club", but it all came to nothing. Deeply disillusioned by his failure to make any progress, he eventually left California for New York on 9 October. He sailed for England on the 13th, never to return.

Once back in England, Fowler Wright began submitting proposals to local movie studios, and continued doing so for the next two years, but the only result of his efforts was a film version of his crime novel *Three Witnesses* (1935), made at Twickenham Studios, for which his own script was again discarded, and whose final product he described as a "ghastly mess". Although he finished *David* and made a start on his continuation of on Sir Walter Scott's unfinished novel *The Knights of Malta*, his productivity in 1933 was way down on previous years; on 31 December he tersely summarized his experiences in the following manner: "Year fundamentally relieved by sale of 'Deluge' film rights (film actually ghastly). All other results poor."

The long-anticipated movie version of *Deluge*, directed by Felix. E. Feist, was eventually released by RKO Radio Pictures late in 1933, but when the studio went bankrupt shortly thereafter the scenes depicting the destruction of New York by earthquakes and a tidal wave—the product of some highly effective and very expensive special effects—were sold to another studio for recycling, with the condition attached that the original had to be withdrawn from circulation. This was accomplished so effectively that the film was lost for many years, and was only rediscovered in 1987 when a version dubbed into Italian was found. Although an English-language version was discovered some years later in the French national cinema archive, it remains unavailable to the public. The meteoric history of the film version is ironically mirrored in the pattern of Fowler Wright's literary career, which had brought him brief fame and one moment of spectacular success, followed by a slow descent into total obscurity after 1933.

Although Fowler Wright instructed his children not to see the movie version of *Deluge*, it is actually much better than he seems to have thought. The special effects footage—which sent the movie way over budget—is quite remarkable, and although the remainder of the film is rather anti-climactic it is reasonably well done. Except for the indulgence of transplanting the action to America, the storyline sticks far more faithfully to Fowler Wright's original than most other movie adaptations of books—especially scientific romances. The ending, although it is not Fowler Wright's (Claire nobly hands Martin back to his wife, then plunges into the water and swims off towards the horizon in search of a community in which she will not have to be continually reminded of her loss) is by no means ineffective. Peggy Shannon's performance as Claire is creditable and Sidney Blackmer is a perfectly adequate Martin.

Had the *Deluge* movie not been lost it might well have sustained interest in Fowler Wright's work far better than the later adoption of his work into the science fiction genre. Republic Studios, which bought and killed the film in order to obtain the images of New York's spectacular destruction, did a considerable disservice to the original in redeploying them in products of a much inferior kind, including the B-movies *SOS Tidal Wave* (1938), *Dick Tracy vs. Crime, Inc.* (1941), and *King of the Rocket Men* (1949).

The list of titles in the 1933-37 diary makes it appear that Fowler Wright was planning to ease up on crime stories—the only one actually listed apart from *The Secret of the Screen* is *Who Else But She?*, written and published in 1934—but it might simply be the case that he was not given to planning his potboilers so far in advance. He was, at any rate, forced to revert to reliance on their income for the greater part of his income. The fact that Fowler Wright's fortunes declined so markedly after his fruitless excursion to America is clearly reflected in a deterioration in the quality of his published works, but that was not symptomatic of the waning of his creative powers. The work into which he poured most of his energy during the late thirties remains mostly unpublished. The books that got into print were mostly potboilers. Nevertheless, his fantasies, in particular, continued to feature material of interest in the context of this essay.

Vengeance of Gwa strongly resembles *Dream* in all important respects. As before, we find an independent, strong-willed heroine who enters into an uneasy alliance with savage folk not of her own kind, and eventually witnesses a destructive war for survival between that tribe and another, more rapacious species. The heroine in this incarnation is Raina, who emerges into the savage world from a great city inhabited by a highly-civilized people resembling the Atlanteans of Captain Sparrow's island. This city is a sterile counter-utopia akin to Heaven in "The Choice" and a forerunner of the world to be described in much more detail in *The Adventure of Wyndham Smith*:

> "They had long conquered all the evils which plague mankind. They had no lack of delectable things. They had vanquished pain, and made death no more than a pleasant dream, that will come to those who begin to yawn for the night. The beatitudes would have had no meaning for them, who neither quarrelled nor mourned.
>
> "Once, in its tenth year, each child was exposed to heat and cold, to hunger and pain, on the outside of the walls, and he would not ask to feel them again, having had enough of the outer things. (p. 9)

Raina, accepting exile from the city because she cannot abide its sterility, comes to the coastal strip where the Baradi live, ruled over by their king Bwene. Their territory is limited and the tribespeople face a resource crisis, but they are hemmed in on one side by a more powerful humanoid tribe, the Ho-Tus, and on the other by a fearful horde of ape-men. The time is approaching when the tribe must fight one or the other, or perish. Bwene also has personal troubles, caused by the fact that his first wife, Bira, is both faithless and, apparently, incapable of bearing him a son. He has, in the past, taken a second wife, Gwa, but she disappeared mysteriously shortly after becoming pregnant. The implication is that Bira has murdered her, but there is no proof of this.

When Raina arrives in the Baradi territory Bwene begins to consider her as a possible new wife, thus placing her in great peril from Bira's jealousy. The plot concerns the working-out of this situation, against a background of bloody conflict as the tribe clashes first with the Ho-Tus and then with the ape-men. As in *Dream*, nature is painted very red in tooth and claw, and a grim realism dictates the actions and decisions of the tribesmen. In the end, Bwene's tribe is almost annihilated, but a few survive, although Bira is destroyed when proof of her crimes is revealed. Bwene's final demand that Raina should become his wife, and her hesitant response, recall the concluding scene in the epilogue of *Dream*, and suggest that Bwene is Stephen Cranleigh, still trying to marry Marguerite Leinster. (A comment in the introduction to *Spider' War* supports this interpretation.)

Like *Dream*, *Vengeance of Gwa* owes nothing to our knowledge of prehistory. The author admits this freely, obliquely in a little prefatory quote attached to the text and more explicitly in a dust-wrapper blurb that he wrote for a reissue of the book in 1946:

> "The book is a fantasy to the extent that it is set in a remote period of the Earth's history, and populates it with races of men, and some other creatures, which cannot be precisely identified with any of which remains or fossil impressions have been discovered. It is realism in that the conditions which it presents are logical and credible, and include nothing which may not quite probably have occurred in the immense period during which the human race has existed.
>
> "It postulates a fundamental morality which is independent of place or period, and it contains a philosophy of life, which is briefly that hazard is better than security, effort than success."

The basic pattern of relationships is less tangled in *Vengeance of Gwa* than in *Dream*. It is basically a triangular situation involving Bwene, Bira and Raina. Triangular situations are, of course, common in Fowler Wright's work, though they differ markedly in kind: the present example is not at all like that containing Martin and Helen Webster and Claire Arlington, or that containing Stanley and Crystal Maitland and Jehane. There is, in fact, a curious "developmental sequence" to be seen in these triangles, if they are considered in chronological order. In the first, the first wife is steadfastly loyal; in the second she is partially disloyal, but is retained without being required to make room for her ostensible rival; in the third she is wholly disloyal but discarded and replaced only with difficulty and after much tribulation. If one considers this sequence, the remarkable opening scenes of *Spiders' War*, which are to be fully discussed in due course, can be seen to have a broader context.

Although the significance of the chain of triangles is something of a puzzle, one thing that might be noted right away is that they cannot reflect any change in Fowler Wright's attitude to his own wives. If *Deluge* probably does relate metaphorically, if rather obliquely, to his own situation, *Vengeance of Gwa* certainly does not—what is being worked out in this exemplary chain is at a much deeper level of philosophical abstraction, having to do with the "fundamental morality" referred to in his description of the story. This point too will be taken up again in connection with *Spiders' War*.

* * * * * * *

Although Fowler Wright's career was definitely on the decline he enjoyed one more brief and muted popular success with a project he had nursed through his time in America and made some attempt to promote while there: a future war novel provisionally entitled *The Splendid Curse*. The great majority of British scientific romances developing post-catastrophe scenarios were tales of destructive future warfare, and it was a natural next step for Fowler Wright to move in that direction. He found a golden opportunity to revive the project in 1935. The proprietor of the *Sunday Dispatch*, probably mindful of the huge success that Alfred Harmsworth had enjoyed in 1906 when he commissioned William le Queux to produce a speculative account of a German invasion of England for the *Daily Mail*, decided—with the active encouragement of the government, according to Fowler Wright—that the time was ripe to repeat the trick. Fowler Wright was commissioned to go to Germany to study Adolf Hitler's rearmament program and assess its likely consequences.

Fowler Wright set off with Truda for the continent on 25 January; they returned on 7 February. He immediately began work on what the *Sunday Dispatch* was determined to call *The War of 1938* (although Fowler Wright's own text stuck resolutely to his conviction that the next war would actually begin in 1939). Although he was perpetually at loggerheads with the editorial staff at the newspaper over the way his copy was edited, Fowler Wright completed both his own text and the heavily-amended serial version. The story correctly anticipated that the spark which would ignite the next war would be Hitler's annexation of the Sudetenland, so the book version appeared as *Prelude in Prague: A Story of the War of 1938*

(1935), although the US publisher retained the serial title and demanded a different ending. It sold moderately well, particularly in translation; it was read all over Europe—except, of course, Germany, where it was understandably banned.

Fowler Wright tried to take advantage of this new success by carrying the story forward in two more volumes, the first of which was initially supposed to recover the original title of *The Splendid Curse*; by the time he had finished it in 1936, however, it was called *Four Days War*. It did not repeat the success of its predecessor and Fowler Wright found the third volume, *Megiddo's Ridge*, much tougher going. He despaired of meeting the deadline given to him by publisher Robert Hale (30 June 1937), but a last ditch effort allowed him to complete it on that day, albeit in a rather abrupt and hurried fashion.

Prelude in Prague is remarkable for several reasons. It has a prophetic dimension in suggesting that Germany would manufacture an excuse to attack Czechoslovakia to regain part of her "traditional territories", and that this would be the prelude to much greater military ambitions. As with many other future war novels of the period, though, it transforms itself in its final chapters from a rather cliché-ridden thriller into a coldly effective horror-story, which recognizes and displays the possible devastations of a new war.

The story begins with an account of Germany's strategy in building up diplomatic pressure on Czechoslovakia, leading to the creation of an excuse to launch her air-fleet against Prague. The actual story-line follows the exploits of two young Englishwomen visiting that city. One, Perdita Wyatt, is visiting her fiancé, a secretary at the British Legation; her companion, Caresse Langton, is the wife of a Foreign Office official. The plot in which they become involved is very conventional, involving secret documents planted on them by a desperate spy, the kidnapping of Perdita, and eventually their desperate attempts to escape from Prague when the bombers come. The other main character in the story is variously known as no. 973 (his identification code in the British Secret Service), Richard Steele and Adolph Zweiss. In this last guise he was once a German air ace in the Great War, but he now appears to be wholly loyal to Britain. His dual identity enables him to move through the convolutions of the plot with great ease.

Fowler Wright assumes in *Prelude in Prague* that the extent of German rearmament has been much greater than is widely known, and that they have large air fleets based in secret underground aerodromes. He also assumes that they have made considerable progress in chemical weaponry, although a new "freezing gas" only makes a peripheral appearance in this first volume before becoming a key agent in the devastation of Britain in *Four Days War*, the second volume of the trilogy, published in 1936.

Prior to the Great War, most future war stories had been jingoistic fantasies boasting about the destiny of the Anglo-Saxon race and promoting a mythology of a war to end war. The actual experience of the Great War transformed the genre, leading to the production of many bloodcurdling tales of world-destruction by high-explosive and poison gas. In the 1920s these fictions seemed distinctly hypothetical in their extremism, but by the time Fowler Wright began to work in the tradition the possibility of a new war was beginning to seem much more real, making accounts of the next war more journalistic and more pessimistic in character. The end of *Prelude in Prague* presents a clinically horrific catalogue of atrocities, and is chillingly careless in the disposal of some of the leading characters. Only Perdita Wyatt and Steele/Zweiss make their way to relative safety. In the last chapter Germany delivers an ultimatum to Britain.

Four Days War takes up the story immediately, with the British rejection of the ultimatum and the consequent attacks of the German air fleets. Events in England are mostly seen from the viewpoint of Eustace Ashfield, a manufacturer of gas masks, and the girl he loves, the aviatrix Imogen Lister. They see the horrors of widespread destruction wrought by explosives and chemical weapons. In the meantime, Perdita Wyatt has been escorted out of Prague by a German officer and has to be rescued from Nurnberg by Richard Steele, who has by now adopted a few other German identities to supplement his real one. He manages to get her back to a much-changed England before setting out to return to Germany as a one-man fifth column.

By this time, England is in a very poor state. Imogen Lister has been shot down and badly injured. Eustace Ashfield has been sent to work in a factory because there is no longer any room in the beleaguered community for capitalists. Chemical warfare has been supplemented by biological weaponry as foot-and-mouth disease is deliberately sown in an attempt to disrupt food supplies. America has joined in the war on England's side (so has Japan, although Russia and France have capitulated with German demands) but the Americans have decided that it is not worth trying to hold Europe. The war now comes to be seen as a kind of Holy War, with the Christian nations arrayed against the forces of a new paganism. Germany has a new military dictator, symbolically titled Prince von Teufel.

There is more authorial commentary in *Four Days War* than either of the other volumes in the trilogy, including one chapter of exposition (chapter XIII, p. 68-73) in which Fowler Wright delivers a scathing commentary on the sad state of contemporary England, which is represented as morally decadent and quite unready for conflict. In a later expository passage Richard Steele lectures Perdita Wyatt on the many mistakes that England's leaders have made since the Great War, and wonders what the outcome might have been had things gone differently. She speaks up for love as an alternative to strife as a force in human affairs, but he is dismissive of the practicality of a society based on love, whether in its Christian version or any other.

Here, briefly, there is a representation of war as the "splendid curse" of the original title as Steele attacks pacifism and argues that there is something in human nature which loves hazard, and rightly so. He concludes that the present war may "clean the world", but this shadowy optimism is rarely glimpsed again as the story proceeds. Fowler Wright remains conscious throughout that the civilization whose destruction he is describing is, in his view, rotten to the core, but the horror of his vision is so overwhelming that he cannot applaud the means of its abolition. *Four Days War* does end with the kind of speculative summary that one often finds at the end of future war stories of the 1930s, with a series of grandiose questions about the shape of the future, but it is significant that *Megiddo's Ridge*, which concludes the trilogy, does not.

In *Megiddo's Ridge* (1937) Richard Steele worms his way into the very highest councils of the new Germany, winning the trust of von Teufel. The Germans propose to exert pressure on their enemies by a mass movement of women from the occupied lands into Germany, where they will become slaves and breeding stock. This seems to be regarded by Fowler Wright as a kind of ultimate horror, by which the Germans break all the rules of human conduct and place themselves beyond the moral pale.

Perdita Wyatt, working on scavenging detail with Eugene Ashfield in England, is captured by invading Germans and becomes part of this mass exportation, eventually being attached to the household of one Professor Sturm, inventor of a new chemical weapon. When an experiment goes wrong and destroys the family Perdita is charged with their murder and condemned to death, but Steele finds her and secures her release, sending her in a plane to pass on a vital message to the British. Although she manages to deliver the message she is killed, and Steele is executed by the Germans.

In the meantime, the rival armies and air-fleets are massing for a crucial confrontation in North Africa; it seems that the decisive battle might actually be fought around the Biblical ridge of Armageddon. The narrative voice promises on the final page that von Teufel will soon die, killed by some innate physical deficiency, but that is the only hint that readers are given to console them regarding the probable outcome of the final battle. The conclusion is deliberately abrupt, and refuses to look forward even to ask questions about the possibility of deliverance.

Megiddo's Ridge is hardly Fowler Wright at his best. It is even less plausible than its extravagant predecessors, and lacks their effective descriptive passages detailing the sufferings of ordinary people under the impact of high-technology war. It does, however, show him at his most relentless and perhaps his most nihilistic. By the time he wrote this third section of the story he had passed through the phase of being horrified by the prospect he was describing, and had almost begun to take a frustrated delight in the business of tearing up the map of the modern world.

* * * * * * *

Alongside the future war trilogy Fowler Wright continued to publish crime stories, but his only other ventures of the period that were successful in finding a publisher were the two lost race stories issued by Robert Hale, the same publisher who produced the latter volumes of the future war trilogy. Even these were not placed without difficulty—Hale initially rejected *The Screaming Lake* on the grounds that it was too short, and Fowler Wright resentfully padded it out to the required length. It is obvious enough where the padding was added, for the early chapters are bloated and the later ones unreasonably terse.

The Screaming Lake combines many elements already familiar in Fowler Wright's work. The hero, venturing up the Amazon to a land from which many others have failed to return in search of the lost treasure of the Incas, meets a wild white girl held captive by an Indian tribe. Her story is much the same as that of Marcelle in *The Island of Captain Sparrow*, but her character is a pale reflection of that model. Together they reach the refuge of the Inca and his few remaining subjects, and the girl is marked down to become the loathsome Inca's new bride. Naturally, they escape, and in an uncharacteristic bow to conventional cliché the girl turns out to be a titled heiress.

The Hidden Tribe, which Fowler Wright had written before *The Screaming Lake* was published, is rather more substantial but structurally similar. Here there is a subterranean city deep in the Libyan desert, which harbors a culture more technologically sophisticated than that of the desert nomads. It appears to be a fragment of the ancient Egyptian civilization, although its inhabitants worship Artemis. The hero and the girl who mistakenly follows him on his adventure become embroiled in a civil war in the city, and rescue another female captive. Although better-paced than *The Screaming Lake*, the book self-consciously refuses to stray from the path of convention, and it is basically an exercise in pastiche.

To anyone following his published works as they appeared, it must have seemed that Fowler Wright's creativity was almost burned out. It would not have been entirely surprising had this been the case—he was, after all, well into his sixties. In fact, however, his career still had some distance to run, and his life-story had not yet exhausted its twist and turns.

Fowler Wright wasted much of 1938 and 1939 in negotiations with the disgraced financier Charles Clarence Hatry. Hatry was one of the first of a new breed of British businessmen who had bought and sold businesses on a prolific scale, attempting to consolidate and revitalize them. The pattern had been set when he bought the City Equitable Fire Insurance Company in 1914 for £60,000 and sold it again within two years for £250,000. In 1916 he took over the Commercial Bank of London Ltd. and converted it into the Commercial Corporation of London Ltd., which became the clearing house for his other acquisitions until it collapsed in 1923. In 1926 he established a municipal loan company called Corporation and General Securities Ltd., which proved very successful until he began to divert its funds to assist a doomed attempt to revolutionize the troubled British steel industry. His entire operation collapsed in 1929 and Hatry—who had a quixotic streak—tried to exonerate his fellow-directors by offering a rather fanciful confession to the Director of Public Prosecutions, in which he took all the blame—as a result of which, he was jailed for fourteen years in 1930.

Fowler Wright was initially asked to visit Hatry in prison by the M.P. for Ayr, Lt-Col Sir Thomas Moore, when Hatry was determined to "set the record straight" by telling his own version of his story. Fowler Wright seems to have ghost-written at least one autobiography on the financier's instructions in order to "reveal the truth" about his downfall, but none was published—Hatry apparently had second thoughts about the wisdom of such a move when the possibility of his early release was raised. A ghost-written book called *Light Out of Darkness* (1939), about the possible economic consequences of the war, did reach print, however. Hatry appears to have made all manner of promises to Fowler Wright, few of which were kept, but following his release from prison early in 1939, he quickly bought the booksellers Hatchards for £6,000, and gave Fowler Wright a job editing *Books of Today*, a periodical produced by the firm.

This appointment was a mixed blessing, partly because commuting between London and the south coast, where Fowler Wright was now living, was so arduous as to make it difficult to write anything at all, and even more so because the office in which Fowler Wright was working was destroyed by German bombs in May 1941, obliterating all his incomplete and unsold projects—which allegedly amounted to something in the region of a hundred manuscripts. The only manuscript of his *Morte d'Arthur*, which he had recently brought to completion after half a lifetime's periodic labor, was among those lost, although he made every effort to reconstitute it and eventually produced a new manuscript version.

Late Works

Fowler-Wright's last imaginative novel of the 1930s was by no means a pure potboiler. It is implausible in its basic premise and is not particularly well-shaped as a story, but it represents a significant return to the task of displaying where the new gods would lead. According to the 1933-37 diary the project began as a short story, "Original Sin", which failed to sell when it was written in 1936 (it eventually appeared in *The Witchfinder* in 1946). It has clear ideative links with the stories in *The New Gods Lead*. Set in the year 2838 it takes the form of a manuscript produced by one XP4378882. This explains how the conquest of disease long ago led to the passing of laws regulating birth, and ultimately to the creation of a pain-free utopia of comfort and ease like the one briefly mentioned in *Vengeance of Gwa*.

Into this settled world has come a new ideology, the Doctrine of Futility, which advances from heresy to sacred writ as mankind passes judgment on its own pointlessness, deciding that mass suicide is an appropriate end for the race. The writer and his friend Stella plan to exempt themselves from the mass suicide, in order to become a new Adam and Eve, and they secure the last places on the line as the last few people take turns to give one another lethal injections. When the narrator has to execute the second-last woman he hesitates, seeing fear in her eyes, but Stella will have none of such prevarication and presses the needle home. This new original sin seems to the hero to be an unpromising beginning to the founding of a new world.

Thinking the idea too good to lose, Fowler Wright set about expanding the theme of "Original Sin" to novel-length, producing *The Adventure of Wyndham Smith*, which was published in 1938. Smith is a medical student of our own day snatched into the future in order to take part in a bizarre and unconvincing experiment in "ego-transplantation". As a result of this the soul of the twentieth century man becomes lodged in the identity of Colpeck-4XP, who is thus subtly altered to become a potential rebel against the collective decision taken by the men of this far future to exterminate themselves.

With great difficulty, Smith/Colpeck makes a plan that will exempt him from the mass suicide along with a girl named Vinette, whose character has a fatal flaw (by the standards of this hyper-rational era). This time the mass-suicide is to be followed by mass-cremation, and there is a dramatic battle as the last few pass into the fiery chamber and Smith's plan is discovered. As in "Original Sin" there is a brief moment when it seems that a second woman might survive, but Vinette passes sentence of death upon her.

The two survivors then go out into the greater world, now left to the dominion of the giant agricultural machines which carry on despite the demise of their erstwhile masters. They are not yet safe, because a precaution has been taken against the possibility of some individuals opting out of the suicide pact: there is a company of mechanical trackers and killers that has been programmed to search for them and hunt them down. In time, these and all the other machines will rust into immobility, but for a while, at least, they will have to be avoided at all costs.

Having taken the same kind of choice as other Fowler Wright characters before them, Smith and Vinette flee into the wilderness to build a new life for themselves in circumstances that are harsh and demanding. The future stretches before them, vast and uncertain, but the author provides a token climax by arranging a crucial confrontation between his hero and the killer automata, whose resolution is made to stand as a conclusion. As with other novels of this period, the ending seems decidedly clipped, as if the author, having lost his imaginative impetus, wanted to conclude it as swiftly as possible. The same criticism might be applied to the last of his historical novels, *Ordeal of Barata*, which was published the following year.

By the time the war began Fowler Wright's most creative phase had come to an end, after a decade of mixed fortunes. One of the last projects he mounted before the war began, dealing with a contemporary *cause célèbre*, was apparently suppressed because the war changed the circumstances of one of its protagonists, and the manuscript was presumably one of those destroyed by the bomb in 1941.

The loss of those manuscripts makes it difficult to weigh up the whole of his endeavor, and undoubtedly contributed to the fact that he seemed thereafter to have reached the end of his tether. His tenure as editor of *Books of Today* only lasted from August 1940 to July 1941—during which time he wrote articles for the magazine on a number of subjects, literary, and political—but he continued to work for its parent company, Books of Today Ltd. for some time thereafter. The imprint published several of his own works, including reprints of *The World Below, Vengeance of Gwa* (this time under his own name), and *Elfwin*. It also issued a small pamphlet reprinting two short stories from *The New Gods Lead*, entitled *Justice and The Rat: Two Famous Stories* and a new collection of more recent stories, *The Witchfinder*; the latter included two speculative stories, "Original Sin" and the eccentric comedy "The Temperature of Gehenna Sue", about a showgirl turned literally frigid by a scientist commissioned to break her romance with a playboy.

Between 1940 and 1944 Fowler Wright still managed to publish six books, but one was the long-completed *Siege of Malta* and the other five were mediocre crime stories, two featuring Mr. Jellipot, and three comprising a trilogy about the exploits of an unlikely association called the Mildew Gang. Paper-rationing ensured that publishers were only willing to issue books that were certain to sell out, and they placed a high priority on crime fiction. In 1945 Fowler Wright published another Jellipot novel, and also tried to sneak an item of speculative fiction out under the Sydney Fowler pseudonym; unfortunately, *The Adventure of the Blue Room* is by far the worst of his scientific romances, and perhaps the worst of all his published novels. As with the future war trilogy, it proceeds from the premise that the transformation of war by scientific discovery will threaten Armageddon. It is set in 1990, eleven years after the third Great War, and deals with a threat to the balance of terror which is preventing further conflicts. The plot quickly deserts the arena of international intrigue to retreat into the house of a scientist, in whose rooms the fate of the world is implausibly settled.

Books of Today Ltd. moved to the Old Brompton Road in 1945 or 1946, where the company shared premises above a bookshop with the publishers C. & J. Temple. When it eventually closed down entirely, in 1949, Fowler Wright and Truda opened a bookshop of their own in Kensington High Street, but it lost money steadily until it closed in 1954. Truda did not live long thereafter, and Fowler Wright spent the last decade of his life traveling between the homes of several of his children, carrying his remaining manuscripts in a battered suitcase, in which they gradually disintegrated, leaving only a handful of complete works and a few fragments to be salvaged by the family for the website they set up in the mid-1990s.

Alongside the bookshop venture, Fowler Wright did contrive to undertake a few other projects. One more crime story appeared in 1947, but his other publication of that year was a new translation of *Marguerite de Valois* by Alexandre Dumas. This was followed up by a "redaction" of Lord Lytton's *The Last Days of Pompeii*, removing some of the padding that the author had put into his famous novel in order to fit it into the three-decker format of its initial publication. At this point in time, Fowler Wright's career as a creative writer appeared to have run its course. He still had a little unpublished work on hand, in spite of the catastrophic loss of his manuscripts in 1941, but it must have seemed unlikely that he would publish anything else of consequence that was wholly new; he was by now well into his seventies. There was, however, one last development still to come in his checkered career.

Fowler Wright's brief period of fame in America was long gone, but he was not entirely forgotten there. *Deluge* had faded entirely from the memory of most of its tens of thousands of readers, but one particular group of its admirers had unusually long memories: the members of the science-fiction fan community, who had found in *Deluge*, *The Island of Captain Sparrow*, and *The World Below* some of the few works published outside the specialist pulp magazines that were of interest to them. *The Island of Captain Sparrow* had already been reprinted in *Famous Fantastic Mysteries* in 1946, while short stories by Wright had been reprinted in the *Avon Fantasy Reader* and in some of the pioneering hardcover anthologies of sf edited by Groff Conklin and August Derleth. *Famous Fantastic Mysteries* also reprinted *The Adventure of Wyndham Smith* in 1950. The really important development in the sf world during the post-war years was, however, the emergence of small specialty publishing houses operated by fans. These publishers were actively looking for classic material to bring back into print, and two came to Fowler Wright. In 1949 August Derleth's Arkham House issued *The Throne of Saturn*, a short story collection including the whole of *The New Gods Lead* plus the two futuristic fantasies from *The Witchfinder*, and Shasta brought out a new edition of *The World Below*. The Arkham House volume was reprinted by an English publisher and the two parts of *The World Below* were reissued again in 1951 as two "Galaxy Novels".

Fowler Wright cannot have made much money out of these reprints. The Shasta edition of *The World Below* sold more than 2,000 copies, but most of these were at generous levels of discount, and

The Throne of Saturn remained in print for many years before the 3,000-copy Arkham edition was exhausted. However, this interest from America did help to reignite Fowler Wright's enthusiasm for speculative fiction, and he decided to make an attempt to become a science fiction writer. Forrest J Ackerman became his American agent, and Fowler Wright began grinding out stories aimed at the American sf market. Unfortunately, very little came of this late burst of effort, and only one new work actually reached print: *Spiders' War*, published in America in 1954.

It is not entirely certain that *Spiders' War* was actually written in the early 1950s. It might conceivably have been written much earlier, though there is one textual reference the dates the published version later than 1945, and if a version had existed before 1941 it would have been destroyed by the bomb, and must have been completely rewritten thereafter. The novel certainly seems much better than Fowler Wright's other early 1950s sf stories, if the few fragments which remain of the latter are typical, but this might only mean that it was the first of them, and that it extracted the best from the new burst of creativity.

Spiders' War is a manifest sequel to *Dream*, and has a brief prologue in which the heroine in her contemporary incarnation—now Marguerite Cranleigh, having obviously married her persistent suitor—asks whether the magician can send her into the future rather than the past. He assures her that there is no difficulty, largely because there is no difference: past, present and future are "all one".

The opening chapters of the story proper have provoked some comment from science fiction readers and critics, though the book as a whole is usually treated dismissively. The heroine wakes into her dream to find herself tied up. She is now Gleda, and has been captured by one Lemno, who intends to kill her and butcher her body for its meat. After seeing Lemno's shrewish wife Destra, however, Gleda suggests that he would do better to change his plans. Lemno, struck by the logic of her argument, kills Destra (without any apparent compunction) and frees Gleda to be his wife. The shock-value of this episode is considerable, and, when cited alongside the ending of *Deluge*, it can be made to suggest—misleadingly—a certain amorality in the author's outlook. Undoubtedly the incident is meant to shock, but it is not an arbitrary piece of nastiness.

Lemno's tribe, like Bwene's, is caught in a desperate ecological squeeze. Its crops and livestock have been devastated by disease. Cannibalism has been reluctantly adopted as an alternative to starvation, but only as an emergency measure. The episode in which Destra is murdered arises from a two-stage argument. Firstly, Fowler

Wright suggests that if people are carnivorous anyhow, then they should be prepared to eat human meat if no other is available. Secondly, given that this is the case, they should therefore be prepared to be realistic in selecting their prey. If no one in the community has conveniently died, then someone must be killed. Gleda is a member of another tribe, and hence fairer game than a member of the immediate community, but Lemno's second thoughts are logical enough given his particular circumstances. Destra is a bad wife, and Gleda promises to be a good one.

Fowler Wright presents this episode as an exemplar of a moral code in action: a code that is neither squeamish nor hypocritical. It becomes the starting-point for a debate about laws, and how the behavior of members of a society should properly be regulated. Lemno argues that if punishment for crimes is legitimate at all, then it should not be carried out impersonally. Rather, members of the community should take responsibility for their own decisions about just deserts. (It is worth noting here that Fowler Wright did not believe in corporal punishment for his children, but required them to design appropriate punishments for themselves when they did wrong.)

This argument about crime and punishment then extends to an argument about the nature of society; it becomes the cornerstone of a manifesto for an idiosyncratic anarchism. More than any other community in Fowler Wright's work Lemno's approaches a state which, if hardly ideal, is as satisfactory as a human society can be. It is, of course, a fantastic society—its political decisions are taken by telepathic plebiscite—but it is the closest Fowler Wright ever came to describing a way of life allegedly fit for human beings. It is highly significant that Marguerite Cranleigh asks the magician whether she may carry into this future dream a memory of what she has been—thus, conscious comparisons can be made between this world and ours, further assisted by the fact that Lemno is a historian researching our time. It is equally significant that there is no epilogue; as far as we know the heroine never returns to the present. In Lemno she has found the one version of Stephen Cranleigh with whom she can be satisfied.

The beliefs of an author must not, of course, be carelessly deduced from the beliefs of his characters. One thing that is certain is that if Lemno had been a mere projection of Fowler Wright, he would have been just as unable to bring himself to kill Destra as Martin Webster was unable to kill the abortionist in *Dawn*. Fowler Wright is not recommending, nor even endorsing, the course of action followed by his hero. He is dealing with a hypothetical case, trying to follow through the logical implications of a general philosophy of life. If this particular instance seems cruel, that is mainly because nature, in Fowler Wright's philosophy, has its cruel side, though it is not to be refused respect—even reverence—on account of it. In the end, Lemno and Fowler Wright both argue, the cruelties of natural justice are less than, and preferable to, the purely human cruelties that are the products of our unnatural way of living.

The plot of *Spiders' War* follows the same formula as that of *Dream* and *Vengeance of Gwa*. Again, the tribe under pressure must fight for new land. Other, more powerful tribes dominate some neighboring lands, and in order to make a bid for virgin territory it is necessary to cross a region which is the habitation of gigantic spiders created long before when a biological experiment went wrong.

Lemno leads a group of his people into the land of the spiders. Gleda is with him, and so also is Jalna, who is ambitious to displace her as Lemno's new wife. After a great deal of action, involving not only the spiders but also the rival tribe from which Gleda came, a new balance is attained. Peace is made between the tribes, although not without great difficulty, largely by virtue of the happenstance that Gleda was a princess in her own land. Jalna is bartered away in marriage to the king, Gleda's brother. The spiders are defeated by the collective efforts of the human tribes, and are all but exterminated. Typically, though, Fowler Wright refuses to allow the victory to be total, and makes sure that a vital cocoon of eggs survives. There can be no lasting peace, no certainty of survival—it would be unfortunate, in his view, if there were.

Although *Spiders' War* has to be read in the context of Fowler Wright's work as a whole, it may offer a clearer version of his underlying philosophy than any other novel. It tells us quite explicitly that civilization is a historical and spiritual dead end, and that despite all the torments and brutalities of living within the system of nature, such a life is nevertheless to be preferred to the attempt to escape from the rule of nature into a technological cage. This is, of course, not a message likely to appeal to many twentieth century readers (science fiction fans, perhaps, least of all) but one thing that can be said for it is that it faces the issue squarely, without the silly tissue of illusions that is used to sugar-coat the pill by other modern followers in the footsteps of Rousseau.

It is not simply a general philosophy of life that is at stake in *Spiders' War*, though, but also a more personal one. Here, Marguerite Leinster Cranleigh apparently achieves the personal fulfillment so enigmatically denied to her previously, and the last of Fowler

Wright's hypothetical triangular relationships achieves an end as clear and definite (and, in its way, as shocking) as the first.

Although it is never actually stated in *Spiders' War* that Lemno is Stephen Cranleigh's *alter ego*, just as Stele was, Marguerite has asked the magician whether she may find in this new dream, as she has before, "one whom I knew well". Her persistence in revisiting the magician is not so much a symptom of a desperate desire to escape from Cranleigh, but rather to transform him. She is perhaps more realistic than she seems in assuming that, if he is to be genuinely transformed, then the entire world which contains him will have to be transformed too. The right man for her is not one that can be found in the civilized world, but one who is too good for it, by virtue of being untainted by it. What she wants is the male equivalent of Charlton Foyle's Marcelle (who came, it will be remembered, along with her own dream-microcosm).

In Fowler Wright's work, therefore, the quest for the ideal personal relationship involves a determined retreat from the artificial to the natural. This is not because he is an advocate of natural sexual passion. Fowler Wright's reaction against Freud may have been as violent as D. H. Lawrence's reaction (in his essays "Fantasia of the Unconscious" and "Psychoanalysis and the Unconscious") but it was a reaction in a very different direction. Passion, indeed, features hardly at all in Fowler Wright's work. The desire that his male heroes feel for his heroines, and *vice versa*, is never expressed in sexual terms, but in terms of protectiveness, desire for companionship, and emotional support. Relationships are always conducted on a pragmatic basis.

Reference to sexual desire is not particularly noticeable by its absence from Fowler Wright's work, because there were still many writers of his time who exercised a severe self-censorship in the interests of "decency". His non-acknowledgement of sexual desire is, however, no mere hangover from the Victorian times in which he spent his formative years. Writers dedicated to Victorian decorum would never have written so many novels in which wild girls run naked through lush tropical jungles, nor any novel in which the hero ends up with two wives, or changes wives by summary execution. Fowler Wright's attitude to sexual desire certainly does not arise from mere prudishness.

The real key to Fowler Wright's handling of personal relationships is not the relative dearth of passion, but rather the heavy emphasis on moral calculation that displaces it. He should be seen as the most ardent champion of the natural marriage contract—the most basic of all social contracts in his estimation, backed (of course) not by law but by honor. For Fowler Wright, living with other people, in particular and in general, is essentially a matter of accepting a whole set of obligations and responsibilities that one is honor-bound to discharge. Enshrined within this set are the principles of natural justice that he contrasted so strongly with the perverted laws of civilized England.

Fowler Wright had a clear idea of what the contract of marriage "naturally" involved. It is in working out the logical consequences of this contract that the various exemplary cases in his works become coherent with one another. Thus, Martin Webster becomes entitled to have two wives simultaneously, and so does Bwene, Bwene is also entitled to discard Bira when her perfidy stands revealed, just as Lemno is entitled to discard Destra. Crystal Maitland's behavior comes to be seen as an example of someone moving into uneasy transgression of the true (as opposed to the legal) terms of her marriage contract, and thus being delivered into a moral whirlpool from which she delivers herself only with difficulty.

All of this helps to explain why the opening chapters of *Spiders' War* are not merely an example of shocking sadism. It would be wrong, though, to regard the episode simply as an element in a hypothetical pattern. To some extent, the episode does reflect an eccentric preoccupation that is noticeable in the brief fragments which survive from two of Fowler Wright's other science fiction stories of the early 1950s. Both "Martian Reception" and a fragment which probably comes from "Outbreak from Earth" dwell on the possibility of humans being used as food, notionally in support of the claim that humans can expect no moral consideration from the inhabitants of other planets. Again, the author is tacitly attacking the squeamishness and hypocrisy of humans who are prepared to eat meat but find the idea of slaughtering animals repulsive (he, it will be remembered, did not eat meat) but there seems to be more than the simple desire to make a point in this frequent repetition. Even in the most light-hearted and amiable of all his works, the unpublished *Inquisitive Angel*, much is made of the sheer delight experienced by the heroine when she can change into a flea and bite somebody. Deeper than the complicated philosophy of life that underlies the puzzling surface of Fowler Wright's scientific romances, there really is a tiny spark of an authentic, stubborn and slightly smug misanthropy.

In the same year that Fowler Wright published *Spiders' War*, two other books appeared. One was *With Cause Enough?*, the last of his crime novels and yet another tale of Mr. Jellipot. It had probably been written some years earlier. The other was the long-delayed and much-revised translation of the *Purgatorio*. These were the last works to see the light of day; in the last ten years of his life he published nothing new, though he presumably kept up attempts to sell his novel about Cortés, sometimes using the title *For God and Spain*, and his other completed works.

The last work of Fowler Wright's that appeared in print in a professional publication while he was still alive was the brief short story "The Better Choice", which he did for Groff Conklin's anthology *Science Fiction Adventures in Mutation* (1955). A mere two pages long, it tells the story of a scientist who turns his wife into a cat for the purpose of experimentation, and loses her because she finds that life as a cat is so much more invigorating than life as the wife of a twentieth century scientist. The story is quite typical of its author.

It might be the case that, just as "Original Sin" was the seed of *The Adventure of Wyndham Smith*, so "The Better Choice" was the seed of *Inquisitive Angel*, the only unpublished fantasy by Fowler Wright to have been preserved in almost-complete form. This tells the story of a visit to Earth by a young female angel, Elya, who can control her form and change into any animal at will—including a cat. In the course of an easy-going and good-natured plot she encounters English etiquette, motor cars, politics and the law, and delivers predictable judgments on all of them, usually by mischievous interference with their course. As with most Fowler Wright heroines she is a free spirit, forthright and uninhibited; she appears for the first time stark naked in London's Oxford Street. *Inquisitive Angel* is not a particularly good novel, and most of the axes it grinds are familiar ones, but it has a light touch and liveliness not seen in the author's other fantasies (although it is glimpsed in one or two of his crime novels, including *Arresting Delia*). It was probably written in 1953 or 1954, and demonstrates that Fowler Wright retained something of his artistry even at the age of eighty.

Today, Fowler Wright is condemned to the purgatory of literary obscurity. Arno Press reprinted *Deluge* and *Dawn* in a single volume in one of their series of library reprints, and Hyperion Books similarly reprinted *The World Below*, but these were small editions. Fowler Wright's son Nigel, who operated Fowler Wright Books Ltd. as a wholesale distributor of religious books, collaborated with the Irish publisher G. Dalton to reprint paperback editions of *The World Below, Deluge*, and *The Island of Captain Sparrow*, but these passed unnoticed because of the lack of facilities for appropriate distribution. Most of Fowler Wright's books—especially the later ones—are extremely rare and difficult to find in second-hand copies. Another reprint of *Deluge* was, however, produced by Wesleyan University Press in 2003, with elaborate scholarly augmentation; and the hard work that various family members put into producing electronic versions of all his texts has permitted the Borgo Press Imprint of Wildside Press to issue a series of fifty-six reprints and original works (a few retitled), which will bring all of the author's books back in print by 2010.

This slide into hopefully-temporary oblivion is not entirely surprising. It has happened to many speculative writers, partly because speculative fiction was not taken seriously as a literary form until very recently and partly because nothing dates quite as fast as images of the future. Nor is Fowler Wright a comfortable writer whose works invite re-reading for pleasant relaxation. He is a thinking person's writer, who always attempts to challenge the reader's intellectual verities. In his own day Fowler Wright was often compared to Wells, but he lacked some of Wells's literary virtues and had not the grandiose imaginative sweep of Olaf Stapledon. Fowler Wright could be brilliant, but only fitfully. *The World Below* is only half-finished and some of his later works are only half-started. Had he been able or willing to lavish the same care on his novels that he lavished on his Arthurian epic and his translations of Dante—had he even been prepared to invest a little more time in preplanning and revising—he might have achieved much more. As things were, the critics and the public were right in concluding that the promise shown by *Deluge* was never fulfilled.

Nevertheless, Fowler Wright occupies an important place in the development of British scientific romance. He was the one person to speak out quite unequivocally against the "new gods": not just science and technology themselves, but the habits of mind that made science and technology attractive. Comfort and Cowardice, it will be recalled, are the names that he once gave to the new gods. In a tradition replete with frightening and pessimistic visions of the future Fowler Wright might almost claim to have been the one wholehearted alarmist. While others argued against occasional or frequent misuses of science, Fowler Wright's skepticism cut more deeply, regarding science—at least in the ideological form it had taken sine the Enlightenment—as a perversion of providence.

Sam Moskowitz, who expressed his judgment in an article on Fowler Wright that he initially titled "The Devil's Disciple", was horrified by this particular kind of pessimism, considering that Fowler Wright was rejecting the one true path to salvation—but Fowler Wright had no time at all for the kind of salvation that led to a well-ordered and comfortable eutopia, whether on Earth or in the

Kingdom of Heaven. Moskowitz, in dubbing Fowler Wright a devil's disciple, took the rejection of Heaven as a perverse acceptance of Hell, but that is to misunderstand the system of theological metaphors upon which Fowler Wright drew: the Hell of eternal punishment has no place at all in his scheme; the choice to be made, as "The Choice" makes clear, is between Heaven and life, not between Heaven and Hell. Heaven and Hell, for Fowler Wright, are both human products—products of the imagination or products of historical progress—and are not to be reckoned poles apart, but rather united in opposition to the state of nature.

On superficial acquaintance one could easily mistake Fowler Wright for a social Darwinist, glorifying the struggle for existence, but that would be wrong. He certainly is not a social Darwinist in the sense of one who attempts to explain social evolution with analogies borrowed from the theory of biological evolution—in that sense he is no kind of evolutionist at all. Nor is he concerned with the doctrine of the survival of the fittest, in any version. What he glorifies, in fact, is not the struggle *for* existence but the struggle *of* existence: the battle between individuals and the vicissitudes of circumstance. For him, this is largely a moral battle: a struggle to create and maintain a moral identity in the face of appalling odds. None of his characters really succeeds in this, and perhaps it is an impossible task, but his heroes and heroines always achieve something in this regard. Mostly, they win personal victories in the arena of marital relationships, but such small successes are certainly not to be despised in his way of thinking.

It is perhaps ironic that such an openly didactic writer should be so easy to misunderstand and misinterpret. Certainly, it requires fairly elaborate analysis to make clear exactly what Fowler Wright was about. This is not, however, simply because he failed to make himself clear, but rather because his imaginative forays are explorations rather than mere allegories. They are accounts of imaginative journeys which he undertook—in the best sense—naively, not knowing quite what to expect; they are not tourist brochures rehearsing argumentative rituals for the nth time. Once the pattern of his ideas is revealed, though, it can be appreciated and admired even by those who could never share it, both for its uniqueness and for the way it fits in with the personality of the man, his moment, and his milieu.

DAVID BRIN

Glen David Brin was born on 6 October 1950 in Glendale, California. He obtained a B.S. in Astronomy from the California Institute of Technology in 1973 and then spent two years on the technical staff of the Hughes Aircraft Research Laboratory at Newport Beach before receiving an M.S. in electrical engineering from the University of California, San Diego. He went on to obtain a Ph.D. in space science from UCSD in 1981. His published scientific papers are distributed across a wide spectrum of topics, including space station design, the theory of polarized light, the nature of comets and the astronomical and philosophical questions implicit in the Search for Extra-Terrestrial Intelligence.

It was while working for his doctorate that Brin completed his first sf novel, *Sundiver* (1980). He went on to teach physics and writing at San Diego State University between 1982 and 1985, during which time he was also a post-doctoral fellow at the California Space Institute, UCSD. He then became a full-time writer, although he spent some time as a "visiting artist" at the University of London's Westfield College, served as a "visiting disputant" at the Center for Evolution and the Origin of Life in 1988-90, and was a "research affiliate" at the Jet Propulsion Laboratory in 1992-93. Between the latter appointments he lived for eighteen months in Paris, where his fiancée Cheryl Brigham was doing research in geochemistry; they returned to California thereafter to marry and raise a family.

It is unusual for a writer to launch a career in science fiction writing with a novel, having served no "apprenticeship" in the magazines, and even more unusual for the novel in question to sell so well as to go through numerous printings. Brin was, however, a writer whose work and career were routinely to defy all kinds of expectations. He rose more rapidly to best-seller status than any predecessor within the genre—and did so, moreover, by working in an arena that had become rather unfashionable: solidly traditional "hard science fiction". The principal agent of his success, the series begun with *Sundiver* and extended through three more increasingly-massive projects, is space opera of a more scientifically-conscientious kind than the colorful comic-strip variety whose popularity had been renewed by *Star Trek* and *Star Wars*.

* * * * * * *

Sundiver introduces a scenario in which humankind has managed to augment the intelligence and communicative ability of dolphins and chimpanzees, thus "uplifting" them to sapience and membership in a common moral community. Having made contact with alien species, however, humans have discovered that their own seemingly-spontaneous evolution of sapience is a dramatic exception to a pattern which extends across the galaxy. It appears that all other sapient species have been artificially uplifted by "patrons" who consider that favor a debt to be repaid by long periods of servitude. Humankind's new neighbors are deeply offended by the notion that humans might have achieved sapience without the aid of patrons, considering *Homo sapiens* to be a "wolfling" species, improperly prepared for galactic civilization, whose members are rendering further insult to galactic norms by neglecting to demand repayment from their own "clients".

This scenario embodies a remarkably ingenious narrative move, preserving for the reader the sense that even on the vastest scale imaginable, the principle of mediocrity does not apply to his own species, and hence to him. Brin's awareness of the cleverness and *chutzpah* with which this conjuration was worked is deftly encapsulated in the short story "Shhhh" (1989), in which the pride of the race is salvaged by a trick of much the same kind, served up with a blatant wink.

The plot of *Sundiver* concerns an investigative expedition undertaken by humans, in the brittle company of resentful alien observers, to determine whether the "Ghosts" allegedly haunting the interior of the sun are actually living beings—and whether, if so, they have any bearing on the vexed question of humanity's uplift. The probe is launched from the caves of Mercury, its journey plagued by the interpersonal tensions among its passengers and by various small acts of sabotage, all of which come to a head as it plunges into the outermost layer of sun.

In a long-drawn-out but remarkably tense climax, which moves smoothly from murder mystery to quasi-gladiatorial combat, it transpires that the alien observers are not quite what they seem, nor as amicably inclined as they pretend.

Sundiver was nearly twice the length that was regarded as standard for genre novels in 1980, but in that respect it was ahead of its time, and Brin's ability not merely to retain but continually to stretch the suspenseful tautness of his narrative over such a long distance was to stand him in good stead as fashions shifted in the marketplace. Because hard science fiction stories work in hypothetical worlds that have to be rigorously defined as well as carefully elaborated, it is very difficult to develop them at length, and exceedingly difficult to maintain dramatic tension while dutifully filling in their details. Brin proved to have an unprecedented talent for that kind of work, and he acquired the craftsmanship necessary to make expert use of that talent with remarkable rapidity.

Following the publication of *Sundiver* Brin began to make an impact in the science fiction magazines. "Just a Hint" (1981), his debut in the pages of *Analog*, juxtaposed images of humans who have understood the impact of fluorocarbons on the ozone layer, but cannot come to terms with their own aggressive tendencies, and aliens who have put war behind them, but cannot figure out why they are suffering a plague of skin cancer. Among other things, the story offers a possible solution to the Fermi paradox, which wonders why we have heard nothing from other civilizations if there really are as many out there in the galaxy as the calculus of probability seems to suggest—an enigma to which Brin was to provide several further hypothetical answers.

"Just a Hint" was followed in Analog's pages by "The Tides of Kithrup" (1981), a novella describing the battle for survival of the crew of a dolphin-commanded spaceship stranded beneath the surface of an alien ocean. Another novella, "The Loom of Thessaly" (1981), was Brin's first departure into fantasy, although an orbital platform plays a crucial role in launching the plot and in providing a wryly calculated *deus ex machina*. The view from orbit reveals a tiny region of Thessaly that is virtually inaccessible; unlike Rome, all roads lead away from it, and it is almost impossible to approach on foot. An intrepid explorer who will not be put off eventually finds that it is the abode of the three Fates, still busy weaving the destiny of humankind—but he, like his author, is solidly on the side of progress, and his encounter becomes a heroic struggle against the tyranny of destiny.

Brin commented in an endnote attached to this story in *The River of Time* (1986) that most of his novellas "deal with myth, or contain mythic themes", and one of the mythic themes which most interests him is the desire of humans to challenge gods, which he consistently overturns in order to stake the claim that hubris is a cardinal virtue rather than a deadly sin.

"Coexistence" (1982), which was renamed to provide *The River of Time* with a title story, is a surreal extrapolation of the classic theme of H. G. Wells's "The New Accelerator" and Jack London's "The Shadow and the Flash", which takes the fundamental idea an important step further. This too was to remain a hallmark of Brin's work; he is rarely content merely to display a fanciful idea, preferring to run with it as far as it can be taken. When he does exercise restraint, as in "The Postman" (1982)—a study of the calculated creation of a myth—he is likely to return to the theme at a later date to move the situation forward. In this novella a lone wanderer in a post-holocaust world appropriates a uniform and a mailbag from a long-dead corpse and uses it to con the paranoid inhabitants of isolated settlements into the hopeful belief that some vestige of social order is in the process of being restored. The story-line illustrates a second aspect of Brin's interest in myth: the manner in which manufactured stories can create a sense of community and a sense of communal purpose.

* * * * * * *

"The Tides of Kithrup" was vastly expanded into the second novel in the Uplift series, *Startide Rising* (1983). The travails of the crew of the starship *Streaker* are elaborately extended and provided with a long-drawn-out but relentlessly tense climax, which combines the effects of internal tensions and external threats. These result from the fact that *Streaker* is forced to take refuge on Kithrup after recklessly reporting the discovery of a vast "graveyard" of derelict spaceships—a treasure trove that might contain valuable information about the mythical Progenitors who began the uplift program. The leakage of this news establishes the starship's salvaged cargo—whose exact nature remains a mystery to the reader—as a valuable object of desire. Fortunately, *Streaker*'s pursuers immediately begin fighting among themselves over the privilege of claiming their prize, exchanging shots above and on the planet's surface, while the dolphins and humans hide in the depths.

Brin devotes a good deal of effort to the description of Kithrup's biosphere. Because the crust is unusually rich in heavy metals the indigenous sea-life uses heavy metals to form skeletal structures and protective scales. Many plant structures, including the coralline roots of "drill-trees" are equipped with metal "tools", while vast masses of floating weed dangling down into the almost salt-free water provide inverted forests, through which gleaming fishes swim. The delight in comprehensive and conscientious "world-building" displayed here was to be extended in all his other planetary romances, giving them a useful depth to complement the extraordinary breadth of their action-adventure sequences. *Startide Rising* won the Hugo and Nebula awards for the best novel of 1983, cementing Brin's reputation as a key writer of hard science fiction. It also won him the first of five Locus Awards.

Brin's next novel was an abrupt change of direction. *The Practice Effect* (1984) is a comic fantasy about a quasi-Medieval parallel world, in which practice really does make artifacts perfect—and lack of usage results in a steady waning of their virtue. Every wealthy man requires an army of hirelings to keep the apparatus of his wealth in good order, thus sustaining a quirky variation of the feudal social order beloved of genre fantasy writers. As with many a Campbellian hero before him, the zievatron-displaced physicist of *The Practice Effect* finds that his technical skills are mistaken for magic by the credulous locals, and he sets out to make the most of his aptitude and reputation. Like the protagonists of L. Sprague de Camp's *Lest Darkness Fall* and H. Beam Piper's *Gunpowder God*, he finds the problem of introducing enlightenment into a Dark Age more vexing than initially seems likely, but his resourcefulness eventually proves equal to the task.

Like its predecessors, the Bantam edition of *The Practice Effect* went through multiple printings, confirming the popularity that allowed Brin to become a full-time freelance writer. It also won the last of the Balrog Awards that briefly served as the fantasy genre's equivalent of the Hugo, before leaving the field to the jury-determined World Fantasy Award. *The Postman* (1985)—an expansion of "The Postman" and its sequel "Cyclops" (1984)—was even more successful, rapidly selling film rights, although the long-delayed movie eventually made by Kevin Costner and released in 1997 was a travesty of the text and bombed spectacularly at the box office.

The extended story explains how the inventive hero, having initially masqueraded as a postman purely in order to obtain a welcome from desperate townspeople who have long forsaken charity, is forced actually to become what he pretends to be. In order to convert the flickering flame of hope that he has kindled into a self-sustaining fire, he has to embellish his fantasy continually, and to accumulate a further supply of symbolic materials—including the computer whose discovery provided the subject matter of "Cyclops"—with which to put flesh on it. His efforts to establish a platform for the rebuilding of democratic society are, however, plagued by "Survivalists" whose intention is to extend an autocratic tyranny throughout the former USA by force of arms. Because the Survivalist leaders are cyborgized super-soldiers, their nomadic hordes are difficult to resist, but the defenders of the true faith have better myths to guide and sustain them.

The Postman won the John W. Campbell Memorial Award for best novel of 1985 as well as Brin's second Locus Award and an American Library Association award for the best "young adult" novel of the year. The central motif of its final sequence—a stand-up contest between right and might—was taken to a further extreme in the fantasy of alternative history "Thor Meets Captain America" (1986), in which America's attempts to win World War II seem to be doomed when Nazi experiments in black magic contrive to secure physical existence for the bloodthirsty Norse gods.

Brin's other short stories of the mid-eighties were remarkably various, considering their relatively small number. "Tank Farm Dynamo" (1983) is a standardized *Analog* account of a near future problem solved by a technological fix. "The Fourth Vocation of George Gustav" (1984) is a quirky fable slyly reflecting upon some classic science-fictional themes, whose protagonist is a robopsychologist avid for monarchical power. "The Crystal Spheres" (1984) offers the unlikeliest of Brin's various solutions to the Fermi paradox, proposing that there might be *cordons sanitaires* around novice civilizations; the story won him a second Hugo. "The Warm Space" (1985) is a fanciful and rather flippant problem story in which excursions into hyperspace require a technological fix if they are to be both useful and survivable. "Lungfish"—one of five stories that made their first appearance in *The River of Time*—offers a more plausible but much darker answer than "The Crystal Spheres" to the question of why the universe presents no clear evidence of alien life. Three of the other original stories—"Senses Three and Six", the brief "Toujours Voir" and "A Stage of Memory"—are grouped together under the heading of "Recollection" because they deal with possible distortions of subjective experience.

The River of Time appeared in the same year as *Heart of the Comet* (1986), written by Brin in collaboration with his fellow Californian hard sf writer Gregory Benford. (The two would have shared the same initials had Brin not opted to use his middle name, further enhancing the coincidence that linked them both to yet another Californian hard sf writer Greg Bear; the three were later to adopt the collective nickname of "the Killer Bs".) *Heart of the Comet* was an attempt to cash in on the long-anticipated re-appearance in Earthly skies of the epoch-making Halley's Comet, which was scheduled to make extra headlines when a NASA space probe intercepted it. As matters transpired, the comet did not provide nearly as grand a spectacle as Hale-Bopp ten years later—it was never more than a pale smudge in the sky, barely visible to the naked eye even at perihelion—but the novel provided some slight compensation to some of those who had hoped for something more dramatic.

Brin and Benford set their story during the comet's next scheduled passage through the inner solar system, in 2061. The plot describes the establishment of a colony in the comet's nucleus, with the intention of moving it into a more convenient orbit. The project runs into unexpected difficulties when the discovery of native micro-organisms is swiftly followed by the appearance of enormous purple worms. Adapted by evolution to take advantage of the comet's widely-separated perihelions, the versatile native life-forms take full advantage of the new resources imported by the humans. As in Brin's Uplift novels, the problems arising from the alien ecosphere are further complicated by ideological differences among the colonists—but by the time the comet returns to the inner solar system the comet-dwellers' problems have been transformed into a host of new evolutionary opportunities.

* * * * * * *

The Uplift War (1987) extends the story begun in *Startide Rising*. Although *Streaker* remains offstage, the derelict space fleet that might conceal the secrets of the Progenitors remains a key bone of contention, over which many different parties are squabbling in the eponymous war. As in the former volume, however, the action of the novel takes place on a very narrow segment of the vast stage of the Five Galaxies, on the old and rather decrepit planet Garth. In addition to their recently-uplifted cousin species, the human heroes are here united in a common cause with the Tymbrini and various other alien allies, all of whom are intent on fighting off the invasion of the brutal Gubru.

The Uplift War follows much the same recipe as its predecessor. The painstakingly-detailed ecosphere on view in this volume is a forest instead of an ocean, so the prominent part played by dolphins in *Startide Rising* is here recapitulated by uplifted chimpanzees. Inevitably, the wilderness in which the heroes take refuge turns out to contain secrets of its own, including the fugitive existence of the eminently-upliftable simian Garthlings. The book is dedicated to

Jane Goodall, Sarah Hrdy, and Diane Fossey, whose work with various primate species provided the basis from which the author's depiction of uplifted chimpanzees and the elusive Garthlings is extrapolated. Brin also lavishes a great deal of care on his presentation of the customs and attitudes of the alien Tymbrini.

As is usual in Brin's novels, *The Uplift War* contrives to maintain a fierce pitch of dramatic tension throughout its latter phases but it is, in essence, merely a replay of *Startide Rising*, which carefully conserves the fundamental mysteries of the Uplift universe for further use and does not provide the sense of closure for which some of its readers must have wished. It confirmed the enduring popularity of the series when it won the Hugo and Locus Awards for best novel of 1987 and reached the short-list for the Nebula.

A gap of three years separated *The Uplift War* from Brin's next novel, the equally massive but rather more ambitious *Earth* (1990). Set fifty years in the future, it examines the plight of the ecosphere under the accumulated stresses of population pressure and pollution. The greenhouse effect has altered the world's climate, the decay of the ozone layer has made direct sunlight dangerous, and the struggle to supply the lifestyles of the developed nations has put an enormous strain on food and mineral resources. The rapid advancement of technology has ameliorated the effects of these threats, but the spectacular march of information technology and the clever application of new biotechnologies, assisted by stringent conservation laws, have only succeeded in keeping the world one step ahead of a final collapse.

In order to present this panoramic image Brin employs a mosaic narrative similar to the one which John Brunner used for a similar purpose in *Stand on Zanzibar* (1968), Brunner having taken his own inspiration from John Dos Passos. Brin, however, anchors his many commentary embellishments to a more robust central plot-thread, in which scientific experimentation with a tiny black hole goes awry, tipping the black hole into the planet's core. There the wayward singularity begins a deadly gravitational *pas de deux* with its natural twin, which has been sitting peacefully in the centre of the Earth for millions of years. The battle to take control of these hungry masses ultimately becomes entangled with another battle fought by an extreme Environmentalist, who is intent on taking control of the world's computer network and using its authority to produce a Draconian solution to the distress of Mother Earth.

The long narrative crescendo typical of Brin's work leads Earth to the usual grand flourish, but the final *deus ex machina*—which is nearly literal as well as providing the metaphor with one of its most extreme paradigm cases—does not sit as well in a grimly realistic novel about the dangers facing our own world as it might have done in a grandiose space opera. As if anticipating this criticism and deciding to fight fire with fire, however, the author inserts between his two afterwords—one of which is explanatory, while the other is devoted to acknowledgements (including suggestions for further reading and the addresses of relevant organizations)—a "special bonus story" which brazenly takes the *deus ex machina* one step further.

Abbreviated versions of parts of *Earth*'s mosaic narrative were spun off as "Privacy" (1989) and "The Secret of Life" (1990), and other short stories Brin produced before and soon after its publication shared its preoccupation with the near future of our own world. They also partook of a similar propensity for dramatic flourishes. "The Giving Plague" (1988) applies an intriguing Darwinian logic to the design of a disease which makes unusual provision for its transmission to new hosts. "Dr Pak's Preschool" (1989) takes the notion of giving children an educational head start to a new extreme, which eventually results in the unborn being put to work with such dramatic economic effect that they become too valuable to be allowed out of the womb. Typically, Brin then took the notion of human wombs as a significant site of industrial activity one step further in "Piecework" (1990).

Although "What Continues....and what Fails" (1991) follows the example of "Piecework" in beginning with its heroine pregnant and in a philosophical mood, the story quickly expands its perspective to take in the more grandiose vistas of possibility glimpsed in *Earth*'s "special bonus story". The widening of perspective continued in "Genji" (1992; reprinted as "Bonding to Genji")—Brin's contribution to the Shared World anthology *Murasaki* edited by Robert Silverberg and Martin H. Greenberg—which offers a painstaking account of the work of a team of Japanese scientists engaged in the exploration of a new world. "Detritus Affected" (1992) returned to Earth in order to follow the exploits of miners and archaeologists working side by side in the excavation of twentieth century garbage dumps, but the story-line quickly takes off into surreal symbolism.

Brin's next novel, also separated from its predecessor by three years, exhibited the same expanded magnitude. *Glory Season* (1993) addresses some of the social problems arising from Earth, but conducts its thought-experiment in a very different laboratory. The story is an exercise in social design, of the kind that Ursula K. Le Guin had dubbed an "ambiguous utopia", couched as a planetary romance. The novel cleverly examines the pros and cons of establishing a society in which the ecosphere-threatening aspects of Earth's near-future society have been carefully suppressed. The society in question is pastoral, its use of advanced technologies having been subject to careful selection and stringent limitation. This restraint has been facilitated by the social marginalization of males, which has also ameliorated the Malthusian pressure of population increase. The story's setting, the remote and hidden world of Stratos, has been colonized by feminists anxious to establish a new mode of reproduction as the central element of their society.

Because *Glory Season* offers an image of female-dominated society written by a male writer, the book's publication was regarded with some suspicion by feminist critics (who tend to hold such works as Poul Anderson's *Virgin Planet* and Mack Reynolds's *Amazon Planet* in utter contempt). Although Brin took care to include a strong plot-line with an appropriately dramatic climax, the fact that the story remains, in essence, an analytical utopian romance meant that many ardent fans of his space operas found it the least interesting of his works. Seen from a critical viewpoint, however, there is no doubt that *Glory Season* succeeds magnificently in doing what it set out to do. Although the Uplift series commands more affection from lovers of action-adventure fiction and *Earth* has more immediate pertinence, *Glory Season* is more likely to be remembered by literary historians as the outstanding item in the opening phase of Brin's career.

The design of the hypothetical matriarchal society of Stratos takes into account numerous pertinent arguments which are dismissed or simply ignored by the vast majority of attempts to imagine female-dominated societies, and takes enormous pains to accommodate them. Brin, conscious of the diplomatic niceties of writing as a male, goes to far greater lengths in trying to present an even-handed account of female ambitions than any female constructor of feminist utopias or dystopias has ever bothered to go in weighing male ambitions. The novel can stand comparison with such classics as Marge Piercy's *Woman on the Edge of Time* and Ursula Le Guin's *The Left Hand of Darkness*, and ought to be included in any serious discussion of the issues raised and the speculative strategies employed by those novels.

The architects of Stratos society, being unable to eliminate males entirely from their society, have engineered them to be fertile for only a brief interval during the summer of the planet's long year. For the rest of the year they are uninterested in sex, although their co-operation has to be won in the conception of "winter children" who emerge as clones of their mothers following the stimulation of female lust by "glory frost". Maia, the heroine of *Glory Season* is a "var"—one of the summer children who are almost as marginal to Stratos society as the males, although she is exceptional in having a natural clone: her twin sister Leie. When the time comes to leave the protective environment home in which they have spent their childhood, the two sisters seek their fortune at sea, where the maintenance of shipping trade provides most of the planet's males and many of its vars with gainful employment. After their separation during a violent storm, Maia runs into further trouble and her fate becomes entwined with that of a visitor from the worlds of the Human Phylum, who has brought news that threatens the stable and peaceful society of Stratos with a drastic upheaval.

Different factions among the vars and clone-families react very differently to the news in question, forcing the visitor—with Maia in tow—to flee across the planet's surface, harassed by several different companies of pursuers. This long chase provides the context in which Maia and the reader gradually come to appreciate the complexity of Stratos society, and all the strengths and weaknesses inherent therein. Brin is conscientious enough to leave both Maia and Stratos with all remaining possibilities lying awkwardly open before them, and all their vital choices as yet unmade, so that the reader might make up his or her own mind about the results of the thought-experiment.

* * * * * * *

Yet another three-year gap followed before the produce of Brin's next major project began to appear, this time in several volumes. In the interim he published his second short story collection, *Otherness* (1994). The collection also includes several contentious essays. An enthusiastic and skilled public speaker, Brin has addressed gatherings as diverse as the Society of Science Educators, the American Library Association, the Southern California Academy of Science, the Oregon Psychological Society and the Los Angeles Junior Chamber of Commerce. He has also been a frequent guest on radio and TV talk shows, usually functioning as an expert "futurist". The amiably combative style of his talks has attracted a considerable following; his personal appearances at sf conventions always draw large crowds and always conclude in lively discussions.

Assertive opinions are rarely in short supply in the various communities to which Brin addresses his talks, and they have been a useful arena for testing and refining newly-emergent analyses and lines of argument. Brin's perennial delight in discovering new wrinkles in old theses, and in turning items of conventional wisdom on their heads, have frequently produced gladiatorial performances that have been greatly appreciated even by those audience-members who only turned up in order to turn their thumbs down.

Although Brin's oratorical style is flamboyant, and his fictional extrapolations of social trends often go to extremes in order to maximize their rhetorical and satirical force, his interest in the issues he raises is always serious and intense. *Earth* was intended as a propaganda piece as well as a melodrama, and Brin has continued to develop its themes in polemical talks and articles, alongside various other hobby-horses. Such publications as "Zero Sum Elections and the Electoral College" (1992) and "The Threat of Aristocracy," (1994), both in *Liberty*, and a 1996 interview in *Wired* entitled "Privacy is History—Get Over It," helped pave the way to his first non-fiction book, *The Transparent Society: Will Technology Force Us to Choose Between Freedom and Privacy?* (1998), which "point[s] out important advantages that candor and openness offer to a confident civilization".

"The Dogma of Otherness", the essay that gives *Otherness* its title, can be seen as an ironic celebration of the kind of "peer review" to which Brin routinely subjects his arguments. It contends that the definitive element of modern Western culture is its insistence on allowing all points of view to be heard and respected—and then wonders whether it might now be time to moderate free speech with voluntary courtesy, lest our pluralistic society should fly apart. The argumentative thread is taken up in more specific terms in "Science versus Magic", then further narrowed in "What to Say to a UFO"—whose niggling element of annoyance is only slightly assuaged by the accompanying story, "Those Eyes" (original to the collection)—and "Whose Millennium?". The arrangement of the stories in the collection is, however, careful to broaden the perspective, placing the three stories that embrace the cosmic perspective in a loving manner—"Bubbles" (1987), "Ambiguity" (1990), and "What Continues...and What Fails"—before the one that brings the argument to a conclusion of sorts, "The New Meme".

Tolerance of Otherness is also the dominant theme of *Brightness Reef* (1995), the first volume of the trilogy comprising Brin's next addition to the Uplift series. The title borrows a stratagem from Gregory Benford, whose "Galactic" series employed titles that combined images of light and water, although its supplementation by *Infinity's Shore* (1996) and *Heaven's Reach* (1998) testified to the fact that Benford had used up the most readily-exploitable resources.

Brightness Reef is set on Jijo, a planet left to lie fallow by its former leaseholders, the Buyur, in accordance with the standardized rules of planetary management. The Buyur dutifully destroyed their cities—although some of the machines left to accomplish this demolition remained operative long afterwards—but, during the million years following the departure of the Buyur, several parties of refugees have arrived on Jijo in "sneakships", providing the seeds of a thriving but illegal colony.

In addition to humans and the centaur-like urunthai, these refugees include four other sapient populations of varying exoticism, ranging from the hoons—some of whom, including one of the novel's chief viewpoint-characters, delight in mimicking human ways—to the wheeled g'Keks, the quasi-crustacean qheuens, and the extremely exotic traeki. There are also post-sapient glavers, which have accepted devolution to animal status as the price of freedom. The six sapient races, having settled their differences in the Great Peace, have established a thriving mini-civilization. Some still cling to the principle that the colony should consent to its own elimination, but others cannot be persuaded of it. The plot of the novel gets under way when the precarious political balance sustained by the Jijo colonists is upset by the arrival of more spacecraft. These are crewed by humans, but they are also carrying members of a race which the crewmen believed by some to be the discreet uplifters of *Homo sapiens*. The precise purpose of the new arrivals is mysterious, and the exiles-in-residence fear that in the course of covering their own tracks the newcomers might find it convenient to exterminate them.

As in the previous volumes of the Uplift series, Brin pays careful attention to the design and development of Jijo's ecosphere, distributing the rewards of that work in the interstices of a complex and steadily-accelerating plot. The profusion of viewpoints, some of which are alien, makes the novel far more of a patchwork than its predecessors and undermines the tension of the developing plot. This effect becomes even more obvious in the middle-section of the sprawling narrative, which is contained in *Infinity's Shore*. This second volume is mostly devoted to the business of further complication. As well as continuing its account of the crisis in the affairs of the exiles of Jijo it takes up the story of *Streaker* following its escape from Kithrup. The multispecific crew of *Streaker* eventually becomes even more multispecific when it takes aboard elements of Jijo's society and carries them off into the final phase of the project.

Both *Startide Rising* and *The Uplift War* had ended with an escape which, however satisfying it might be in climactic terms, left all the fundamental mysteries of the series tantalizingly unaddressed. Each of those volumes had produced an image of the Uplift universe refracted through the affairs of a relatively small group of characters trapped in a single location. *Brightness Reef* and *Infinity's Shore* recapitulated this pattern in a more fragmented fashion, but *Heaven's Reach* sets forth into new territory, with the apparent intention of settling all outstanding questions as well as offering a panoramic view of the complex civilization of the Five Galaxies. It is substantially shorter than either of the first two volumes of the trilogy, but this is not entirely surprising; the dramatic expansion of breadth could not possibly have been complemented by the same kind of depth that was added into the earlier volumes.

The extravagant tour of the Five Galaxies contained in *Heaven's Reach* testifies to Brin's consciousness of the fact that the bedrock of his own enterprise is the tradition of fantastic voyages through the cosmos founded by E. E. "Doc" Smith, John W. Campbell Jr., and Jack Williamson. In the course of providing a summary account of the distribution, organization and evolutionary dynamics of universal life and civilization, Brin accommodates and reassesses many of the key clichés of that tradition: the metabolically-exotic species whose atmospheres are poisonous to human beings; the societies of intelligent machines that have outlasted their makers; the societies of beings who have transcended the limitations of vulgar matter. The tour is further enlivened by the advent of the Time of Changes, whose imminent advent had been teasingly mentioned in earlier volumes; no mere social upheaval, this involves devastating "space quakes," which disturb every star and planet—although there are some alien races which regard the crisis as a precious opportunity to further their exotic agendas. Although provisional answers are provided to many long-dangling questions, Brin also takes care to preserve sufficient mystery for future exploitation.

As usual, most of the short stories Brin published while the three volumes of the trilogy were in production offer different takes on similar concerns. Further space opera clichés are re-examined in the first contact stories "Fortitude" (1996), in which the human species must be examined lest its ancestry prove insufficiently noble to permit assimilation to the greater galactic community, and "An Ever-Reddening Glow" (1997), in which members of the intergalactic Corps of Obligate Pragmatists beg human beings to stop polluting the universe with the noxious effluvia of their space-drive. "Paris Conquers All" (1996 with Gregory Benford), re-examines an even earlier cliché, looking at the alien invasion of H. G. Wells's

The War of the Worlds from the pragmatic perspective of Jules Verne.

Brin also agreed—after initially proving reluctant—to join the other Killer Bs in providing a trilogy of novels extending and re-examining the narrative backcloth which began the process of sophistication that eventually made space opera a fit medium for thought experiment: Isaac Asimov's Foundation series. His nonfiction, meanwhile, continued the development of his other major line of speculation, trying hard to figure out what kind of social adaptations might be forced by technological advancement, and which might be necessary—however difficult of achievement—to stave off the ecocastatrophic Time of Changes that seems to be fast approaching.

* * * * * * *

In an era when genre science fiction has been overtaken, in purely commercial terms, by the heroic fantasy that once eked out a frugal living on its margins, Brin is one of a handful of writers who have contrived to sustain its market potential, demonstrating that its concerns and methods still have best-selling potential. He has shown that space opera can be written with a good science-fictional conscience without compromising its potential to excite readers, and he has shown that one can bring a similar conscientiousness to accounts of the near future and to social-scientific thought-experiments with productive results. Were he to curb his tendency to excess—which sometimes makes his visions rather garish and his arguments a trifle Procrustean—he might find that a few more people would be willing to take him a little more seriously, but he might also lose the unique edge and flair that embellish his narrative verve and rhetorical thrust.

Although Brin's occasional deployment of *deus ex machina* stretches credulity, it is not altogether a bad thing that credulity should occasionally be stretched, even to the point at which it snaps. The court in which the question of what constitutes human progress, and how that progress can best be sustained, needs a ready supply of trained and practiced devil's advocates; Brin's skills of that argumentative kind are as finely honed as anyone's.

JONATHAN CARROLL

Jonathan Samuel Carroll was born in New York City on 26 January 1949. His father Sidney Carroll (1913-1988) was also a writer, most of his work being stories and scripts for films. Sidney's greatest success was the Oscar-nominated screenplay for *The Hustler* (1961), starring Paul Newman, although the only award he won was an Emmy for a documentary film about the Louvre in Paris. (Jonathan has written several screenplays himself, including treatments of some of his novels, but none has yet reached the screen.) Jonathan's mother, June Sillman, was a lyricist, dancer, and actress who did a great deal of work for Broadway musical comedy shows, including the "New Faces" series of revues which ran haphazardly from the late 1930s to the early 1960s. She appeared in two movies, having a small part in the fantasy *An Angel Comes to Brooklyn* (1945) before appearing—as June Carroll—in the 1954 film version of the 1952 *New Faces* show.

Carroll's early life was rather unsettled; although he regarded Dobbs Ferry in New York State as his home town he lived a rather nomadic existence, continually moving back and forth between the east and west coasts. He became something of a juvenile delinquent before being sent to the Loomis School in Connecticut. He then attended Rutgers University, graduating *cum laude*. In June 1971 he married the artist Beverly Schreiner; their son, Ryder Pierce Carroll, was born in 1980. He worked for a year as an English teacher at North State Academy in Hickory, North Carolina before obtaining a scholarship to study for a master's degree at the University of Virginia. After teaching in the US for a while longer he obtained a position as an English language teacher at the American International School in Vienna, where he and his family settled.

Carroll began publishing articles and stories in various small press magazines in the early 1970s, the first being an essay on "Reading My Father's Story" in the Cimarron Review (1973); the story in question was Sidney's "The Shining Thing", about the pioneer of Dandyism "Beau" Brummell. His own short fiction included "Hand me Downs" (1974) in the *Roanoke Review*, "All the Angels Living in Atlanta" (1975) in Caret Magazine, "Skip" (1975) in *Iron Magazine* and "The Party at Brenda's House" (1976) in the *Transatlantic Review*, the last-named being a semi-autobiographical piece set in Dobbs Ferry in 1968.

Carroll's first published novel, *The Land of Laughs* (1980), introduced a narrative pattern that he repeated in several other novels, using a distinctive narrative method that makes almost everything he has written since then readily identifiable as his. The majority of his novels commence with a leisurely introduction to the key characters, whose everyday lives and hopes are deftly detailed in such a way as to captivate the sympathy of the reader. Carroll is a remarkably seductive writer; no matter how leisurely the opening chapters of his novels are, they are invariably gripping, so beautifully styled that it is easy for unwary readers to assume that little will be required of them but to savor the texture of the prose. There is, however, something a trifle untender about the way they grip the reader, and there comes a point in most of his plots when the narrative flips—sometimes very abruptly—into a much more demanding phase. Some readers find these transitions profoundly uncomfortable, but others find a unique thrill in the subsequent transformations that no other contemporary novelist delivers.

Often overlapping substantially in terms of their *dramatis personae*, Carroll's novels are set in a narrative space of their own, whose deceptively close resemblances to the reader's world make unceremonious intrusions of the supernatural startling—but on reflection, these narrative twists always serve the purpose of rendering explicit a creeping but nebulous unease that has quietly possessed the plot since its inception. It is significant that many of his central characters are writers, and that many of those who are not are connected with the media in some creative capacity; even Frannie McCabe, the policeman who plays an increasingly prominent part in the novels set in Crane's View (a clone of Dobbs Ferry), owes his unusual wealth to an idea he contributed to a TV show produced by his ex-wife. The prominence of such figures in Carroll's work recalls Gustave Flaubert's oft-quoted judgment that artists are—or, at least, ought to be—monstrosities, positioning themselves outside nature, because, if they involve themselves too much with ordinary life, they risk being absorbed or broken by it. Carroll's artists always do get too mixed up with life, one way or another, but none of them can long resist the pressure of the monstrosity that lurks outside nature and inside them.

Thomas Abbey, the teacher and would-be writer who is the main protagonist of *The Land of Laughs*, introduces himself on the first line as the son of a famous father—a movie actor—who explains regretfully that he hardly knew the man. Encouraged by his meeting with a fellow fan, Saxony Gardner, he sets off on a quest to find the father-substitute who transformed his childhood with magical books: the author Marshall France. With a view to writing France's biography, Thomas and Saxony go to the small town of Galen, where the writer's daughter Anna still lives. They are delighted when their tentative approach receives a far warmer welcome than they had anticipated—but their delight ebbs away and is finally transmuted into a peculiar *angst* when they discover that Galen, let loose by his death from the excessively powerful grip of Marshall France's abundant imagination, is desperate to discover a replacement and savior. The quality of France's imagination turns out to be far more oppressive than his heart-warming children's books had implied, but its power and sternness derive nevertheless from the capacity those fantasies have to provide an avenue of escape for alienated readers.

Joseph Lennox, the protagonist of *Voice of Our Shadow* (1983), is also a writer, whose big break comes when his short story is turned into the successful play that gives the novel its title. Like Thomas Abbey, he begins his story with reminiscences of his childhood: his parents, and his bullying brother Ross. Much later, while living in Vienna, Joe is befriended by Paul and India Tate, a happily-married couple, and inconveniently falls in love with India. The sudden death of Paul Tate does not serve to make this situation any less complicated; instead, the consequent increase in the shame that Joseph cannot help feeling serves as a trigger to release a torrent of long pent-up guilt, left over from his relationship with his brother. Penitent though he is for all his present and past sins, Joseph is exposed for a second time to the merciless but curiously ambivalent oppression he suffered in his youth. Death has not tempered Ross's malevolence at all, nor made its studied peculiarity any easier to comprehend.

Bones of the Moon (1987) strikes a more delicate balance between unease and sentimentality. Its heroine, Cullen James, seems to have a perfect relationship with her husband Danny, in spite of a long and slightly turbulent hiatus between their first meeting and their eventual marriage. Cullen becomes pregnant while they are traveling in Europe, and begins to have vivid dreams. In her dreams she has a son named Pepsi, and the focal point of their relationship is the magical island of Rondua, which becomes real as she invents it for his amusement, quickly obtaining its own identity. Like the books of Marshall France, Rondua provides a wonderful escapist fantasy—and Cullen eventually publishes stories set there—but, as in *The Land of Laughs*, it is only one expression of a creative force that cannot be fully contained or controlled.

When Danny and Cullen's child is born it turns out to be a girl, named Mae, and it then seems that Pepsi must be the envious "ghost" of a child Cullen had aborted before cementing her relationship with Danny. It is after Mae's advent that Cullen's dream self finds the first of the eponymous Bones of the Moon—an artifact of allegedly-tremendous power. Her real world relationships expand, troublesomely, to embrace the wayward film director Weber Gregston—who also begins dreaming about Rondua. She begins receiving letters from the imprisoned killer Alvin "Axe Boy" Williams, who killed his mother and sister in an apartment below the one where she once lived. Rondua, inevitably, becomes an increasingly disturbing psychological presence, the creative energy embodied therein eventually overflowing to impact on reality—although the ultimate impact is cushioned, in a slightly less-than-convincing manner. (The American edition has a slightly different ending, but the difference is not significant.)

Had Danny and Cullen James' child been a boy they would have called him Walker. The protagonist of *Sleeping in Flame* (1988) is Walker Easterling, a foundling who grows up to be an actor-turned-writer resident in Vienna. The novel tells the story of his relationship with the sculptress Maris York, interrupted by a long detour in which he returns to the USA to work with Weber Gregston. There he meets the actor Philip Strayhorn and the talented "shaman" Venasque, whom he consults about the troublesome mystery of his own slowly-evolving supernatural powers. Venasque's attempts to help Walker are tragically interrupted, but Walker gains sufficient moral rearmament to enable him to meet his long-lost father face-to-face when he returns to Europe, and to cope with the astonishing revelation of who his parent was and whence he came.

Weber Gregston reappears in *A Child Across the Sky*, this time taking centre stage as an investigator of the reasons behind the suicide of Philip Strayhorn. A series of videotapes left to Weber by Strayhorn reveal that the heart of the mystery is a set of horrific slasher movies about a fictitious incarnation of evil called Bloodstone, which Strayhorn wrote, directed and starred in when his career was in decline. The content of the films is described very obliquely; what the reader learns about them is mainly concerned with the childhood experiences that Strayhorn plundered for inspiration. The key to the mystery is Strayhorn's imaginary childhood playmate, the "angel" Pinsleepe, who manifests herself to Weber in the mock-innocent guise of a nine-year-old girl, and claims to be paradoxically pregnant with the dead man's cancer-stricken girlfriend.

The first thing Weber does after hearing about Strayhorn's death is to visit Cullen James, thus forging a strong thematic link between *A Child Across the Sky* and *Bones of the Moon*. What binds the two books together is a shared conviction that, if the things people most delight in imagining were somehow to become real, the actuality would be nightmarish. Carroll might have had difficulty bringing the earlier book to a satisfactory conclusion, and the bizarre double twist at the end of the intervening *Sleeping in Flame* is hard to swallow, but *A Child Across the Sky* contrives a climax that is neater as well as nastier than any of those attained in his earlier works. In so doing, it raises some intriguing questions about authorial responsibility. In reprocessing the substance of his own and his friends' childhood nightmares into cinematic horrorschlock, did Strayhorn make evil so glamorous that his films became a corrupting force? Did he, tacitly or formally, sell his soul to the devil in return for the gift of showing people the hidden horrors of their own inner nature? And did he, in a fortuitously missing scene from his last movie, succeed so well in pleading Satan's case that he went beyond the permission granted by God for the devil's Earthly endeavors?

The central character of the novella *Black Cocktail* (1990) is Ingram York, the brother of the heroine of *Sleeping in Flame*. He strikes up a friendship with the charming Michael Billa, who gradually reveals the secrets of his unhappy childhood, when he was protected from bullies by the charismatic Clinton Deix—a protection that culminated in murder. When Deix reappears, he is still fifteen years old, having been cast into existential stasis after the murder, and his motives with regard to Ingram are perversely unclear. They are clarified by a narrative move every bit as wild as that which concluded *Sleeping in Flame*: a near-literal *deus ex machina* so difficult to justify or follow that the story simply falls apart.

Outside the Dog Museum (1991) compensates for the misfiring of *Black Cocktail* by introducing its surreal element immediately. Its protagonist, Harry Radcliffe, a friend of Venasque, the shaman whose death was recorded in *Sleeping in Flame*, is an acclaimed architect. The plot gets under way when he is approached by an enigmatic Sultan, who wants him to design a billion-dollar Dog Museum. He resists the idea until he is caught in an earthquake that kills the aspiring client. The Sultan's son and heir is determined to complete the project, although he transfers the intended site from the Arabian desert to the Austrian Alps.

Drawn into it in spite of himself, Harry eventually learns that the Dog Museum is merely a disguise for an erection no less strange and seemingly no less absurd: the Tower of Babel. Rather than using this revelation as an abruptly conclusive narrative ambush, however, Carroll attempts to run with the idea. Like Weber Gregston in *A Child Across the Sky*, Harry is forced to wonder what it would actually mean—psychologically, mythically and historically—for himself and for the world, were he to complete his commission. Again, the responsibility of the Secondary Creator, who operates godlike power in building worlds-within-texts, but cannot entirely control the forces they exert thereafter, is called into question.

Although a careful reference to Cullen James establishes that the novel belongs to the same fictitious heterocosm as its predecessors, *After Silence* sets up an entirely new cast of characters. Its early phases are, in some ways even warmer than those of *Bones of the Moon*, telling the story of cartoonist Max Fischer, who falls in love with Lily Aaron, a single parent with a nine-year-old son, Lincoln—but all this is flashback, the first paragraphs of the story having already informed us that Max will shoot Lincoln in the head. As the story unfolds it seems less and less likely that such a thing could ever come to pass—Max becomes as fond of Lincoln as he is of Lily—but Lily's past contains an ugly secret, which Max cannot let alone. His determination to penetrate it, even though he determines to keep it, wrecks everything—far more comprehensively than he could ever imagined possible.

After Silence is one of the most reflective of Carroll's novels, replete with philosophical reveries and aphoristic observations, but its protagonist is as unreliable a narrator (and hence as unreliable a creator) as any of his predecessors; if his blithe failure to unravel the appeal of his own cartoons does not suffice to make that point, the final phase of the story comprehensively undermines the credibility of his earlier self-analyses.

From the Teeth of Angels (1994) concludes the loosely knit series that had begun with *Bones of the Moon*. Weber Gregston makes a brief reappearance, and so does the dead Philip Strayhorn, but the central characters are children's TV star Wyatt "Finky Linky" Leonard (who played bit parts in *A Child Across the Sky* and *Outside the Dog Museum*) and the actress Arlen Ford, who quit stardom for a quiet life in Vienna. Although *From the Teeth of Angels* is more awkward in its construction than the earlier novels in the series, employing multiple first-person narratives—frequently recomplicated by laid-in letters—it is also the most deeply moving, and the one that reaches the most satisfactory conclusion. The adversary here claims to be Death, operating in a metaphysical framework in which God and the Devil do not exist, but he is a liar—and even though he has both the license and the power to harass, mock and eventually destroy the cancer-afflicted Wyatt and the hapless Arlen, Wyatt eventually figures out the crucial limitation of his power and personality. *From the Teeth of Angels* is Carroll's finest book to date, and it brought his first major sequence to a deft and highly effective end.

Publication of *From the Teeth of Angels* was followed by *The Panic Hand*, a collection of stories that updated and considerably expanded the German language collection *Die Panische Hand* (1989) by adding in several more recent stories. It contains none of his work from the 1970s; the earliest item in it, "The Jane Fonda Room"—in which new entrants to Hell choose their own "torments", thus being compelled to have their most cherished affections spoiled by infinite repetition—first appeared in 1982. By virtue of their relative brevity, only a few of the items included in the collection are able to reproduce the characteristic pattern of Carroll's longer works, although *Black Cocktail* is reprinted and a second novella, "Uh-Oh City" (1992) also has sufficient space to lay the pattern out.

Interestingly, only a few of the short stories collapse the pattern in the most expectable fashion, by using the narrative flip as a surprise ending; the greater number move the moment of surrealization to a much earlier point in the narrative, so that the balance between sentimentalized naturalism and metaphysical adventurism is tipped in favor of the latter. "Postgraduate" (1984), "The Dead Love You" (1990), "A Quarter Past You" (1990), and "The Life of my Crime" (1992), are further accounts of eccentrically horrific damnation, while the World Fantasy Award-winning "Friend's Best Man" (1987) imagines a Day of Judgment that is no less brutal for seemingly excluding the possibility of Hell.

The responsibility of Secondary Creation is absurdly re-emphasized yet again in "The Sadness of Detail" (1989), whose heroine is threatened with dire eventualities if she cannot produce the drawings which—for unfathomable reasons—keep God sufficiently entertained to prevent the real Creation evaporating for lack of divine attention. The over-efficient cleaning-lady in "Uh-Oh City" actually turns out to be one thirty-sixth of God, but her role is still intermediary. "Mr. Fiddlehead" (1989), which was subsequently adopted for exemplary purposes into the text of *A Child Across the Sky*, is perhaps the purest statement of Carroll's ambivalent fascination with imaginary friends. He has a similar fascination with dogs, which play a considerable range of cameo roles in his works and occasionally move to centre stage—again, the most extreme example of all is to be found here, in "Friend's Best Man".

Having set the seal on the heterocosm in which his previous six novels had been set, Carroll began developing the new background of the small town of Crane's View in *Kissing the Beehive* (1998). Bestselling author Sam Bayer, casting around for inspiration while blocked on his new novel, decides to write the story of a girl whose murdered corpse he found there when he was a teenager. He is assisted in his research by Veronica Lake, a fan of his work with whom he has just started an affair, and Francis "Frannie" McCabe, a close boyhood friend who is now Crane's View's police chief. The investigation soon becomes complicated, firstly by the gradual revelation of Veronica's tawdry secrets—which bring an ominous desperation into her attempts to help Sam—and by two further murders, whose perpetrator seems to be prepared to take any measures whatsoever to hasten Sam's inquiries along.

Kissing the Beehive has no supernatural component, although it bears all the other hallmarks of Carroll's work. Its successor, *The Marriage of Sticks* (1999), also starts quietly in its scrupulous examination of the life of Miranda Romanac, a dealer in rare books. She does not arrive in Crane's View until she and her lover Hugh Oakley are given a house there, after Hugh leaves his wife, but as soon as the action shifts to that location the ghosts of Miranda's exceedingly checkered past and future begin to arrive in profusion— enough of them, ultimately, to fill a sports stadium. It is in Crane's View, with the ambiguous assistance of Frannie McCabe, that Miranda is belatedly able to recognize herself for what she really is, and is forced to make the hard decision as to what to do about it.

McCabe is the protagonist of *The Wooden Sea* (2000). Having already been carefully and respectfully introduced by his appearances in the previous novels, he is immediately hurtled into confrontations with his past and future, which are even more urgent and demanding than those afflicting Miranda Romanac. Like Harry Radcliffe in *Outside the Dog Museum* and the protagonist of "Uh-Oh City", Frannie appears to have been drafted into some kind of Divine Plan, the road to whose fulfillment is by no means clear— although it seems that the urgency of the problem will require very extraordinary things of him. In this respect the novel is closely allied with the hectic novella *The Heidelberg Cylinder* (2000), in which a naïve family man finds that his neighbors are being dispossessed of their houses because Hell is full and Satan is relocating damned souls to Earth. The hapless protagonist discovers that Hell is a much nicer existential option than its enemies had ever let on, because the damned get to choose their own decor, so the decision to prefer life is an authentically heroic one—all the more so because its purpose is so stubbornly enigmatic.

Dogs, though everpresent in Carroll's work, play a particularly prominent part in both *The Wooden Sea* and *The Heidelberg Cylinder*; in the latter story, the protagonist's soul is externalized in a quasi-canine form. Like Friend in "Friend's Best Man", the dogs in *The Wooden Sea* give the impression that they might well hold the key to the intractable mystery of what life really requires of humans, if there is, in fact, a key to be found. They are, after all, gifted with instincts—not to mention a capacity for unconditional loyalty—which humans seem to lack.

The Crane's View novels are less sentimental in their initial representation of loving relationships than such novels as *Bones of the Moon* and *After Silence*. The seductiveness of the stories owes more to their mystery elements, but even in *Kissing the Beehive* mystery is employed as a Trojan Horse in much the same fashion as the romantic subplots of the earlier novels. As Weber Gregston and Harry Radcliffe had already demonstrated, a determination to get to the bottom of mysterious things is no more innocent than a desire to find fulfillment in loving relationships; it leads just as inexorably to nightmarish processes of self-re-examination.

There is a sense in which all Carroll's protagonists get to choose their own torments, thus shaping the pattern of their own damnation (and, occasionally, discovering means to resist damnation) but the worst aspect of this process—in all its various forms—is that it does not really matter whether they choose foolishly or wisely, or how much virtue they have stored up in advance. In Carroll's heterocosms neither love, nor honest curiosity, nor creative flair—no matter how faithful the love, how determined the endeavor or how ingenious the creativity might be—can save anyone from the effects of spiritual pollution. On the contrary; love, curiosity and artistic creativity only serve to bring such effects more fully, or at least more monstrously, into the open. This is a bleak prospect, but it is a difficult argument to refute—especially when it is offered by a writer of such seductive artistry and seemingly-transparent sincerity.

SAMUEL R. DELANY

Samuel Ray Delany was born in New York City on 1 April 1942. His father, also named Samuel, was an undertaker who ran a prosperous funeral parlor on Seventh Avenue in Harlem. After leaving kindergarten he attended a private elementary school, Dalton, which he described in his autobiographical memoir "Shadows" as "progressive, and extremely eccentric". He was afflicted by a mild dyslexia which made both reading and writing difficult, but the difficulty only intensified his resolve to get to grips with both practices, and the subsequent struggle conferred upon his engagement with all manner of texts a determined and intimate involvement that seems to be quite unique.

After Dalton, Delany attended the prestigious Bronx High School of Science. While he was there, and with the encouragement of fellow student Marilyn Hacker—who also had ambitions to be a writer, and became a talented poet—he wrote several novels, one of which obtained him a scholarship to the Breadloaf Writers' Conference in Middlebury, Vermont in 1960. After returning therefrom he began attending the College of the City of New York. He dropped out in 1961, having neglected his classes in favor of other pursuits; as well as writing more novels he had joined the staff of the college literary journal, *The Promethean*, had become the director of *Perseus*, a verse play by Marilyn Hacker, and had formed a folk-singing group called the Harbor Singers. He might have made a living as a musician—"Shadows" recalls that he made as much money as a "basket musician" in Greenwich Village as he did from his early sf novels between the crucial ages of nineteen and twenty-two—had he not eventually decided that his literary interests were paramount.

Delany's relationship with Marilyn Hacker resulted in her becoming pregnant in 1961; although he expressed some slight puzzlement about the decision in his partial autobiography, *The Motion of Light in Water*, on the grounds that he, a black homosexual man, and she, a white Jewish girl, were not conspicuously well-matched, there is nothing particularly surprising in the fact that they were married in August 1961. His birth into a relatively privileged family and his experiences as an extraordinarily intelligent and multi-talented child had already established him as an exotic individual who casually cut across virtually every conventional social and intellectual boundary he ever encountered.

The couple remained together for nearly twenty years, and eventually did have a child, even though the pregnancy that initially prompted the marriage ended in a miscarriage in October. Delany had by then taken a job with Barnes & Noble, while Marilyn had become an editorial assistant at Ace Books; soon after, as a result of a series of obsessive dreams, he began work on what would become—thanks to her employers—his first published novel, *The Jewels of Aptor* (1962).

Although Delany's early novels were all published under the sf label, many of them were as exotically chimerical as he seemed to be himself. They were immediately established as the most significant modern exemplars of the hybrid subgenre of "science fantasy". Like the standard models of genre fantasy established in the 1970s they are quest stories conducted in lush and gaudy settings, whose margins and interstices are occupied by godlike powers and where technology is frequently indistinguishable from magic. Their futuristic locations range from post-holocaust Earths to sprawling galactic empires, but rational plausibility is only one issue relevant to their design; their quasi-mythical quality is at least as important. They are, however, taken very seriously as arenas for the growth and development of their main characters, whose existential discomforts are modeled with a scrupulousness and creativity rarely encountered in the multitudinous formularistic fantasies that soon came to dominate the modern fantasy genre.

From the very beginning, in *The Jewels of Aptor*, the enlightenment sought by Delany's questing heroes was an authentic—and genuinely scientific—understanding of the fabric of reality and the quality of experience. Delany was also sensitive from the very beginning to the intimate interrelationships between myth and language and between myth, language and perceived reality. The quests mapped out in his early works are both personal and social, genuine progress in the one sphere being seen as inseparable from genuine progress in the other; this is another significant feature marking his works as science-fantasies, because it is one that tends to be absent from genre fantasies where quests for personal fulfillment are often conducted within static and fundamentally unchangeable social frameworks.

Delany built up a substantial body of ground-breaking work with astonishing rapidity, supplementing the colorful quest fantasy *The Jewels of Aptor* with the intricately-developed trilogy collectively entitled *The Fall of the Towers* (1963-5), the novellas *The Ballad of Beta-2* (1965), *Empire Star* (1966), and "The Star Pit" (1967), and the novels *Babel-17* (1966), *The Einstein Intersection* (1967), and *Nova* (1968). He also began an unprecedentedly exhaustive analysis of the kind of endeavor constituted by these works, generalizing his conclusions into an account of distinctive ways in which meaning is generated in texts that refer to imaginary worlds. This was to remain a central preoccupation of his academic writing, and it played a vital part in shaping his later fiction. *The Einstein Intersection* was the first of his novels to make the creator visible within the text, and to link the process of fictional creation to the parallel life-experiences of the author.

Of the many images from Delany's first fertile period that recommend themselves for extensive analysis, the central image of *Empire Star* may figure as a key exemplar. The eponymous object is a human habitation established at the gravitational center of the most massive multiple star in the galaxy, whose many components perform an intricate dance around it. The awesome strain to which space-time is subjected parts the fibers of reality, so that the temporal present becomes entangled with both the spatial past and the possible future. Only "multiplex" minds can hope to maintain their spatiotemporal situations and perspectives within it; "simplex" or "complex" minds (like ours) are likely to suffer radical disorientation and displacement. It is a hypothetical ultimate of all potentiality: a multiplex forge upon which psychological and physical reality are constantly worked and shaped into something humanly usable.

The short novel's hero, young Comet Jo, is the product of a simplex culture, who comes into possession of a Jewel—the story's narrative voice—which is actually a multiplex consciousness that requires him to complete its interrupted delivery to Empire Star. In order to do that, Comet Jo must take a crash course in the differences between simplex, complex and multiplex thinking and confront some of their many manifestations within the many-layered and multifaceted galactic civilization centered on Empire Star. No other science fiction story packs such awesome richness and complexity into such a narrow narrative space.

Babel-17 employs the same narrative background as the earlier works—the image of a "galactic empire" standardized in the wake of Isaac Asimov's *Foundation* trilogy as a sort of all-purpose container for imaginative contracts of every sort—in a more sophisticated fashion than any other user had ever done. The story describes spacefarer Rydra Wong's heroic attempts to come to terms with the alien by cracking a linguistic code created by aliens. Inevitably, the progress she makes distances her gradually from her own human roots, threatening to recapitulate the Biblical legend on Babel in a more intimate and decisive fashion.

The Einstein Intersection carried conceptual experimentation even further, imagining a future Earth abandoned by human beings, who have evolved beyond any further need of it but have left their bodies and minds behind for newcomers to occupy. These inheritors embark upon an intensive recapitulation of their predecessors' mythologies, aided by an ancient computer system employed by humans for Psychic Harmony Entanglements and Deranged Response Associations (PHAEDRA), which now resides in a radioactive Underworld but is still capable of providing illusory gratifications for any and all desires.

The myths recapitulated by PHAEDRA and transfigured as they are acted out by the characters in he novel are very various, ranging from the classical (Orpheus and Jesus) to the ultra-modern (Billy the Kid and Jean Harlow), but they are all subject to the same process of calculated adaptation to a species whose existential situation is different from human nature in several ways—most significantly, the fact that the species has three sexes rather than two. As usual, the novel's hero, Lobey—its Orpheus—starts off with all kinds of misconceptions regarding himself and his world, and his learning process is a difficult and painful one.

Delany quickly moved on from this Orphean quest to set the ultimate quest—for the grail—within the framework of an unorthodox item of space fiction, in *Nova*, whose autobiographical inserts relate to the extensive travels in Europe upon which Delany had recently embarked. He was based in London for some time, during which he became peripherally involved with Michael Moorcock's quest to remake the British sf magazine *New Worlds* as an *avant garde* publication; it was there that Marilyn Hacker gave birth in 1973 to a daughter, responsibility for whose upbringing Delany continued to share after the marriage was dissolved in 1980.

In *Nova*—which Delany wanted to describe as a "space opera", although he was advised against it on the grounds that the term, however apt it might have been in terms of the novel's echoes of Richard Wagner's *Parsifal*, had too many negative connotations— space captain Lorq von Ray sets out on a quest for the "grail" that will enable him to seize economic control of the galaxy from his ambitious rivals: the mysterious element Illyrion, formed in the heart of exploding stars, from which it is understandable difficult to recover. The novel's narrative voice is provided by one of his helpers, the relatively innocent artist Katin, who gradually gets to grips with the inordinately complicated web that binds the story together with the galactic culture that is at stake in the plot.

His early work won Delany a large adulatory audience. *Babel-17* and *The Einstein Intersection* both won Nebula Awards, as did the fine short stories "Aye, and Gomorrah..." and "Time Considered as a Helix of Semi-Precious Stones" (1969), which also won a Hugo. These successes won him the time to devote several years to the long and extremely ambitious novel *Dhalgren* (1975). *Dhalgren* is set in the city of Bellona, which has been detached from the USA both socially and geographically by some unspecified cataclysm, perhaps sparked by a race riot. The cataclysm has disturbed the passage and patterns of time, forcing the city's inhabitants to abandon the use of clocks and calendars and accept that their environment might be temporally as well as physically self-enclosed, thus establishing a new anarchic frontier. The richly abundant and vividly violent street-culture of Bellona co-exists with a small but extremely sophisticated high culture, maintained by an aesthetic elite.

The amnesiac protagonist of *Dhalgren*, the Kid, initially goes to work for the Richards family, whose members are trying (in vain) to maintain a semblance of the old normality. He helps them to move upstairs in their apartment complex, away from a "nest" of "Scorpions," the street gangs who wander through the city. In the meantime, he begins to write poetry in a notebook he has found. When his "employment" peters out he becomes a Scorpion himself, and eventually the leader of a nest. His poetry is published, and he becomes famous, at least locally. Near the end of the novel, The Kid believes that he has discovered his real name, but when he leaves Bellona, his fate is still obscure. The world-within-the-text of *Dhalgren* became a crucible for Delany's self-analysis, comparable to that of the autobiographical essays that he now began to produce in some profusion.

The intensely introspective analysis of *Dhalgren* was inverted once more into a gaudy science-fictional setting in *Triton* (1976; reprinted as *Trouble of Triton*). *Triton* has some significant similarities to *Dhalgren,* but turns the premises of the earlier novel inside out. Once again, a protagonist is introduced into a society of near-total freedom, but this time the setting is an established and elaborately-planned society on Neptune's moon Triton in the year 2112; the protagonist, Bron Helstrom, is a worker in "metalogics" for a company (termed a "hegemony") located there. On Triton, people are not only free to behave and live in almost any social, sexual, or religious pattern; they also may change their residences, their physical sex, and their psychological sexual orientation almost at will—but not everyone can cope with the responsibilities that these freedoms entail, and Bron, a recent immigrant from Mars, is one of those who cannot.

In the course of the plot, Triton becomes allied with the other Outer Satellites of the worlds beyond Jupiter in a highly destructive war against Mars and Earth, but the book's main focus is Bron's obsession with an itinerant roaming actress and theatrical producer called The Spike. Her rejection of him drives him into a psychological crisis, precipitating a sex-change operation that does not have the desired result. Triton's social system, designed to accommodate anyone and everyone—one of its rules requires a subsidiary location where the rules do not apply—still cannot accommodate someone like Helstrom, who does not share the presuppositions on which this system is founded.

Triton is subtitled *An Ambiguous Heterotopia*—a riposte to the subtitle of Ursula K. Le Guin's *The Dispossessed* (1974), *An Ambiguous Utopia*. Although *Triton*'s society is quasi-utopian, offering a near-ideal model of future society, the model it provides, like all utopias, is inherently insufficient. In contrast to utopias, which attempt to provide solutions to social problems and consolation to their readers, heterotopias are deliberately disturbing and disruptive. Triton cannot "hold together" metaphorically or literally; it cannot accommodate a Helstrom, just as it might lose its artificial gravity by virtue of a random incoherence of the subatomic particles in its energy field. *Triton* also includes two appendices, one of them comprising notes on, and omitted segments from, the novel, and the other excerpts from "lectures" by a Martian scholar, entitled "Some Informal Remarks Toward the Modular Calculus, Part Two." These additions are integral to the novel, serving to remind the reader of the book's own artificiality and inevitable incompleteness.

The year of *Triton*'s publication, 1976 was, however, the year the genre fantasy took off commercially, offering a new milieu for the kind of experimentation in which Delany had become interested. His next major fictional project was a series of stories set in the imaginary prehistoric empire of Nevèrÿon, which eventually extended over four volumes: *Tales of Nevèrÿon* (1979); *Neveryóna* (1983); *Flight from Nevèrÿon* (1985) and *The Bridge of Lost Desire* (1987).

As issued by its publishers, the Nevèrÿon series begins and ends with the novella "The Tale of Gorgik", whose first version opens the first volume and whose revised version closes the fourth. The first volume has four other stories, "The Tale of Old Venn", "The Tale of Small Sarg", "The Tale of Potters and Dragons," and "The Tale of Dragons and Dreamers"—the first and third of which are also novellas—and an appendix describing the discovery and translation of the series' (imaginary) root text by one K. Leslie Steiner. The second volume, subtitled "The Tale of Signs and Cities", is a novel. The third includes two tales of Nevèrÿon, both novellas, and two appendices, the first of which is a near-novel-length hybrid of fact and fiction about the advent of AIDS in New York City called "The Tales of Plagues and Carnivals". The second appendix offers some explanation of the series, laconically observing that: "Clearly the Nevèrÿon series is a model of late twentieth-century (mostly urban) America," but only providing an elliptical and rather cursory answer to the obvious question "What kind of a model is it?"

As its name suggests, Nevèrÿon might easily be regarded as New York writ large rather than a parallel version of America as a whole. Its capital port of Kolhari is no metropolis, being primarily significant as the site of the Bridge of Lost Desire—a quasi-archetypal location where sexual encounters of all kinds may be sought and negotiated. The Bridge of Lost Desire is a fantasized version of Brooklyn Bridge, which has a somewhat muted but not dissimilar significance in "The Tale of Plagues and Carnivals". Brooklyn Bridge crops up as a symbolically-loaded location in several other Delany works, ranging from *Empire Star* to the naturalistic title-piece of *Atlantis: Three Tales* (1995).

Delany's original intention had been to end the Nevèrÿon series after three volumes, and he had already begun a projected two-volume novel that would transplant its themes into a milieu expanded from that of *Triton* to the dimensions of a galactic empire. The first volume appeared as *Stars in My Pocket Like Grains of Sand* (1984) but he did not finish the second, provisionally entitled *The Splendor and Misery of Bodies, of Cities*, having lost his impetus when an intimate relationship that was carefully transfigured in the plot broke up (perhaps the first catastrophe in his life since the death from lung cancer of his father in 1960 that he felt helpless to control or manage constructively). Instead, he began work on a volume that he intended to call *Return to Nevèrÿon*, although the title was changed to *The Bridge of Lost Desire* at the behest of an editor. It consists of two long novellas, "The Game of Time and Pain" and "The Tales of Rumor and Desire", plus the revised "Tale of Gorgik" and a flirtatiously ironic appendix signed by the fictitious K. Leslie Steiner, which insists on describing itself as a preface despite its sternward position.

The central thread running through the Nevèrÿon series is the history of Gorgik the Liberator, the slave-turned-statesman who brings about the abolition of slavery in the empire but retains a powerful interest in the apparatus of slavery—embodied and symbolized in a shackle worn as a collar—as an accessory in homosexual intercourse. Gorgik's early biography, described in the first tale, is carried forward in "The Tale of Small Sarg" and "The Tale of Fog and Granite"; he plays a subsidiary role in *Neveryóna*, and then looks back on his life in "The Game of Time and Pain". The counterpoint to Gorgik's slightly-ambiguous career as a liberator is a complementary series of narratives with female protagonists—or female objects of desire—which explore and develop the author's fascination with feminist aspects of sexual politics.

The Nevèrÿon series is far more naturalistic than the promiscuously syncretic mock-Medieval background that has been standardized by genre fantasy. Indeed, some observers might dismiss it from the genre on the grounds that a key definitive feature—workable magic—is missing. Although the native fauna of Nevèrÿon includes dragons, which are occasionally encountered in the stories, that inclusion seems calculated to emphasize by its singularity that all the other inventions featured in the series are cultural. It would, however, be quite wrong to attempt to relocate the series within the science-fictional subgenre of prehistoric romance; it is a fantasy not merely because it abstracts cultural elements from a more considerable chronological range than could ever have been brought together in one place at one time, but also because it uses their alchemical fusion for both analytical and creative purposes. The series is, in essence, a genre fantasy from which the customary froth of wish-fulfillment has been carefully skimmed, precisely in order that the psychology of wish-fulfillment can be taken back to its roots.

Given the kinds of metafictional games played in the Nevèrÿon series, whose publication *Stars in My Pocket Like Grains of Sand* interrupted, it is not entirely inappropriate that the larger work of which it was intended to form a part remained frustratingly incomplete. Its two major protagonists are Rat Korga and Marq Dyeth, the former an illiterate slave who is filled with knowledge by technological information devices, the latter a descendant of an ancient family and "industrial diplomat". The reader is deliberately tantalized with uncertainty regarding the sex of the two lovers, because the denizens of this future universe classify all humans as "women" and refer to them as "she" regardless of actual sex. Although travel and communication cut across vast distances between planets and galaxies, the social complexities and contradictions within the populations of individual planets can make worlds seem both large and strange. Although Marq can communicate with the inhabitants of many other planets with relative ease, it is much harder for him to travel on his own home planet and communicate with other members of his own "family".

The loving relationship between Marq and Rat is complicated by the social and political structures within which they exist. There is an all-embracing power struggle between the Family, which seeks universal dominance to impose a restrictive, authoritarian system of belief and behavior, and the Sygn, an anarchic alliance that seeks power only to abnegate its use in any restrictive sense. Complicating this conflict are the Web, the information link that connects the planets, and the Xlv, a nonhuman species capable of space travel, which might have destroyed Rat's home planet. As the first half of the diptych ends, though, everything still awaits the remotest possibility of resolution.

Soon after the publication of *The Bridge of Lost Desire* Delany became a full-time teacher in the Comparative Literature Department of the University of Massachusetts, Amherst. He remained in academia thereafter, moving briefly to the State University of New York at Buffalo in 1999-2001 before taking up a new appointment as Professor of English and Creative Writing at Temple University, Philadelphia. His subsequent publications were mostly issued by university presses, and include far more criticism than fiction. The move coincided with a policy change in the US publishing industry, which resulted in many of Delany's early books going out of print in 1987—a change that Delany discussed at some length in an interview with Jayme Lynn Blaschke conducted in April 2001 (posted at ww.sfsite.com). In that interview Delany explains the relative dearth of his fiction publications during the 1990s with the observation that:

> "Fiction—at least for me—requires long, relatively uninterrupted time stretches in which to bring it to fruition.... For me, a novel requires weeks of living in a largely mental and wholly internal landscape.... Sadly, however, uninterrupted time blocks are not what life doles out to any of us with regularity."

Delany made only one fleeting return to fantastic fiction, when he completed a new version of a story he had first written in 1962, *They Fly at Çiron* (1993). Like the *Nevèrÿon* series, it is set in a fantasy realm where civilization is just getting started. Çiron is a peaceful, pastoral region whose inhabitants are suspicious of the Winged Ones, flying humans who inhabit the nearby mountains, but when its idyllic way of life is brutally disturbed, the Çironians join forces with the Winged Ones to resist the invasion. A crucial friendship develops between a Çironian, Rahm, a Winged One, Vortcir and a renegade officer of he Empire, Kire, which enables the defenders to prevail, but the Çironians' innocence is lost; the "virus" of civilization has infected them, and they are already planning to strike back.

After his virtual abandonment of fantastic fiction Delany continued to dabble in other kinds of "paraliterature", including graphic novels and pornography (the only genres regarded with even greater contempt than science fiction and genre fantasy by many academic critics). His first pornographic novel, *The Tides of Lust* (1973), is a dreamlike fantasy, but *Mad Man* (1994) and *Hogg* (1994) are as naturalistic as the form permits. One of the respects in which Delany's work is unique is that he invariably enters into such projects as wholeheartedly and as meticulously as he enters into any others, always determined to make the most of whatever opportunities the form may present.

Delany added further depth to his interest in pornography in the short novel *Phallos* (2004), which makes up for its lack of length by its awesome complexity. The central narrative has two frames, one briefly recording the external narrator's quest to locate a "lost" pornographic novel published in the late 1960s, the other describing an admittedly-false historical context making out the text to be an ancient document known to the likes of Walter Pater and "Baron Corvo". The text itself—only described in synopsis, with excerpts—tells the story of Neoptolemus, a youth from Syracuse whose elaborate sexual odyssey, which begins in the company of a Roman merchant, involves him in the murder of Antinoüs, the favorite of the Roman emperor Hadrian. The murder is somehow linked to the worship of a "nameless god," whose worship is linked to the prehistory described in the Nevèrÿon series. The process of synopsization removes most of the novel's alleged pornographic content and thus (in the context of its supposed 1969 publication) its presumed *raison d'être*, while preserving the material that is (in the context of Delany's work) its true heart and soul.

Delany's next fiction publication, *Dark Reflections* (2007), is compounded out of three novellas that offer snapshots of the life of

Arnold Hawley, an African-American poet. The three are presented in reverse chronological order, the snapshot of his middle age and youth being seen from his viewpoint at the age of sixty-seven. Delany was sixty-five when the novel was published, but its first part is set twenty years before publication, so Hawley belongs to a generation preceding the author's, and that is the whole point of the text; it is, in essence, an account of what Delany's life might have been like had he not been fortunate enough to be born in his own time.

Although Delany was not untouched by racial and sexual prejudice, they did not hold him back in his life and career; Hawley, born into a poorer family in a more hostile era, suffers their full stifling effect. In the first section he has just won a prize for the poetry he has been publishing from small presses for many years—a welcome belated acknowledgement, but one of insufficient value to allow him to retire early from his job teaching at a community college. The second section describes a brief and horribly disastrous marriage that he was unwisely led to contract in his mid-thirties, after many miserable years living in the closet, too frightened and ashamed of his homosexuality to express it. The third describes his formative years and details the manner in which his potential as an artist and human being was ruthless expunged by evil (but commonplace) circumstance. Read in juxtaposition with Delany's own experiments in autobiography, the novel provides a deft and thorough analysis of the sometimes-unsung benefits of the historical changes that have overtaken America—or, more specifically, New York—in the latter half of the twentieth century.

Delany's removal from the popular fiction marketplace occasioned a certain amount of resentment as well as a good deal of regret on the part of his erstwhile fans. The trajectory of his career seemed to some critics to be a retreat into obscurantism, but its transitions were smooth as well as penetrative. He used the freedom granted him by the commercial success of his early works to follow the interests outlined therein to a perfectly natural, if rather esoteric, limit. If this was self-indulgent, it was certainly not lazy or narcissistic; indeed, the hallmark of all Delany's self-analytical work—which includes his fantastic fiction as well as more obvious vehicles—is a remarkable determination to be thorough, in every possible way.

There is nothing self-aggrandizing in Delany's unusually frank examinations of his own life or the imaginary lives of characters in whom he has fervently interested himself; his curiosity about his own experience as a gay black man is utterly scrupulous in its quest for honest expression and true explanation, and his attempts to understand and explain the different experiences of others are marked by a great generosity of spirit as well as a keen critical insight. His unembarrassed adventures in pornography demonstrate that his attempts to understand the erotic workings of the human mind are uninhibited by any fear of stigmatization.

As a writer of fantastic fiction—which is only one of the many things that he has been and become—Delany is the most intensely devoted modern explorer of the linguistic and imaginative possibilities inherent in the description of imaginary worlds and ways of life. If he is a more esoteric writer now than he was when he started out, that is because he has obtained a much fuller understanding of the multiplexity of his task as he has grown older and wiser, and cannot be content to approach that task in a contentedly complex. Let alone a simplex, manner.

JOE HALDEMAN

Joe William Haldeman was born in Oklahoma City on 9 June 1943; he was the younger brother of Jack Carroll Haldeman II—born 18 December 1941—who also became a science fiction writer. Joe Haldeman obtained a B.S. in Physics and Astronomy from the University of Maryland, College Park in 1967, two years after marrying Mary Gay Potter. He was drafted after graduation and sent to Vietnam, where he served as a combat engineer, in 1968.

Haldeman was seriously wounded in 1969 by the shrapnel from a massive booby trap bomb, sustaining extensive damage to the left leg and the right foot. After returning to the USA he continued his education, initially returning to the University of Maryland to study computer science and later obtaining an M.F.A. from the University of Iowa, Iowa City in 1975. He had written poetry for some years but switched to writing prose after his return from Vietnam, deciding as soon as he was confident of his ability to make a career of it. He took part in several workshops, including the Milford science fiction workshop run by Damon Knight and a literary workshop in Iowa whose luminaries included Raymond Carver, John Cheever and Stanley Elkin.

Although his earliest sales were routine magazine science fiction of the kind that he had read avidly throughout his teens, Haldeman's experience in Vietnam was a powerful influence on his work from the very beginning. His first novel, *War Year* (1972), is a naturalistic account of combat in Vietnam which drew heavily on his own experiences, although it also attempted to place them in a wider context. His third magazine sf story, "Time Piece" (1970), is a brief meditative account of a future war against alien "snails", narrated by a ranker who comments in laconically acidic terms on the logistical and psychological consequences of the time-dilatation effects of near-light-speed travel and the situational logic that insists that humankind cannot possibly win. This was essentially a thumbnail sketch for the novella "Hero" (1972), which was the platform on which *The Forever War* (1975)—the multi-award-winning sf novel that secured Haldeman's critical reputation and commercial success—was built. *The Forever War* continued to overshadow his subsequent productions to such an extent that he was eventually compelled to provide it with a companion-piece in *Forever Peace* (1997); publication of the latter novel was likewise preceded by a naturalistic novel in which the Vietnam War was a central concern, *1968* (1994).

Discussing *Forever Peace* in a 1997 Locus interview, Haldeman reflected on the nature of the impact that Vietnam had made on him:

> "Being in combat changes your life completely, usually for the worse. It's not specific things that happen in combat, it's a kind of gestalt—living with horror for day after day after day, and finally you've sort of moved away from the human condition. And you never quite get back, no matter how many years go by. I've seen this in old, old men who were in World War I. I look in their eyes and I see myself. They can never be completely kind, they can never be completely humane." (*Locus* 438, p. 69)

Haldeman visited a duplication of his own wounds upon the central character of "A Mind of His Own" (1974), but the introduction to the story in the collection *Infinite Dreams* (1978) explains that he was moved to do so by his reaction to an abruptly-disabled man, whose angry bitterness in the face of disaster drove away his wife, family and friends—including Haldeman, who understood how the man felt but had no solution to offer.

In a 1989 *Locus* interview Haldeman recalled how a peculiar incident in Vietnam had sparked the idea for *The Hemingway Hoax* (1990), and how another such incident—in which his evacuation in a CIA plane from the hospital where his leg had been patched had briefly made him a fellow-passenger of a man strapped down and tranquillized, with a tag on his collar reading "paranoid schizophrenic"—had become the seed of *1968*, which he had begun in 1974 but did not complete until 1992.

A 1994 interview adds a corrective comment to the latter anecdote, to the effect that although he had started out wanting to tell the main story of 1968 from the viewpoint of a clear-sighted paranoid schizophrenic his research into the disease eventually convinced him that it would be implausible to do so: "So I gave the guy a stress-related disorder instead, shell shock or PTSD or whatever you want to call it. That I could do accurately, because I've had problems along those lines myself. It turns out that in extreme cases, the symptoms parallel paranoid schizophrenia for short periods of time." (*Locus* 400, p. 4-67)

The idea that war is so innately insane that only deeply crazy people can see it clearly is not, of course, original. Like the look that Haldeman could see in the eyes of old, old men, it goes back at least as far as Robert Graves' reflections on having to appear before a military court during World War I to testify that Siegfried Sassoon was insane—and therefore ought not to be shot for cowardice—when it was perfectly obvious to him that Sassoon was actually the only sane man in the room.

Haldeman, like Graves, subsequently took pride in writing many different kinds of books, exercising considerable care in the avoidance of obsession, but in much the same way that Graves' experiences colored everything he wrote—returning him again and again to the consideration of the predicaments of sane individuals heroically failing to cope with an insane world whose inexorable forces of destruction are unwinding lethally and chaotically all around them—the effects of Haldeman's wounding resound constantly within his work. Few writers exact such a heavy tax of pain and distress from their main characters as Haldeman, and few wreak such wholesale and stomach-churning havoc upon their bystanders, innocent and guilty alike.

* * * * * * *

Haldeman's first published story was "Out of Phase" (1969), in which a strangely-assorted band of starfaring explorers have second thoughts about the wisdom of assigning their only crew-member capable of imitating human form to the job of exploring Earth when they recall that he is in the "aesthetic phase" of his development, and thus highly likely to render the human population into works of art by ingeniously murdering every last one of them. Fortunately, his father persuades the shapeshifter that it is time to move on to the next phase of his development—although the casual exit-line dutifully suggests that his entry into the "power phase" might not bode too well for humankind either. This suggestion is, however, considerably ameliorated in the sequel "Power Complex" (1972), where the shapeshifter is compelled by his dutiful father to work under severe restrictions.

Haldeman did not take the series any further, although his decision to omit the stories from his collections may imply that he considered extrapolating them into a mosaic novel. He did complete a mosaic novel based on "To Fit the Crime" (1971) and "The Only War We've Got" (1974), which feature a human drafted into service as an interplanetary spy, whose shapeshifting powers are forced upon him by surgery and augmented by hypnotic techniques that continually modify his personality. The third story in the series became the title element of *All My Sins Remembered* (1977).

The galactic culture introduced in "To Fit the Crime" is based on a future history in which a twenty-first-century war between the superpowers results in the devastation of the entire northern hemisphere, leaving the southern nations to lead the way to the stars. They establish a "Confederación" which is little more than the political arm of the Australia-based Hartford Corporation, which ruthlessly exploits its monopoly on faster-than-light travel. Although Otto McGavin, the hero of *All My Sins Remembered*, appears to be defending a protective Charter of Rights, he eventually realizes that the Charter is merely one more instrument of oppression, suppressing warfare only because warfare is bad for business, and defending aliens from local exploitation only to conserve them for exploitation by the greater powers.

Haldeman was to return to the Confederación whenever he needed a stable galactic culture as a setting for his stories, although "The Mazeltov Revolution" (1974) sketched out in a comic manner the means by which the Hartford monopoly might eventually be broken. In collaboration with his brother Jack he began to write a Confederación-set series of tales apparently aimed at younger readers, launched with "Starschool" (1979) in the short-lived Asimov's *SF Adventure Magazine*. The full series appeared in the mosaic novel *There Is No Darkness* (1983), but the uncompromising brutality of the stories—which involve the hapless young hero in loaded gladiatorial contests before having him press-ganged into a war—forced the book to be redirected towards an adult audience. "A Tangled Web" (1981) employed the backcloth for a black comedy of commercial double-dealing, but "Seasons" (1985) offers a far more sophisticated account of the slow and bloody destruction of a team of xenologists by enigmatic aliens, concluding with a far more brutal account of Confederación *realpolitik*.

Haldeman's other early stories include the brief "I of Newton" (1970), in which a careful logician thwarts the designs of a rule-bound demon. Haldeman later rewrote it as a TV script aimed (unsuccessfully) at *Night Gallery*, and recouped something of his investment by selling that version to *Fantastic*—where the first had appeared—as "The Devil His Due" (1975). More typical of the directions in which his imagination would take him, however, were "Counterpoint" (1972), in which the careers of two men born in very different circumstances are dramatically transformed by a brief intersection in Vietnam, and the scathingly sarcastic "26 Days on Earth" (1972), in which a young example of the carefully-engineered *Homo mutandis* records his impressions of the society of his primitive cousins. Transformation by war is the central theme of the stories which made up the mosaic of *The Forever War* but no consideration of that work should neglect the sarcastic edge that all the stories contain.

* * * * * * *

"Hero" and its sequels, "We Are Very Happy Here" (1973) and "End Game" (1975), deliberately recapitulate the theme and narrative pattern of *Starship Troopers* (1959), the somewhat controversial but undeniably definitive future war novel written by the sf author who had been Haldeman's favorite during his early teens: Robert A. Heinlein. The early phases of *Starship Troopers* are based on Heinlein's own experiences as a career officer in the US Navy during the 1930s, but Heinlein was invalided out before Pearl Harbor, so the later phases are the imaginative construct of a man who deeply regretted the fact that his physical deficiency had made him unfit for combat. Haldeman was very conscious of the fact that his own novel was a corrective text, based in the experience of being rudely thrust into war and forced to suffer the next-to-worst effect of actual combat.

Whereas Heinlein's book willingly endorses conventional self-justifying accounts of military endeavor—representing military discipline as productive of a valuable camaraderie, military service as something that fits a man for citizenship, and wars as direly unfortunate evils which, being inevitable, must at all costs be won—Haldeman's is a demythologizing exercise, which subverts all these dicta.

The Forever War tracks the career of William Mandella as he rises through the ranks from trainee to major (given that his eventual partner's name is Marygay Potter, Mandella's surname is presumably a modified anagram of Haldeman). He loses all his comrades-in-arms except the belatedly-introduced Marygay in the process, but he does play a key role in the human breakthrough that turns the tide of the war against the Taurans. Here, military camaraderie is an awkward defense mechanism against the frequently-lethal oppressions of orders from above. Time-dilatation effects exaggerate, but do not materially alter, the alienating effects of military service that make all soldiers outcasts from the civilian body politic. (This point was more firmly made by the Earth-set episode eliminated from the mosaic on the advice of *Analog* editor Ben Bova, which was subsequently rewritten as "You Can Never Go Back", 1975). In the end, the cost of bringing the war to a conclusion—it is not, in any meaningful sense, "won"—is so exorbitant as to question the value of survival.

Comparing and contrasting *The Forever War* and *Forever Peace*, Haldeman remarked in his 1997 interview that some readers had construed the conclusion of the earlier book to be a happy ending, adding "I don't know where they learned to read!" His own description is that the war ends "when humanity is turned into this bunch of faceless clones, all with one personality, which is the way the enemy was set up, so they could finally communicate." Mandella and humankind, having looked into the abyss and found monsters, have—as per Nietzsche's famous warning—become monstrous themselves. This ultimate catch-22 is the horror that lurks in the background of almost all Haldeman's work, frequently moving into the foreground to provide bitter climaxes.

It is worth noting that, despite the images of desolation and second-stage savagery that dominate "You Can Never Go Back", the future history of *The Forever War* is more optimistic in several significant ways than that of the Confederación. Before running into the Taurans, Earth's nations have established a viable multinational government whose member states have surrendered their nuclear arsenals. The tachyon-based technology that operates as a stepping-stone to the black hole "Stargate" also produces unlimited power. These were the foundations that the scientifically-conscientious Haldeman thought necessary to set up a situation in which interstellar war could actually occur. The extrapolation of likelier near-future situations always led him to scenarios in which such conflicts would be impossible. In the Hugo-winning short story "Tricentennial" (1976) he felt compelled to make a similarly-unlikely facilitating move in order to set up the notion that interstellar space flight might be conceivable at all, inventing a dark companion for the sun that happens to be a matter/antimatter binary—an idea he was to use again in the Worlds trilogy.

* * * * * * *

The Forever War was turned down by eighteen publishers before Ben Bova persuaded St Martin's Press—which had not previously dabbled in science fiction—to take a chance on it. It is hardly surprising, therefore, that Haldeman's ardent desire to be a professional writer led him to take on a considerable amount of hackwork in the late 1970s. He subsequently referred back to these exploits as "adventure novels" and even included his two *Star Trek* tie-ins in lists of his previously-published works, although he declined to make the same gesture in respect of the two novels he wrote under the house pseudonym Robert Graham or the later novelization of the movie *Poltergeist* to which he laid claim in the 1997 Locus interview (*The Encyclopedia of Science Fiction* credits it to James Kahn). The book that was marketed as his second novel, *Mindbridge* (1976) was, however, much more ambitious.

Although it is not a mosaic novel in the sense that *The Forever War* is, *Mindbridge* is even more fragmentary in its structure. Its fragmentation is excused as a calculated adaptation of a literary method invented by John Dos Passos and previously science-fictionalized by John Brunner, but all Haldeman's longer works are fragmented in one way or another and he seems far more comfortable working in short bursts to produce staccato narrative effects. He also cited the influence of Dos Passos in the introduction to "To Howard Hughes: A Modest Proposal" (1974) in *Infinite Dreams*, and the next story in the collection, "A Mind of His Own" (1974) trailed one of the key motifs of *Mindbridge*: an intrusive technique of personality-modification. In the short story, the technique is an irresistible force, which meets its match in the immovable central character, but Jacque Le Favre, the hero of *Mindbridge* applies it so successfully as to qualify himself for membership in an elite corps of interstellar explorers and for communication—via an intermediate "mindbridge" species—with an advanced alien race.

Mindbridge carefully re-examines the cynical assumptions of *The Forever War* and the Confederación series, searching for a more optimistic outlook not merely on the near future of humankind but also its ultimate destiny. It seems, however, that the creature which serves as the bridge that makes human/alien communication possible without the radical adjustments of *The Forever War* was too convenient a facilitating device to receive the author's wholehearted support, and his eventual treatment of its implications is wryly sarcastic.

In *Worlds*, Haldeman returned a much bleaker view of political probability. He was later to refer back to the books and its two sequels as a "long novel", claiming to have had the end in mind before he began—and the publisher was certainly expecting a third volume when the jacket copy for *Dealing in Futures* was written—but he seems to have got badly stuck after finishing *Worlds Apart* (1983) and published three more novels before bringing the story to a belated close in *Worlds Enough and Time* (1992).

The protagonist of the trilogy is Marianne O'Hara, a citizen of the space-habitat New New York, which—by virtue of being solid, hollowed out of the asteroid Paphos—is one of the few orbital Worlds to survive the strike launched from the surface in the course of a late twenty-first-century war, which also devastates the Earth, and the only one to remain viable thereafter as a habitat. The heroine's descent to Earth to further her education provides the travelogue-plot of the first volume, whose narrative tension is enhanced by her peripheral involvement with the Third American Revolution, which precedes the war by a matter of hours, and is then turned up an extra notch by her kidnapping, rescue and desperate rush to Cape Canaveral in order to catch the last shuttle home.

The second volume tracks O'Hara's involvement with the Janus Project—the building of a starship by the people of New New York—and the exploits of her former rescuer, Jeff Hawkings, who is one of only a handful of adults to survive the artificial plague that has devastated the Earth. As with other wars described by Haldeman, the aftermath of this one is so bloodcurdling as to suggest that those who died were the fortunate ones, but a very tenuous bridge enabling some communication to take place between Earth and New New York eventually provides the means by which the life spans of a few of the child-survivors are restored to near-normalcy. The fact that the project had run into difficulty is signaled by the author's inability to generate any kind of a sub-climax, giving perfunctory treatment to the two events intended for that purpose: the launching of the starship and the restoration of contact between New New York and Jeff Hawkings.

These difficulties continued to afflict the third volume, which never manages to pick up any narrative pace while the Newhome makes its painstaking way to Epsilon Eridani, crippled by a computer virus whose activation precedes loss of contact with New New York and further disabled by a plant virus that devastates its ecosystems. It is not until the colony established on the new world makes painful contact with the greater galactic community that the story really takes off. Although Haldeman used contact with advanced alien races as a "solution" to the problem of human self-destructiveness in other stories—"Passages" (1990) conjures up a similar epiphany for the Confederación and "Images" (1991) a personal gift for a Vietnam vet existentially becalmed by his wounds—he could never inject much conviction into it; it is plain that he thinks it rather cowardly as well as absurdly convenient.

* * * * * * *

The first of the three novels that Haldeman wrote between *Worlds Apart* and *Worlds Enough and Time* must have been undertaken as a change of scene and method. *Tool of the Trade* (1987) is a calculatedly lightweight tale of a spy—a Russian sleeper on the brink of being turned by the CIA—whose attempts to extricate himself from trouble are aided by a quasi-magical watch, which can be made to transmit a signal compelling the obedience of anyone to whom he speaks. Carelessness reveals to his adversaries that he must have some such device, but also equips him with the means of getting in amongst them without leaving any memory-trace. The plot is complicated by the necessity of rescuing his kidnapped wife before a notorious KGB torturer can go to work on her, and then by the attempt to use the watch's power for one highly effective good deed without providing other potential users with sufficient information to allow them to duplicate the trick, hence unleashing chaos. The story is divided into multiple first-person viewpoints, fragmenting it as comprehensively as any of Haldeman's works, although the taut plot-line is enhanced rather than undermined by the device. (The method had also been tried out in "Seasons", where it did not work nearly as well.)

The Long Habit of Living (1989)—retitled *Buying Time* by its US publisher—is also a chase thriller, this time on an interesting interplanetary stage in which the asteroid belt is a lawless quasi-Communist frontier. The lovers on the run, accompanied by a computerized "Turing Image" of a friend whose murder has urged them to flight, are beneficiaries of the Stileman Process: a technology of rejuvenation that has to be renewed every twenty years or so, at a price of a million dollars plus everything else the recipient possesses. The "immortals" who use the process repeatedly must use ingenious means to make their millions over and over again, while the wealth of the super-rich is recycled—a situation ripe for corruption, and far too precarious to endure forever. The science-fictional elements of the story are fascinating, but the plot has too few twists to make it a wholly satisfactory thriller.

The Hemingway Hoax (1990) won Hugo and Nebula awards as a novella, and the book version is only slightly expanded. As with its predecessors, it is more thriller than mystery, although the invocation of enigmatic "time police," who keep murdering the hero in the hope of preventing him from forging Hemingway's lost early works, certainly succeeds in convoluting the plot to an extraordinary degree. It is difficult to perceive any rationale within the plot; no explanation is offered for the motive or method of the individual who finally stands revealed as its prime mover, and the story's climactic dissolution smacks of sweeping the dust under the carpet.

While he was writing these books, Haldeman diverted some of his creative effort into teaching a course in science fiction writing and a more general writing course at MIT—a part-time arrangement set up in 1983. Some of his best subsequent short stories, including "More Than the Sum of His Parts" (1985) and the Nebula- and World Fantasy Award-winning "Graves" (1992), follow patterns derived from exercises which he habitually set his students. He also began writing poetry again in some profusion, much of which was reprinted in *Saul's Death & Other Poems* (1997). The three interviews published in Locus between 1989 and 1994 refer to several projects whose completion was considerably delayed, including a novel about first contact with aliens, provisionally titled *The Coming*, but his work appeared to take on a new lease of life after the completion of *Worlds Enough and Time*, when a new burst of sustained creativity produced *1968*, the fine novella "For White Hill" (1995)—which is about the aftermath of an interstellar war that seems to have been won but still has its most destructive phase to come—and *Forever Peace*.

Forever Peace is not a sequel to *The Forever War* but it does re-examine all of the concerns raised in that novel and in other stories reflecting upon the question of whether humankind can possibly outlive its addiction to war. The war is a mid-twenty-first century affair, which opposes the USA—whose economic hegemony has been firmly secured by its monopoly of "nanoforge" technology—and the puppet governments of the Third World to a loose alliance of "rebel forces". The US forces do most of their fighting by remote control, teams of ten "jacking in" to heavily-armed "soldierboys", reconnaissance units alternating ten-day shifts with squads of "hunter/killers". While they are linked up to their machines and to one another, the military personnel share their thoughts, feelings and memories—but the camaraderie thus engendered has costs as well as benefits. Some civilians pay to be fitted with jacks for private reasons, although they mostly have to go to clinics outside the USA and the procedure is risky. The religious fundamentalists known as Enders—because they are expecting the imminent end of the world—strongly disapprove of the technology.

The novel's hero, Julian Class, is a draftee who alternates tours of duty with an academic career as a physicist, in which connection he is involved with the Jupiter Project, building a massive supercollider in the orbit of Io, which will be able to duplicate the initial conditions of the Diaspora (formerly known as the Big Bang). When he and his co-workers discover that switching on the supercollider will blow up the solar system, their attempt to warn the world is quickly subverted by the military, launching them into a hectic chase-thriller plot whose ultimate aim is not merely to save the world from summary execution but also to create the conditions in which world peace might finally be secured and sustained.

Like its predecessor, *Forever Peace* was a multi-award winner, and deservedly so. It capitalizes on all the experience Haldeman had gained in the interim, eclectically selecting out the most useful of the many narrative methods he had tried out. Although it alternates first-person and third-person viewpoints, it is the least fragmentary of all his novels. It brings into unprecedentedly clear focus an ideology that gives the impression of being fully mature, having finally moved beyond the suffocating effects of sarcastic cynicism and nihilistic bitterness. Some doubt must remain as to whether the ending of the novel is really so very different, in objective terms, from the ending of *The Forever War*—but Haldeman does seem to offer it as the best hope imaginable, barring the intervention of aliens too benevolent to command belief.

* * * * * * *

Although Haldeman, in the 1997 interview, chose to emphasize the fact that combat changes people forever, Julian Class prefers to call attention to the other side of the coin. Referring to someone else's crucial trauma he says: "But that's not who you are. We go through these things, and then we more or less absorb them, and we become whatever we are becoming." (*Forever Peace*, p. 65) If Haldeman's career were to be reduced to the most brutal summary possible, that would do as well as any other formulation. Combat changes everyone, but it does not change everyone in the same way. Haldeman went to Vietnam a scientist and a poet, a man of intelligence and artistry; he came back badly wounded, but essentially the same. His contemplation of likely futures and actual pasts has consistently urged him in the direction of cynical desperation, but his work has never been completely unkind, or completely inhumane.

ROBERT IRWIN

Robert Graham Irwin was born in Guildford on 23 August 1946. He was educated at Epsom College and the University of Oxford, from which he graduated in 1967 with a degree in history. He worked for five years thereafter as a researcher in the School of Oriental and African Studies. After marrying Helen Taylor in 1972 he became a lecturer in history at St Andrews University in Scotland, but when they moved to London in 1977 he gave up full-time work, continuing to teach on a part-time basis while also working as a househusband and writing his first novel, *The Arabian Nightmare* (1983).

At a creative writing workshop Irwin met two other writers equally ambitious to publish their first novels, Eric Lane and Geoffrey Smith. Lane, who had qualified as a barrister but was not enthusiastic to pursue that career, suggested that they should set up their own publishing company for that purpose. The company in question, Dedalus, issued the three books in November 1983. Lane's novel was naturalistic but the other two were both offbeat historical fantasies. Smith's *The Revenants*, issued under the pseudonym Geoffrey Farrington, is an exercise in vampire existentialism somewhat akin to Anne Rice's *Interview with the Vampire* (1976); it seemed to the company's founders to be more commercial than Irwin's novel, but it was *The Arabian Nightmare* that greatly enhanced the company's fortunes dramatically when reprint rights were sold to Eugen Diedrichs in Germany and then to Viking Penguin for a considerable sum.

With Lane at the helm, Dedalus went from strength to strength, reprinting a great deal of classic literary fantasy and some contemporary material from continental European sources, and publishing the first novels of several notable British writers of defiantly unorthodox fiction, including Pat Gray, Andrew Crumey, and David Madsen. Although Irwin's second and third novels were not initially issued by the company, he has remained associated with it throughout its remarkable history, and his own produce may be regarded as an exemplary microcosm of its remarkably eclectic and exuberantly inventive list.

Alongside his novels Irwin has published a number of academic works. Although these derive from his expertise as a historian of the Middle East, they manifest a strong interest in Arabic folklore. His definitive book on *The Middle East in the Middle Ages: The Early Mamluk Sultanate, 1250-1382* (1986) was followed by an article on "The Arabic Beast Fable" (1992), the monumental *The Arabian Nights: A Companion* (1994), and *Night and Horses and the Desert: An Anthology of Classical Arabic Literature* (2000). His fascination with the method, substance and historical context of the Arabian Nights is fundamental to *The Arabian Nightmare*, a tale of the never-ending manufacture of intricately interwoven fantasies even more ingenious, and considerably more macabre, than those spun by Scheherazade.

When Antoine Galland first introduced the *Mille-et-Une Nuits* into Europe between 1704 and 1717 its imaginative apparatus was so widely borrowed as to color the temper and manner of French literature for more than a century, and composing tales according to "the Galland method" remained in vogue well into the nineteenth century. The most intricate and extensive of these pastiches was a gaudy picaresque patchwork nowadays known as *The Saragossa Manuscript*, written by the Polish count Jan Potocki (1761-1815) and published in a series of fragments—the earliest in the original French and the last recovered from Polish manuscripts—over a period of nearly two hundred years. Rediscovered in the 1960s, this was the second key influence on *The Arabian Nightmare*, having introduced the motif of a man who seems to wake repeatedly from frightful nightmares only to find that his "waking" experience decays over and over again into the same awful confusion.

In Irwin's novel, sufferers from the so-called Arabian nightmare are cursed to suffer appalling torments when they dream, only to forget all about them when they awake—which adds a further dimension to the confusion of the protagonist, Balian of Norwich. Balian keeps telling himself that he cannot be afflicted by the Arabian nightmare because he can remember his dreams—an argument that fails every time his most recent apparent awakening proves to have been merely a further extrapolation of his dream.

Irwin also takes care to import a good deal of twentieth-century thought into his account of the Arabian nightmare, enlivening his consideration of the nature of dreams with ideas drawn from modern psychological theory and experimentation as well as filling out his descriptions of fifteenth century Cairo and its dream-analogue with details drawn from the illuminating perspective of modern historical studies.

Balian's existential confusion is further reflected by a teasing game in which the reader is continually invited to wonder who, within the tale, is its supposed author and actual teller; every time a conclusion seems to be reachable it is quickly confounded. The text is thus engaged in a constant game of self-deconstruction, which links it to the fancies of the latest generations of Gallandesque French Romance-mongers, including Barthesian mythologists and Derridaesque post-structuralists.

There never was another tale as self-conscious in its convolutions as *The Arabian Nightmare*, nor one that eases the unease of the dream-state into such seductively sinister intercourse with the intelligence of the reader. The network of tales-within-tales reminds us, unremittingly, of the precariousness of our identity in the face of a world whose solidity and predictability can never be wholly certain, and sets us upon the subtle rack of deepest anxieties. Even while he undermines his readers with cognitive vertigo, however, Irwin writes with great charm and suave wit; the novel always maintains a vibrant sense of wonder, which recognizes and applauds the fact that nightmares, no matter how horrid they are, are magnificent feats of the imagination of which dreamers can be legitimately proud.

There is a uniquely glorious triumph in making one's literary debut with a novel of such manifest brilliance that it becomes an instant classic, but it can cast a shadow over subsequent endeavors. Perhaps *The Arabian Nightmare* will not prove, in the end, to be unsurpassable, but it was certainly an exceedingly hard act to follow. Anything else was bound to seem narrow limited by comparison, so it is entirely appropriate that Irwin's next novel made necessity into a virtue by concentrating its attention on the discomforts and psychological politics of narrowly-confined experience and imaginative limitation. *The Limits of Vision* (1986) makes a stark and frankly absurd contrast with *The Arabian Nightmare* in shrinking its horizons to a opposite extreme, focusing intently on the paranoid fantasies of Marcia, a housewife engaged in a continuous war against the household dirt that—according to her defiantly arcane understanding—is actually the empire of the incarnate spirit of evil, Mucor.

The Limits of Vision is a calculatedly silly book, whose packaging is replete with warnings against the awful dangers to health and hygiene posed by "dirty books". It is very funny, but its sparkling humor overlays a serous discourse about the constant struggle of the human imagination to break free from the fetters of limited vision.

Marcia's imaginary dialogues with various intellectual giants, and her bold plan to add a corrective sequel to Dostoyevsky's *The Brothers Karamazov*, are not only brave but intellectually substantial. The novel's denouement provides a timely reminder that anyone who isn't paranoid in today's world must be stark raving mad. Whether the novel actually succeeded in providing moral rearmament to those modern prisoners of conscience who stay home to do the housework, while their spouses sally forth into the world, remains unknown—but it certainly has that precious potential.

Irwin's third novel, *The Mysteries of Algiers* (1988), was a political melodrama exploring more recent trends in north African politics, but he returned to the margins of fantasy in *Exquisite Corpse* (1995), a delicate and poignant account of a doomed love affair set against the background of the Surrealist Movement. In keeping with the spirit of the exercise, the text represents itself as the second (1952) edition of a novel whose first (1951) edition was entirely fictitious, updated by additional material which shows the contents of that first edition in an entirely new light. Its readers are, therefore, invited to imagine themselves not only reading the text that is but also the text that (hypothetically) was, appreciating the transformation and illumination that has been gifted by the "new" information.

Caspar, the protagonist of *Exquisite Corpse* looks back, with the aid of this curious binocular vision, on the heady days of his involvement with the ill-fated Serapion Brotherhood (named after the tale-tellers in another of the classic portmanteau works by which Irwin is fascinated, E. T. A. Hoffmann's *Die Serapions-brüder*, 1819-21). Membership of the Serapion Brotherhood involves Caspar with Oliver Sorge, author of *The Vampire of Surrealism*—who, according to the dedication "taught me all I know about writing"—and MacKellar, author of *The Girlhood of Gagool*. It is while working on his illustration to the latter masterpiece that Caspar meets up with the archetypally ordinary typist Caroline, with whom he falls in love—according to his own conscientiously surreal fashion—and whose mysterious disappearance is the subject-matter of the text.

The hypothetical first edition of the novel is said to have presented this vanishing act as an enigma, surreal in itself; the second presents it as an enigma solved, in a bathetically mundane manner—but that interpretation too has to be taken with a pinch of salt, because Caspar's vision and memory may have been permanently confused by his experiments with hypnagogic imagery. Caspar takes these experiments very seriously—as did his author, who admits to consulting the hypnagogic images cast upon his closed eyelids from within when seeking inspiration for the continuation of the plot. Although Caspar has no idea how profoundly his hypnagogic adventures have altered his consciousness, and the reader can only guess, they undoubtedly create an arcane kinship linking him to dreaming Balian, hallucinating Marcia and the drugged protagonist of Irwin's sixth novel, *Satan Wants Me*, which significantly increases his unreliability as a narrator.

When the Serapion Brotherhood arranges the first Surrealist Exhibition in England—briefly bringing Caspar into contact with the presiding genius of surrealism, André Breton—the contact proves explosive and the Brotherhood disintegrates. Caspar's career thereafter, doubly blighted by the vanishment of Caroline and the advent of World War II, goes rapidly downhill. As with Marcia in *The Limits of Vision*, Caspar's ruminations on the theory and practicality of art-work are assisted by other—perhaps much wiser—minds, whose fleshly envelopes make brief but effective guest appearances. Like Marcia, Caspar retains his defiant individuality to the end, but in his case the stubbornness of that insistence proves more corrosive and ultimately tragic.

As in both Irwin's earlier novels, the readers of *Exquisite Corpse* are expected to develop a keen but never-quite-reliable sense of the extent to which the unreliable narrator is fooling himself, but, as in both earlier cases, those readers are eventually invited to wonder whether they have been a little too ready to assume the superiority of their own judgment. That game continues, played with considerably more aggression, in *Satan Wants Me* (1999), which tracks the further evolution of the modern fascination with occultism briefly celebrated by the surrealists.

Like *The Limits of Vision*, whose subject-matter harks back to Irwin's days as a househusband, *Satan Wants Me* has a quasi-autobiographical element, recalling Irwin's student days; it is set in 1967, the year of his graduation. The novel's protagonist, Peter Keswick, finds himself caught in a limbo between student life and wholehearted labor, contemplating the bottom rungs of a potential career ladder while cherishing the remnants of a glorious freedom from responsibility. The text takes the form of a diary, which he is instructed to keep by Dr. Felton, the Master supervising his instruction in the mysteries of the Black Book Lodge—a descendant organization of Aleister Crowley's Ordo Templi Orientis, which maintains its headquarters in Horapollo House. It is understood from the beginning that the diary is to be consulted on a regular basis by Dr. Felton, and the alert reader is expected to deduce that, although it will strive mightily to give the impression of absolute honesty, there might well be matters that will go surreptitiously unrecorded for diplomatic reasons—although the most alert reader in the world would find it difficult to estimate the exact extent of this dissimulation.

Peter's unreliable narration is not the only source of mystery in the plot. The Black Book Lodge is, by its nature, the ostensible custodian of many-layered secrets, and it has hidden agendas within its own hidden agendas. The reader is expected to deduce—although Peter is much slower on the uptake—that the Lodge has a particular interest in him, and that its members' careful interventions in his love life are aspects of a cunning plan. Although he is given Crowley's *Moonchild* (1929) to read by way of homework, Peter is not sufficiently attentive to that novel's plot to notice either the crucial similarities or the crucial differences between the scheme there outlined and the one that is gradually enveloping him. Distracted by the strain of keeping his own secrets, he is insufficiently wary of the spider-web that has been constructed to catch, entangle and consume him.

It may seem to be a rather back-handed compliment to say that the greatest strength of *Satan Wants Me* is the bathos that ultimately reduces the mock-sublime elements of the story to common folly, but that is what the text intends. Writers who try to treat Crowleyesque magic with deadly earnest, like Dennis Wheatley, who was reaching the end of his best-selling career in 1967 and makes a dutiful cameo appearance in *Satan Wants Me,* only succeed in making it seem ridiculous—a fact fully appreciated by Crowley, who included a reading list for would-be initiates in *Magick in Theory and Practice*, which blithely recommends such puritan melodramas as comedies while emphasizing that *Alice in Wonderland* is "invaluable to those who truly understand the Kabbalah".

It is far more effective, if one is ambitious to disturb sophisticated readers, to present that kind of magic dismissively and parodically, displaying its absurd pretensions as absurd pretensions, while granting it an insidious power in spite of that fact. Irwin's treatment of magic is sufficiently delicate to allow the interpretation that its effects are due to drug-distorted perceptions and the power of suggestion, but it is also sufficiently robust to permit real horrors to creep into its action. The text continually moves from the high-flown rhetoric of Felton's instruction to the ham-fisted crudity of Peter's obedience, but the implicit irony of such bathetic moves gradually becomes infected with a genuine unease—and when the plot makes its final precipitous descent, from brief drug-assisted high to enduring brutal mundanity, the tragic dimension of the comedy is fully revealed.

As quasi-autobiographical novels go, *Satan Wants Me* is unusually unself-indulgent—less so, in fact, than its predecessor. Marcia may be mad, but she is an authentic heroine, and it would be difficult even for the most churlish reader not to side with her in her struggle; her fantasizing is bold and brilliant, recording a flamboyant triumph of the imagination over adversity. By contrast, even a charitable reader is bound to find Peter Keswick hard to like; outside his uncontrolled bouts of chemically-assisted hallucination he is depressingly sane, and his sanity has a distinct yellow streak. His whole story, especially its climax, is a cruel record of the triumph of adversity over imagination. The story whose protagonist he provides is, however, far cleverer and much subtler than he is. The diary's last entry, dated October 1997, hammers home the message that any middle-aged baby-boomer reckless enough to think, in 1967, that adolescence was the winter of his discontent knows far better now.

Between *Exquisite Corpse* and *Satan Wants Me*, Dedalus issued another novel by Irwin, which had been commissioned and then aborted by a commercial publisher. *Prayer-Cushions of the Flesh* (1997) is a stylish exercise in pornography: a deft and skilful addition to a noble tradition launched in French by such novels as Pierre Louÿs' *The Adventures of King Pausole* (1901) and carried forward by such pioneers of surrealism as Guillaume Apollinaire. Its protagonist, Orkhan, is the son of a Sultan who has been raised alongside his brothers in a cage, from which the only prospect of release seems to be succession to the sultanate or murderous disposal. When he eventually emerges, however, he is brought into the labyrinthine halls of his father's harem, where he soon discovers that authentic temporal power does not reside where he had always supposed—in the throne and the phallus—but in the ingenious machinations of the women of the harem.

The winsomely mercurial Anadil, the philosophically captivating Mihrimah and the energetically masochistic Roxelana, under the instruction of his mother, the Valide Sultan, undertake a strenuous program of re-education in order to prepare Orkhan for his allotted fate: a program which, in spite of its many exotic and exhausting couplings, he relishes only in part. Mercifully, though, whenever Orkhan is forced by circumstance or exhaustion to rest for a while, there are dwarfs, eunuchs and washerwomen on hand to tell him wonderful stories, all of which are marvelously implausible, deliciously dirty and very probably false.

Although *Prayer-Cushions of the Flesh* is a literary confection, intended purely for amusement and the nourishment of pheromonal appetites, it is by no means a negligible work; as Voltaire one remarked, the superfluous is a very necessary thing, and there is a special delight in such fabulous superfluities as these.

Irwin's *oeuvre* also includes four short stories: "The Persistence of False Memory (1989) "Waiting for the Zaddik" (1991) and "Singing Underwater" (1992) and "An Incident at the Monastery of Alcobaca" (1992). "Waiting for the Zaddik", a stark meditation upon the historical significance of the Holocaust, is a bleak *conte philosophique*.

There is a sense in which all Irwin's subsequent work can be seen as a series of footnotes to *The Arabian Nightmare*, carefully extrapolating the fundamental unease of that novel's blurring of the boundary between fantasy and reality. Many other contemporary writers delight in blurring that boundary, but very few who write in English are as interested in Irwin in the way in which confusions within stories—especially those that relate to stories-within-stories—can reach out of the text to embrace the reader's own involvement, not merely with the text at hand but with the texts referenced within it, and with all the tangled tales that comprise the intricately-interrelated fabrics of fiction and reality.

GRAHAM JOYCE

Graham William Joyce was born into a mining family in a colliery village in Warwickshire on 22 October 1954. He was educated at Nicholas Chamberlaine Comprehensive School in Bedworth and Bishop Lonsdale College of Education, from which he graduated with a B.Ed. in 1978. He subsequently attended Leicester University, where he obtained an M.A. in English and American Literature in 1981, the same year in which he won a George Fraser Poetry Award. He worked thereafter in various short-term jobs, including teaching, before becoming a development officer for the National Association of Youth Clubs. In 1988 he married Suzanne Johnsen, a solicitor.

Joyce did a good deal of traveling while pursuing his ambition to write, and completed his first novel, *Dreamside* (1991), on the Greek island of Lesbos before going on to the Middle East. After returning to England he became a Writing Fellow at Wolverhampton University, and then, in 1997, a part-time tutor in creative writing at Nottingham Trent University. He and Suzanne settled in Leicester; their daughter Ella was born on 6 August 1996 and their son Joseph on 18 October 1998.

Although Joyce's later work was to draw extensively on his experience of other countries and cultures, *Dreamside* draws upon earlier experiences. The lives of its four central characters are profoundly affected by an experiment undertaken while they are university students in the mid-1970s, in association with a professor of psychology, L. P. Burns. Burns is researching the phenomenon of lucid dreaming, and under his tutelage Lee Peterson, Ella Innes, Honora Brennan and Brad Cousins become so adept at taking control of their dreams that they are able to meet up "dreamside", in the dreamworld equivalent of a holiday cottage in the Brecon Beacons owned by Burns. After the professor's death they continue their dream-adventure for a while, but it turns increasingly sour and is utterly spoiled when the volatile Brad "rapes" Honora within their shared dream. The four go their separate ways, all their lives having been blighted in one way or another.

Honora, the only devout religious believer in the group, comes off worst of the four, because she carries the loss of her virginity and her pregnancy into the real world. Although the real baby miscarries, its dreamside equivalent is successfully delivered, and grows up there as a kind of phantom, whose demands on her creators' real lives become increasingly onerous, until they begin to warp reality. Reunited after ten years by bitter necessity, the four have to find a way to repair the damage they have done to themselves and the connective fabric binding the world of their dreams to the world that is—at least in one mode of representation—God's dream.

Dark Sister (1992) is also set in England. It presents a meticulously compiled and carefully supernaturalized study of the fragmentation of a marriage. Maggie, the wife of archaeologist Alex Sanders, discovers an old diary, which introduces her to the world of witchcraft, into which she delves progressively deeper as her trouble relationship comes apart. Although the diary is full of ominous warnings, Maggie finds the assistance she needs in order to prepare potions, lay curses and teach herself to "fly"—but she needs all the contemporary help she can get when the train of dark sisterhood that she has extended back into the past begins to imperil her and her two children. Her estranged husband makes his own contribution to the solution of the mystery as he excavates anomalous findings from his current dig, but bringing the pieces of the puzzle together is as fraught a business as the attempt to salvage something from the ruins of the fractured marriage.

The intensity of the story is cleverly maintained in spite of the fact that Joyce frequently departs from Maggie's central consciousness in order to employ other viewpoint characters—a method that he was to deploy with equal success in most of his subsequent novels, in which the characters often give the impression of being participants in marionette shows whose miscellaneous superhuman puppeteers are only partially apprehended. *Dark Sister* won Joyce the first of three British Fantasy Awards, the others being awarded in relatively quick succession for *Requiem* (1995) and *The Tooth Fairy* (1996).

Joyce was to use witchcraft as a metaphor again in "The Apprentice" (1993), which examines a less conventional relationship against the troubled political background of the Second World War. His first short story sale had been "Last Rising Sun" (1992) to an eccentric theme anthology lamenting the disappearance of the seven-inch vinyl single, *In Dreams*, edited by Paul J. McAuley and Kim

Newman, but that tale of a jukebox which utters curses by spontaneously playing "The House of the Rising Sun" was dramatically upstaged by "The Careperson" (1992), a stark *conte cruel* extrapolating Joyce's experience as a youth worker into a harsh future.

House of Lost Dreams (1993) is similar to *Dark Sister* in using supernatural devices to trace and dramatize the stress put upon his marriage by the revelation of Mike Hanson's adultery with his wife's best friend. Mike and his wife Kim have settled on the Greek island of Mavros, where the head of Orpheus is alleged to have washed up after being cast into a river by the Maenads who murdered him, but the villa they have taken is even more profoundly haunted than the rest of the troubled isle. With the aid of the enigmatic shepherd Manoussos, Mike eventually discovers the nature of the most recent atrocity to have occurred at the house, but the roots of the turbulence afflicting Mavros go much deeper. Occasionally expressed as earthquakes, and consistently underlined by the activity of hostile wildlife, that turbulence gradually consumes Mike's relationship with Kim, and threatens to destroy Mike. There is no sanctuary to be found in the various churches that litter the landscape, whether or not they are still in use—quite the reverse, in fact. It is the Christian mythos that provides Mike's most urgent tormentor with the inconveniently substantial guise of the steel shod warrior-saint Mikalis.

Like Maggie in *Dark Sister*, Mike Hanson is eventually enabled by his contemporary advisers to confront his demon and to extricate himself from the predicament into which sin has delivered him; in his case, though, there is no greater settlement to be won on behalf of the spirits that swarm around the island. This pattern of evolution was continued; as Joyce's work has progressed the victories available to his troubled protagonists have become smaller and smaller, though never negligible. As the superhuman forces featured in his work have become gradually less explicit, they have become proportionately less resistible, assuming the role of a gnomic but implacable fate. The pattern is further developed in several short stories exploring various facets of marital distress, including "Gap-sickness" (1993) and "The Mountain Kills People" (1998).

Like Mike Hanson, Tom Webber, the protagonist of *Requiem*, is driven to flight by guilt. His futile bid for escape, after losing his wife Katie in a freak accident and quitting his teaching job, takes him to Jerusalem to meet up with an old friend, Sharon, who works with mentally-disturbed addicts at the Bet Ha-Kerem Rehabilitation Centre. He also meets an elderly scholar named David Feldberg, who entrusts him with the care of one of the Dead Sea Scrolls, which he has possessed for many years. Sharon and Tom take the scroll to one of her ex-patients, an Arab named Ahmed el-Asmar, who believes himself to be afflicted by djinn. Tom is similarly afflicted, by a phantom that sometimes manifests itself as his wife's ghost and sometimes as Mary Magdalene, the author of the document.

The scroll turns out to be Mary's account of the death of Jesus, her husband, and the subsequent hijacking of the movement that became the Christian faith by "the Liar", Saint Paul. (This version of Mary Magdalene had been trailed in *Dark Sister*, where she is named as one of the avatars of the stigmatized mother goddess.) As the plot of *Requiem* unfolds, the convoluted reasons for Tom's distress become clear, but his condition worsens as his relationship with Sharon intensifies and his demons become more insistent. The haunter eventually takes possession of one of the patients at Bet Ha-Kerem, subverting the counseling Tom receives there from Sharon's employer and precipitating a violent crisis.

The earnest employment of religious faith as a key element in the plot of *Requiem* is supplemented by an unusually harsh scheme of judgment, which regards sins committed in thought as seriously as sinful thoughts translated into action—an attitude that dramatically narrows the scope for poetic justice to operate in bringing matters to a conclusion. Tom's redemption, such as it is, can only be an emollient applied to a wound that will never entirely heal.

The Tooth Fairy takes up the other thread established in *Dark Sister*, focusing on the difficult experiences of childhood while tangled adult lives are consigned to the background. Sam Southall, Clive Rogers, and Terry Morris are three children growing up in a village near Coventry not unlike the one in which Joyce grew up. Sam encounters the Tooth Fairy of local superstition, but finds the filthy, foul-mouthed and androgynous figure much more ominous than he could ever have expected. Stigmatized even by his first encounter, his predicament gets worse as the monster's intrusions into his life become increasingly—though not unambiguously—troublesome. To some extent, the Tooth Fairy represents the conventional hazards and challenges of male adolescence, but takes all of them to such a dark and dangerous extreme that Sam's *rite de passage* becomes a matter of life and death, whose scars are unlikely to heal.

The Tooth Fairy is as redolent of bitter disillusionment as "The Careperson", but as a novelist, Joyce is always careful to conserve the hope that even the direst threats might be overcome, and the darkest of potential futures lightened. Another group of three friends on the threshold of adolescence is featured in *The Web: Spiderbite*

(1997), Joyce's contribution to a series of futuristic novellas aimed at a teenage audience. Restricted by the format, however, Joyce was not able to capitalize on his greatest authorial strengths. The plot is a conventional thriller in which the three teenage "tech-rats" stumble upon a plot orchestrated by the Web series' resident supervillain, the Sorceress, to plant false memories in millions of young people in order to recruit them to her own designer cult, the Planetologists.

The Stormwatcher (1998) has no explicitly supernatural component, although it makes much of the common analogy between human emotions and weather. It tracks the languorous development of a cathartic storm within the tangled relationships of a party of holidaymakers in the Dordogne. Although it features yet another guilt-ridden husband in James (the text offers no surnames) and yet another smoldering wife in Sabine, the main focus of the story is their daughter Jessie, who is being taught to see things in a new way by a mysterious and seemingly-insane instructor—obviously one of the other adult women in the party of five, although the reader is not told which until the crisis actually breaks.

The relationships between the five adults are unusually tangled; Matt and Chrissie, the second couple, are nursing resentments because James once made Matt redundant for less-than-honorable reasons, and the spare female, Rachel, once had an affair with him. The addition of two children means that, when an explicit arithmetic calculation of all the binary relationships within the party is made, the total is far in excess of that obtained by the similar calculation made when Mike and Kim Hanson were entertaining friends in *House of Lost Dreams*—and that is the very essence of the gathering storm. The absence of active supernatural forces reduces the melodramatic aspect of the eventual climax of *The Stormwatcher*, relative to all of its predecessors, but there is ample compensation in the depth and complexity of the carefully-entwined relationships and their curious histories.

Indigo (1999) is the most original and most intriguing of all Joyce's novels. Like *The Stormwatcher* it has no explicit supernatural component, but the beliefs held by several of its key characters are so extraordinary that the entire narrative is possessed of an ominous quality that is quite unique. Jack Chambers, whose life has been subtly but profoundly blighted by occasional contact with the father who deserted him as an infant, must execute certain aspects of the dead man's will in order to claim his share of the inheritance.

In order to locate another beneficiary, Natalie Shearer, and dispose of properties in Chicago and Rome, Jack is obliged to contact his half-sister Louise, to whom he experiences a problematic sexual attraction. She and her infant son Billy go with him to Rome, where they begin to penetrate the mysteries of Tim Chambers' coterie of young artists, many of whom have come to sticky ends. In the meantime, Jack reads the book whose publication is the last of his executive duties: a guide to the dangerous art of becoming invisible, whose first step is to discover and learn to see the phantom color of the Newtonian spectrum, indigo.

Like Jessie in *The Stormwatcher*, Jack finds himself being instructed in a new way of seeing, which promises much but threatens even more—and, as with Jessie, it is by no means clear to the reader whether the intentions of his seemingly-insane tutor are benign or malign. There seems to be little scope for Jack to win any kind of victory, other than figuring out what motivated his mysterious father, and even in that mission his penetrative "bobby's eye" is of very limited use. The metaphors of sight and color deployed within the story are, however, far more subtle and complex than the weather metaphors deployed in *The Stormwatcher* or the witchcraft featured in *Dark Sister*, and the story is much richer as well as much stranger in consequence. The extraordinary elaboration of the peculiar theory of superior sight advanced in Tim Chambers' book makes *Indigo* a more imaginatively far-reaching novel than any of its predecessors, but the problematic relationships orchestrated and illuminated by means of the metaphor are no less intense or sharp-edged; the novel is, in consequence, a remarkable *tour de force*.

Joyce's steady progress—or regress—towards unembellished naturalism continued in the novella *Leningrad Nights* (1999), which follows the exploits of an orphaned child during the siege of Leningrad in the winter of 1941-42. The shell-shocked and psychologically-fragmented Leo appoints himself the protector of a pregnant prostitute named Natasha, and delivers her baby son, Isaac, but Natasha is a secret Christian and when she discovers the origin of the meat that he has used to keep her alive she rejects him. Although she repents of her wrath, he sets out for the front, where his eventual fate is allowed to remain provocatively uncertain.

Smoking Poppy (2001)—the first of Joyce's novels to focus on the experience of a single first-person narrator—begins in even more restrained fashion and proceeds for most of its narrative distance as a naturalistic drama, but eventually allows a quantum of mysticism to intrude upon the plot. Its narrator, Danny Innes, is jerked out of a morass of sullen self-pity when he is told that his once-beloved daughter Charlotte has been jailed in Thailand on charges of drug-smuggling. He sets off to find her, accompanied by his son Philip—a fanatical Christian—and a market trader named Mick Williams, who insists on helping out even though his taciturn relationship with Danny has been limited to serving on the same pub quiz team and the occasional game of snooker.

The forceful Mick proves invaluable in getting Danny rapid access to the British Consul and the imprisoned girl—who turns out to have stolen Charlotte's passport. In order to find the real Charlotte the three must go deep into the jungle, into a lawless region near the Burmese border. When they find her, living in a remote village under the ambiguous protection of the local opium baron, they discover that she cannot leave her hut, believing herself to have been cursed in consequence of an accidental violation of the village's Spirit Gate. In order to have the curse lifted, Danny has to go to extremes himself, not merely in terms of violent action but in making his own opium-induced hallucinatory journey to an uncomfortable confrontation with his imperfect fatherhood.

Marketed as an item of literary fiction rather than a horror story, *Smoking Poppy* seemingly completed a repositioning process that had begun with *The Stormwatcher*, leaching out all but the dregs of the fantastic suffusions that had fuelled Joyce's earlier dramas. The process involved a parallel reduction in the erotic element of his plotting, which flared up briefly and rather perversely in the highly-decorated *Indigo* but otherwise faded gradually into the background while conceding centre-stage to troubled relationships between parents and children (or, in the case of *Leningrad Nights*, a tortuous compact between a pseudo-parental child and an adopted child-parent). Parent-child relationships are also to the fore in the short story "Black Dust" (2002), which retains a small but crucial supernatural element. The replacement of erotic relationships by parental ones did not serve, however, to eliminate or substantially transform the themes of guilt-ridden betrayal and difficult penance that ran through the earlier novels, even though the "demons" associated with the featured betrayals became more enigmatic and ambiguous in character.

The strength of all Joyce's unorthodox melodramas lies in his ability to attribute the utmost seriousness to moral transgressions that many other writers would regard as trivial, or at least easily forgivable, and to impress that seriousness upon his readers. Joyce's work is authentically and creatively disturbing because it examines rather ordinary sins with such an extraordinary scrupulousness that it denies everyone—even steel-shod saints—the comforts of presumed innocence, while still offering hope of an eventual existential compromise, if not a manifest salvation.

MICHAEL SHEA

Apart from the facts that he was born in Los Angeles in 1946—probably the Michael Allen Shea born on 3 July of that year—and attended the University of California, there is little biographical information about Michael Shea available as a matter of public record. When invited to elaborate these data, he observed that "writers often have boring lives" and suggested the following additions: "After post-university years of transcontinental hitchhiking and European travel (more hitchhiking) Shea settled into a life of scrabbling for a living. He has done the usual: construction, carpentry, house-painting, flophouse night-clerking [and] has even descended to teaching (adults). His most precious possessions (and nearly his only ones) are his dear wife, the holographer/artist Linda Cecere Shea, his firstborn Della and second-born Jake." (Personal correspondence, 6 March 2002).

Shea's first-published novel, *A Quest for Simbilis* (1974), is set in the far future scenario devised by Jack Vance in *The Dying Earth* (1950), and describes further adventures of one of Vance's characters, Cugel the Clever, whose original appearance was in *The Eyes of the Overworld* (1966).

The use of the far future as a venue for fantasy fiction had been pioneered in the 1930s by Clark Ashton Smith in a series of stories set in Zothique. Smith had set earlier stories of much the same type in prehistoric sunken continents such as Hyperborea and Atlantis, but had decided that the exaggeratedly Decadent trappings of such settings were compromised by the reader's knowledge that the future of their neighbors must have been one of progressive evolution to modern civilization. Zothique, by contrast, is the perfect milieu for Decadent fantasy, because the entire solar system containing its world is doomed to perish when the sun dies; everything that happens there is cursed with a magnificent futility. Individual humans may retain the hope that they will live out their lives before oblivion claims everything, but the lack of any guarantee exacerbates their existential *angst* and they know that there is no point in building any kind of heritage for the sake of generations to come.

The tales of Zothique are possessed of an inherent black comedy, which Smith elected to embellish with fabulously gaudy prose. Vance's adaptation of the scenario differed little in its physical detail, although he was careful not to remain dependent on the obsolete theory by which Lord Kelvin had calculated the likely age of the sun on the assumption that its heat was being generated by gravitational collapse. Stylistically, however, Vance preferred to decorate his black comedies with a more delicate and more explicit wit. Of all the characters he developed for the dying Earth, Cugel is perhaps the most carefully-fitted to the tone of the stories: a casual liar, dyed-in-the-wool cheat and opportunistic thief, who is not quite as clever as he thinks he is. He often comes through his picaresque exploits as much by luck as judgment, and is all the more sympathetic because of it.

Shea's Cugel, who is still pursuing a feud with Iouconnu the Laughing Magician, the earlier phases of which had been mapped by Vance, has suffered a mishap, by virtue of mispronouncing a spell that has left him stranded on a barren shore of the Sea of Cutz. There he meets Mumber Sull, the Thane of a fishing-village that lies in territory once claimed by the legendary magician Simbilis, whose long absence has created an opportunity for usurpers to move in and take over. Sull persuades Cugel that they might benefit from teaming up to find Simbilis, whose power would be more than adequate to return Cugel to a more hospitable place, as well as ridding his own village of its new governors.

Their journey takes them through a series of challenging encounters, including a gruesome escapade in the vaults beneath Cannibal Keep, a hazardous game that wins them the right to use a narrow bridge across a vast chasm, and a failed attempt to do a favor for the obese rulers of the strange city of Waddlawg. Worse misfortune befalls them in the city of Millions Gather, which is a centre of trade between the upper world and the demonic underworld, and they are taken as prisoners into the demons' realm—but this is a necessary step, because the underworld is where Simbilis is allegedly to be found, campaigning against the demon hordes from his beleaguered citadel. As things turns out, the great magician is engaged in a rather different and much more ambitious project, which puts the petty concerns of Mumber Sull and Cugel into a broader context.

The bizarre underworld of *A Quest for Simbilis*, whose hyper-Boschian imagery adds an extra order of magnitude to the exotic surfaces pictured by Smith and Vance, became Shea's key contribution to far-futuristic fantasy. His next few stories set in similar scenarios abandon the trappings of Vance's dying Earth and substitute Nifft the Lean for Cugel. Initially a kind of literary clone, Nifft soon began to develop a more rounded character of his own, and a legendary status within his own world—which led to the tales of his adventures being collected and collated by one Shag Margold, who serves as an ironic and wryly skeptical commentator thereon.

Two of the four adventures assembled in the World Fantasy Award-winning *Nifft the Lean* (1982)—the novellas "Come Then, Mortal, We Will Seek Her Soul" and "The Fishing of the Demon Sea"—involve journeys into netherworlds undertaken by Nifft and his bulkier companion-in-arms Barnar Hammer-Hand. The former story is an elegant sarcastic fantasy, which carefully recomplicates and mercilessly subverts the basic plot of Orpheus' descent into Hades. The land of the dead featured therein is by no means comfortable, but it pales when set beside the gloriously phantasmagoric demon realm featured in "The Fishing of the Demon Sea".

Whereas the first descent undertaken by Nifft and Barnar was a willing one, the second is undertaken under the sternest compulsion—as it would have to be, given that no sane person would ever enter such an Inferno willingly, despite the awesome treasures it contains. They are dispatched to rescue a fool, and in order to do so they must find and recruit the aid of Gildmirth, a resident magician stranger by far in his capabilities and ambitions than Simbilis. Laying hands on the object of their search and freeing him from captivity is, however, merely a prelude to further hazards; getting such an inconvenient burden back to the surface in one piece doubles the difficulties faced during the descent, especially as their route brings them into intimate contact with a titanic refugee from a further and even more Hellish underworld: a demon's demon, interrupted in his attempt to burst out into the greater universe but not rendered entirely harmless.

By comparison with these two items, the shorter tales of "The Pearls of the Vampire Queen" and "The Goddess in Glass" are modest. The former is an account of ingenious thievery, which would be almost conventional were it not for its breezy ostentation. In the latter, Nifft is a virtual bystander observing a minor crisis in the affairs of an insectile "goddess"—actually an extraterrestrial visitor—whose vast size and exceedingly long reproductive cycle contrive a dramatic reversal of familiar existential comparisons between man and insect. This was a theme that Shea was to develop at considerable length, with ingenious variety and great effect, in further phantasmagoric fantasies and a sequence of brilliant horror stories.

Shea's third novel, *The Color Out of Time* (1984), is a sequel to H. P. Lovecraft's "The Color Out of Space", detailing occurrences following the resurgence of the exotic alien entity featured in the earlier story. The valley containing the farm whose well was blighted in Lovecraft's story has been dammed and the diseased terrain submerged beneath a man-made lake. The narrator and his companion are the first tourists camping by the lakeside who notice that anything is wrong; their attempts to alert the authorities and warn their fellow campers are thwarted by the increasingly-intrusive entity, but they are aided in their attempt to tackle it head-on by a resident of the area who remembers the initial infestation and has spent her life—with a little help from H. P. Lovecraft—gathering armaments against exactly such a resurgence.

In a Lovecraft story there would be no possibility of any resistance capable of winning more than a temporary respite, but Shea was already well-used to pitting his heroes against seemingly-impossible odds and bringing them out alive. The three allies contrive a robust and thrilling response to the demonic invader of which no Lovecraftian protagonist would ever have been capable; another Lovecraftian fantasy by Shea, the delectably nasty-minded, "Fat Face" (1988), is far less lenient.

Shea followed *The Color out of Time* with another ambitious far-futuristic fantasy, *In Yana, the Touch of Undying* (1985), which introduces a new anti-hero in Bramt Hex, an uncommitted student of arcana who gives way to a momentary romantic whim and decides to court a rich widow. The decision is unfortunate; he is quickly embroiled in a scheme to sell a local brothel to demons—a move requiring a translocation to the underworld and certain changes in working practices to which the resident whores strongly object. The botched deal does, however, put Hex on the trail of the legendary land of Yana, where the secret of immortality is rumored to be had for the taking, and he sets off to find it.

The quest is, inevitably, a very difficult one, involving numerous bizarre phases and many ironic misfortunes, but in the end Hex does reach his destination, and contrives to make the inevitable descent into the underworld that attainment of his goal requires. Once there, however, he is forced to recognize that the realization of his heart's desire is by no means as simple and straightforward as it once seemed. The imagery of the story is a little restrained by Shea's standards (though not, of course, by anyone else's) but it contains some marvelous set-pieces; its relaxed humor and its calculatedly languid flavor combine into a unique piquancy and it is one of the finest examples of modern Decadent fantasy.

The aquatic monster of *The Color out of Time* has distant kin in Nifft's Demon Sea, and on the alien world where human explorers meet the eponymous titan in the science fiction novella "Polyphemus" (1981), one of several stories Shea published in *The Magazine of Fantasy & Science Fiction*. Monsters extrapolated from marine life-forms by vast inflation were, however, sidelined in subsequent work in favor of insects and arachnids. Other alien visitors featured in Shea's *F&SF* stories include the inquisitive arachnid anthropologist in "The Angel of Death" (1979), whose benevolence is tested to an ironic limit by its encounter with a psychotic serial-killer, and the desperate castaway in the uncompromisingly gruesome "The Autopsy" (1980), whose tiny size does not diminish the threat it poses in its determination to survive. The most distinctive of the set is, however, "The Horror on the #33" (1982), an exceptionally fine existentialist fantasy in which Death rears an ugly insectile head in deeply discomfiting circumstances.

"Uncle Tuggs" (1986) is a more conventional *conte cruel* about a vengeful ghost, remarkable mainly for its moral cynicism. A similarly non-judgmental cynicism was cleverly extrapolated into a satirical account of the future of mass-entertainment in "The Extra" (1987) before reaching a new apogee in the fine novella *I, Said the Fly*, which appeared in *The Sixth Omni Book of Science Fiction* in 1989 before the separate publication of an expanded version. *I, Said the Fly* is yet another tale of alien invasion, this time as part of an exercise in colonization, whose human protagonist takes less inspiration than he might from the media project in which he is involved as he is gradually brought to see things from the insectile invaders' point of view. The brief "Delivery" (1987) is cut from the same cloth.

There was a considerable hiatus in Shea's publications in the early 1990s, although the blurb accompanying "Fat Face" when it was reprinted in the first in the series of *The Year's Best Fantasy* (later *The Year's Best Fantasy and Horror*), edited by Ellen Datlow and Terri Windling, announced that he had two novels forthcoming, entitled *Momma Durtt* and *The Plunderers*. Shea reports that the as-yet-unsold *Momma Durtt* is "a contemporary supernatural thriller (comic horror) about a pollution-poisoned Earth gone murderously mad" and that "*The Plunderers* is a novel that has been first drafted...about alien parasites, quite elaborate, [with a] contemporary setting" (personal correspondence 2 March 2002). He began publishing short fiction again in 1994, and began publishing novels again shortly thereafter. *The Mines of Behemoth* (1997) and *The A'rak* (2000) continue the adventures of Nifft the Lean, the former explaining how he eventually came to part company with Barnar Hammer-Hand and the latter linking him with a new and rather reluctant partner in Lagademe the Nuncio, who serves within the story as an alternate narrator.

The Mines of Behemoth is set in a region of the far future Earth insulated from demonic activity by the vastly-extensive nest of an alien hive whose members are nourished on demon flesh. Although the nest is in the underworld its neighborhood has been all-but-purged of demonkind by ruthless predation; only unusually clever and unobtrusive demonic parasites can thrive in close proximity thereto. The humans living on the surface, ever-anxious to exploit economic opportunities, have sunk a series of shafts into the nest in order that the gargantuan larvae may be "milked" of their "sap"—which to say, their fluid flesh.

This would not normally be the kind of work to which Nifft would stoop, but Barnar's nephew Costard has run into trouble while trying to ruin a sap-mine and Barnar is duty-bound to help him out. Nifft becomes more enthusiastic when an entrepreneur named Ha'Awley Bunt offers to pay a huge sum for a quantity of ichor exuded by the Queen, whose collection is a more dangerous enterprise. Then again, the demonic netherworld is strewn with treasures, which are less well-guarded in this region than in any other—although that situation is complicated by the presence of another ultra-demonic titan from the lower regions interrupted in his upward drive towards the light. The expedition is a great success—but in Shea's universe, even the greatest success is likely to turn to horridly ironic failure, and the disasters that befall Costard and Bunt affect Nifft and Barnar too.

Like "The Goddess in Glass" the Behemoth Queen and her entourage are probably extraterrestrial in origin, and although it poses many practical problems for its human neighbors the net effect of the nest's presence is relatively benign. There is no puzzle relating to the origin of *The A'rak*, which is definitely extraterrestrial, but there is a great deal of ambiguity about the relationship that the giant arachnid forges with its human associates on the island of Hagia. It agrees to serve as their god, to reward them with gold, and to maintain their prosperity by providing unassailable protection for the vaults in which the gold is kept (thus gifting Hagia with the only safe banks in the entire pirate-ridden world). All it asks in return is a few discreet human sacrifices, offered on a regular basis, with which to feed its children—but the number of the A'rak's children have grown as the island's people have thrived, and the witches who inhabit the neighboring islands of the Astrygal chain take the view that its discretion has been merely a preparatory phase.

Lagademe the Nuncio is a messenger hired by the witches to make a seemingly-innocent delivery to North Hagia; although suspicious of him from the first, she hooks up with Nifft, who has come to make a secret investigation of the possibility of making a withdrawal from the island's supposedly-impregnable banks. Borne by rumors of imminent disaster, thousands of other thieves gather in his wake, ready and willing to take advantage of any sudden depopulation.

There is a sense in which *The A'rak* is less adventurous than *The Mines of Behemoth*, being merely one more addition to the great tradition of menacing monster stories, unembellished by any account of the phantasmagoric underworld; its plot has more in common with *The Color out of Time* than "The Fishing of the Demon Sea". It is, however, a remarkably fine example of the "giant bug" subgenre, perhaps the best of all. The painstakingly slow revelation of the monster is handled with great dexterity, and the climactic confrontation is vividly horrific as well as providing a golden opportunity for bold and uncompromising heroics.

Michael Shea has always been the kind of writer more likely to win the fervent loyalty of a limited number of connoisseurs than the approval of a mass audience, because he cannot resist the urge to go to the limit—and then beyond—of any theme he adopts. The subgenres in which he prefers to work—far-futuristic fantasy and existentialistically-sophisticated horror—are unfashionably extreme in themselves, and he has done sterling work in further extending their extremes, with hectic flamboyance and the relish of a gourmet. He is, for this reason, a uniquely precious resource within the field of imaginative fiction: an authentic pioneer.

The fact that Shea has occasionally found it convenient to appropriate materials to which others have staked a prior claim—he describes his current project as "a very delicately Lovecrafted pastiche called *Mr. Cannyharme*, set in the pimp-whore-drug addict heartland of the Mission" (personal correspondence, 2 March 2002)—has served to obscure the fact that he is actually a highly original writer, with an eye for bizarrerie that no one else can presently match. Unlike Nifft the Lean, he is by no means a thief; he has more in common with Oscar Wilde, who could not see a thing of beauty produced by someone else without wanting to produce something akin to it that would be even more glorious—and Oscar Wilde, who bitterly lamented "The Decay of Lying", would surely have approved of a man who could envisage such a rich variety of maleficent and monstrous demons with such awesome clarity.

BIBLIOGRAPHY

WORKS BY S. FOWLER WRIGHT

The Adventure of the Blue Room (as Sydney Fowler). London: Rich & Cowan, 1945; as *The Blue Room*. Borgo Press, 2009.
The Adventure of Wyndham Smith. London: Herbert Jenkins, 1938.
The Amphibians: A Romance of 500,000 Years Hence London: Merton Press, 1925.
The Ballad of Elaine. London: Merton Press, 1926.
The Bell Street Murders (as Sydney Fowler). London: Harrap, 1931.
Beyond the Rim. London: Jarrolds, 1932.
David. London: Thornton Butterworth, 1934.
Dawn. New York: Cosmopolitan, 1929.
Deluge. London: Fowler Wright, 1927.
Dream; or, The Simian Maid. London: Harrap, 1931.
Elfwin. London: Harrap, 1930.
Four Days War. London: Hale, 1936.
The Hidden Tribe. London: Hale, 1938.
The Island of Captain Sparrow. London: Gollancz, 1928.
The King Against Anne Bickerton. London: Harrap, 1930.
[As ghost-writer] Hatry, Charles C. *Light Out of Darkness.* London: Rich & Cowan, 1939.
Lord's Right in Languedoc. London: Jarrolds, 1933.
Megiddo's Ridge. London: Hale, 1937.
The New Gods Lead. London: Jarrolds, 1932.
Ordeal of Barata. London: Herbert Jenkins, 1939.
Power. London: Jarrolds, 1933.
Prelude in Prague; a Story of the War of 1938. London: Hale, 1935.
Red Ike (with J. M. Denwood). London: Hutchinson, 1931.
The Riding of Lancelot. London: Fowler Wright Ltd., 1929.
Scenes from the Morte d'Arthur (as Alan Seymour). London: Erskine Macdonald, 1919.
The Screaming Lake. London: Hale, 1937.

The Secret of the Screen. London: Jarrolds, 1933.
Seven Thousand in Israel. London: Jarrolds, 1931.
S. Fowler Wright's Short Stories, Fowler Wright Books, 1996.
The Siege of Malta (completion of unfinished novel by Sir Walter Scott). vol. 1 *St. Elmo*; vol. 2 *St. Angelo*. London: Fredrick Muller, 1942.
The Song of Songs and Other Poems. Birmingham: Merton Press, 1925.
Spiders' War. New York: Abelard, 1954.
Three Witnesses. London: Thornton Butterworth, 1935.
The Throne of Saturn. Sauk City, WI: Arkham House, 1949.
Vengeance of Gwa (as Anthony Wingrave). London: Thornton Butterworth, 1935.
The Witchfinder. London: Books of Today, 1946.
The World Below. London: Collins, 1929.
[Translation]: *The Inferno* by Dante Alighieri. London: Fowler Wright Ltd., 1928.

(All of the above works, and the texts of various unpublished works, are available for consultation at www.sfw.org.uk)

WORKS BY DAVID BRIN

Brightness Reef. New York: Bantam, 1995. London: Orbit, 1996.
Earth. New York: Bantam, 1990. London: Macdonald, 1990.
Glory Season. New York: Bantam, 1993. London: Orbit, 1993.
Heart of the Comet (with Gregory Benford). New York; Bantam, 1986.
Heaven's Reach. New York: Bantam, 1998. London: Orbit, 1998.
Infinity's Shore. New York: Bantam, 1996. London: Orbit, 1997.
Otherness. New York: Bantam, 1994. London: Orbit, 1994.
The Postman. New York: Bantam, 1985. London: Bantam, 1986.
The Practice Effect. New York: Bantam, 1984. London: Bantam, 1986.
The River of Time. Niles, Illinois, Dark Harvest, 1986. London: Bantam, 1987.
Startide Rising. New York: Bantam, 1983. Revised London: Bantam, 1985.
Sundiver. New York: Bantam, 1980. London: Bantam, 1985.
The Transparent Society: Will Technology Force Us to Choose Between Freedom and Privacy? New York: Addison Wesley/Perseus Books, 1998.

The Uplift War. West Bloomfield, Michigan: Phantasia Press, 1987. London: Bantam, 1987.

WORKS BY JONATHAN CARROLL

After Silence. London: Macdonald, 1992; New York: Doubleday, 1993.
Black Cocktail. London: Legend, 1990; New York: St Martin's Press, 1991.
Bones of the Moon. London: Century, 1987; New York: Arbor House, 1988.
A Child Across the Sky. London: Legend, 1989; New York: Doubleday, 1990.
From the Teeth of Angels. London: HarperCollins & New York: Doubleday, 1994.
The Heidelberg Cylinder. Mobius New Media, 2000.
Kissing the Beehive. New York: Doubleday, 1998.
The Land of Laughs. New York: Viking, 1980; London: Hamlyn, 1982.
The Marriage of Sticks. London: Gollancz, 1999.
Outside the Dog Museum. London: Macdonald, 1991; New York: Doubleday, 1992.
The Panic Hand. London: HarperCollins, 1995; New York: St Martin's Press, 1996.
Sleeping in Flame. London: Legend, 1988; New York: Doubleday, 1999.
Voice of Our Shadow. New York: 1983; London: Arrow, 1984.
The Wooden Sea. London: Gollancz, 2000.

WORKS BY SAMUEL R. DELANY

The American Shore: Meditations on a Tale of Science Fiction by Thomas M. Disch—"Angouleme". Elizabethtown, NY: Dragon Press, 1978.
Atlantis: Three Tales. Seattle, WA: Incunabula, 1995
Babel-17. New York: Ace, 1966.
The Ballad of Beta-2. New York: Ace, 1965.
The Bridge of Lost Desire. New York; Arbor House, 1987; revised as *Return to Nevèrÿon*, London: Grafton, 1989; Hanover, NH: University Press of New England for Wesleyan University Press, 1994.
The Complete Nebula Award-Winning Fiction of Samuel R. Delany. New York: Bantam, 1986.

Dark Reflections. New York: Carroll & Graf, 2007
Dhalgren. New York: Bantam, 1975; revised, Boston: Gregg Press, 1977; London: Grafton, 1992.
Distant Stars. New York: Bantam, 1981.
Driftglass: Ten Tales of Speculative Fiction. New York: Doubleday, 1971; London: Gollancz, 1978.
The Einstein Intersection. New York: Ace, 1967; London: Gollancz, 1967; revised, London: Sphere, 1969; Boston: Gregg Press, 1976.
Empire Star. New York: Ace, 1966.
The Fall of the Towers: A Classic Science Fiction Trilogy. Initially published in three volumes as *Captives of the Flame*, New York: Ace, 1963; revised as *Out of the Dead City*, London: Sphere, 1971; *The Towers of Toron*, New York: Ace, 1964; revised, London: Sphere, 1968; *City of a Thousand Suns*. New York, Ace, 1965; revised, London: Sphere, 1969; omnibus edition New York: Ace, 1970; London: Sphere, 1971.
Flight from Nevèrÿon. New York: Bantam, 1985; revised, London: Grafton, 1989; Hanover, NH: University Press of New England for Wesleyan University Press, 1994
Heavenly Breakfast: *An Essay on the Winter of Love*. New York: Bantam, 1979.
Hogg. Boulder, Col.: Black Ice, 1994.
The Jewel-Hinged Jaw: Notes on the Language of Science Fiction. Elizabethtown, NY: Dragon Press, 1977.
The Jewels of Aptor. New York: Ace, 1962; revised, New York: Ace & London: Gollancz, 1968; further revised, London: Sphere, 1971 & Boston: Gregg Press, 1977.
The Mad Man. New York: Masquerade, 1994.
The Motion of Light in Water: Sex and Science-Fiction Writing in the East Village 1957-1965. New York: Arbor House, 1988; revised, London: Paladin 1990.
Neveryóna; or, The Tale of Signs and Cities: Some Informal Remarks toward the Modular Calculus, Part Four. New York: Bantam, 1983; revised, London: Grafton, 1989; Hanover, NH: University Press of New England for Wesleyan University Press, 1993.
Nova. New York: Doubleday, 1968; London: Gollancz, 1969.
Phallos. Flint, Mich.: Bamberger, 2004.
Silent Interviews: On Language, Race, Sex, Science Fiction, and Some Comics: A Collection of Written Interviews. Hanover, NH: University Press of New England for Wesleyan University Press, 1994.
Stars in my Pocket Like Grains of Sand. New York: Bantam, 1984.

The Straits of Messina. Seattle, WA: Serconia Press, 1989.
Tales of Nevèrÿon. New York: Bantam, 1979; revised, London: Grafton, 1988; Hanover, NH: University Press of New England for Wesleyan University Press, 1993.
They Fly at Çiron. Seattle, WA: Incunabula, 1993.
The Tides of Lust. New York: Lancer, 1973; Manchester: Savoy, 1979; reprinted as *Equinox*, New York: Masquerade, 1994.
Triton. New York: Bantam, 1976; London: Corgi, 1977; revised as *Trouble on Triton*, Hanover, NH: University Press of New England for Wesleyan University Press, 1996.

WORKS BY JOE HALDEMAN

All My Sins Remembered. New York: St Martin's Press, 1977; London: Macdonald, 1978.
Buying Time. Norwalk, Conn.: Easton Press, 1989; as *The Long Habit of Living*, London: New English Library, 1989.
Dealing in Futures. New York: Viking, 1985; London: Futura, 1986.
Forever Peace. New York: Ace, 1997.
The Forever War. New York: St Martin's Press, 1975; London: Weidenfeld & Nicholson, 1975.
The Hemingway Hoax. New York: Morrow, 1990; London: New English Library, 1990.
Infinite Dreams. New York: St Martin's Press, 1978.
Mindbridge. New York: St Martin's Press, 1976; London: Macdonald, 1977.
1968: A Novel. London: Hodder & Stoughton, 1994; New York: Morrow, 1995.
None So Blind. New York: Morrow AvoNova, 1996.
Planet of Judgment. New York: Bantam, 1979; London: Corgi, 1979. (Star Trek novel.)
Saul's Death & Other Poems. Palo Alto, CA: Anamnesis Press, 1997.
There Is No Darkness (with Jack C, Haldeman II). New York: Ace, 1983; London: Futura, 1985.
Tool of the Trade. New York: Morrow, 1987; London: Victor Gollancz, 1987.
War Year. New York: Holt Rinehart, 1972; original version, New York: Pocket, 1978.
World without End: A Star Trek Novel. New York: Bantam, 1979; London: Corgi, 1979.

Worlds: A Novel of the Near Future. New York: Viking, 1981; London: Macdonald, 1982.
Worlds Apart. New York: Viking, 1983; London: Macdonald, 1984.
Worlds Enough and Time. New York: Morrow, 1992; London: New English Library, 1992.

WORKS BY ROBERT IRWIN

The Arabian Nightmare. Sawtry, Cambs.: Dedalus, 1983; revised London & New York: Viking, 1987.
The Arabian Nights: A Companion. London & New York: Viking, 1994.
Exquisite Corpse. Sawtry, Cambs.: Dedalus, 1995.
Islamic Art in Context: Art, Architecture, and the Literary World. New York; Harry N. Abrams, Inc & London: Laurence King, 1997.
The Limits of Vision. London: Viking (in association with Dedalus), 1986.
The Middle East in the Middle Ages: The Early Mamluk Sultanate, 1250-1382. London: Croom Helm, 1986; Carbondale IL: Southern Illinois University Press, 1986.
The Mysteries of Algiers. London: Viking, 1988.
Prayer-Cushions of the Flesh. Sawtry, Cambs.: Dedalus, 1997.
Satan Wants Me. Sawtry, Cambs.: Dedalus, 1999.
[editor and translator] *Night and Horses and the Desert: An Anthology of Classical Arabic Literature.* London: Penguin & New York: Overlook Press, 2000.

WORKS BY GRAHAM JOYCE

Dark Sister. London: Headline, 1992.
Dreamside. London: Pan, 1991.
House of Lost Dreams. London: Headline, 1993.
Indigo. London: Michael Joseph, 1999.
Leningrad Nights. PS Publishing, 1999; reprinted in *Foursight* edited by Peter Crowther, London: Gollancz, 2000 and in *Binary 1: Leningrad Nights* by Graham Joyce/*How the Other Half Lives* by James Lovegrove, London: Gollancz, 2000.
Requiem. London: Creed, 1995; New York: St Martin's Press, 1996.
Smoking Poppy. London: Gollancz, 2001.
The Stormwatcher. London: Penguin, 1998.
The Tooth Fairy. London: Signet, 1996.
The Web: Spiderbite. London: Orion, 1997.

WORKS BY MICHAEL SHEA

The A'rak. New York: Baen, 2000.
The Color Out of Time. New York: DAW, 1984; London: Grafton, 1986.
In Yana, the Touch of Undying. New York: DAW, 1985; London: Grafton, 1987.
I, Said the Fly. Seattle, WA: Silver Salamander Press, 1993.
The Mines of Behemoth. New York: Baen, 1997.
Nifft the Lean. New York: DAW, 1982; London: Granada, 1985.
Polyphemus. Sauk City, WI: Arkham House, 1987; London: Grafton, 1990.
A Quest for Simbilis. New York: DAW, 1974: London: Grafton, 1985.

WORKS BY OTHER AUTHORS

Allen, Grant. *The British Barbarians.* London: John Lane, 1895.
Anderson, Poul. *Virgin Planet.* New York: Avalon, 1959.
Baker, Frank. *The Birds.* London: Peter Davies, 1936.
Ballard, J. G. *The Drowned World.* London: Gollancz, 1962.
Beeding, Francis [J. L. Palmer & H. St G. Saunders]. *The One Sane Man.* London: Hodder & Stoughton, 1934.
Bell, Neil [Stephen Southwold]. *The Lord of Life.* London: Collins, 1933.
Beresford, J. D. *A Common Enemy.* London: Hutchinson, 1941.
——. *Goslings.* London: Heinemann, 1913 (abridged as *A World of Women*, London: Collins, 1920.
——. *The Hampdenshire Wonder.* London: Sidgwick & Jackson, 1912.
Bowen, John. *After the Rain.* London: Faber & Faber, 1958.
Brunner, John. *Stand on Zanzibar.* New York: Doubleday, 1968.
Burroughs, Edgar Rice. *Tarzan of the Apes.* Chicago: McClurg, 1914 (originally in *All-Story* October 1912).
Butler, Samuel. *Erewhon; or, Over the Range.* London: Trübner, 1872 [published anonymously]
Collier, John. *Tom's a-Cold.* London: Macmillan, 1933 (US title *Full Circle*).
Connington, J. J. [Alfred W. Stewart]. *Nordenholt's Million.* London: Constable, 1923.
Crowley, Aleister. *Magick in Theory and Practice.* Paris: Lecram, 1929.

——. *Moonchild: A Prologue*. London: Mandrake Press, 1929.
De Camp, L. Sprague. *Lest Darkness Fall*. New York: Henry Holt, 1941 (originally in *Unknown* October 1941).
Desmond, Shaw. *Ragnarok*. London: Duckworth, 1926.
Doyle, Arthur Conan. *Pheneas Speaks: Direct Spirit Communications*. London: Psychic Press, 1927.
Egbert, H. M. [Victor R. Emanuel]. *Draught of Eternity*. London: John Long, 1924 (previously *Draught of Eternity* by Victor Rousseau, All-Story Weekly, 1-22 June 1918).
England, George Allan. *Darkness and Dawn*. New York: Small Maynard, 1914 (comprising "Darkness and Dawn", *Cavalier* January-April 1912; "Beyond the Great Oblivion", *Cavalier* 4 January-8 February 1913, & "The Afterglow", *Cavalier* 14 June-19 July 1913.)
Farrington, Geoffrey [Geoffrey Smith]. *The Revenants*. Sawtry, Cambs.: Dedalus, 1983.
Forester, C. S. *The Peacemaker*. London: Heinemann, 1934.
Gloag, John. *Artifex; or, the Future of Craftsmanship*. London: Kegan Paul, Trench & Trübner, 1926.
——. *It Makes a Nice Change*. London: Nicholson & Watson, 1938.
——. *The New Pleasure*. London: Allen & Unwin, 1933.
——. *99%*. London: Cassell, 1944.
——. *Sacred Edifice*. London: Cassell, 1937.
——. *Tomorrow's Yesterday*. London: Allen & Unwin, 1932.
Golding, William. *The Inheritors*. London: Faber, 1955.
Graham, P. Anderson. *The Collapse of Homo Sapiens*. London: Putnam, 1923.
Haldane, J. B. S. *Callinicus; a Defence of Chemical Warfare*. London: Kegan Paul, Trench & Trübner, 1925.
——. *Daedalus: or, Science and the Future*. London: Kegan Paul, Trench & Trübner, 1924.
——. *Possible Worlds*. London: Chatto & Windus, 1927.
Hamilton, Cicely [Cicely Mary Hamill]. *Theodore Savage: A Story of the Past or the Future*. London: L. Parsons, 1922; revised as *Lest Ye Die: A Story from the Past or of the Future*. New York: Scribner's, 1928.
Heard, Gerald. *The Great Fog and Other Weird Tales*. New York: Vanguard, 1944.
Heinlein, Robert A. *Starship Troopers*. New York: Putnam, 1959.
Houghton, Claude [C. H. Oldfield]. *This Was Ivor Trent*. London: Heinemann, 1935.
Hudson, W. H. *A Crystal Age*. London: Unwin, 1887.
——. *Green Mansions*. London: Duckworth, 1904.

Huxley, Aldous. *Brave New World*. London: Chatto & Windus, 1932.
Jefferies, Richard. *After London; or, Wild England*. London: Cassell, 1885.
Jensen, Johannes V. *The Long Journey*. New York: Knopf, 1923.
Lamb, William [Storm Jameson]. *The World Ends*. London: J. M. Dent, 1937.
Le Guin, Ursula K. *The Dispossessed*. New York: Harper, 1974.
———. *The Left Hand of Darkness*. New York: Ace, 1969.
le Queux, William. *The Invasion of 1910*. London: Eveleigh Nash, 1906.
Lewis, C. S. *The Great Divorce*. London: Geoffrey Bles, 1945.
London, Jack. *Before Adam*. New York: Macmillan, 1906.
———. *The Scarlet Plague*. New York: Macmillan, 1915 (previously in the *London Magazine*, 1912).
Louÿs, Pierre. *The Adventures of King Pausole*. Paris: Fasquelle, 1901.
Lovecraft, H. P. "The Color out of Space" *Amazing Stories* September 1927.
McDougall, William. *Janus; or the Conquest of War*. London: Kegan Paul, Trench & Trübner, 1925.
Marvell, Andrew [Howell Davies]. *Minimum Man; or, Time to be Gone*. London: Gollancz, 1938.
———. *Three Men Make a World*. London: Gollancz, 1939.
Miles [Stephen Southwold]. *The Seventh Bowl*. London: E. Partridge, 1930.
Mitchell, J. Leslie. *Gay Hunter*. London: Heinemann, 1934.
———. *Three Go Back*. London: Jarrolds, 1932.
Phillpotts, Eden. *Address Unknown*. London: Hutchinson, 1949.
———. Saurus. London: John Murray, 1938.
Piercy, Marge. *Woman on the Edge of Time*. New York: Knopf, 1976.
Piper, H. Beam. *Lord Kalvan of Otherwhen*. New York: Ace, 1965; reprinted as *Gunpowder God*, London: Sphere, 1978.
Potocki, Jan. *The Manuscript found at Saragossa*. London: Viking, 1995.
Priest, Christopher. *An Infinite Summer*. London: Cape, 1979.
Reynolds, Mack. *Amazon Planet*. New York: Ace, 1975.
Rice, Anne. *Interview with the Vampire*. New York: Knopf, 1976.
Rosny, J. H. aîné. *La Guerre du feu*. Paris: Charpentier, 1911.
Serviss, Garrett P. *The Second Deluge*. New York: McBride, Nast, 1912; London: Grant Richards, 1912 (previously in *Cavalier* July-6 January 1911).

Shanks, Edward. *The People of the Ruins: A Story of the English Revolution and After*. London: Collins, 1920.
Shiel, M. P. *The Purple Cloud*. London: Chatto & Windus, 1901.
——. *The Young Men Are Coming!* London: Gollancz, 1937.
Smith, Clark Ashton. *Zothique*. New York: Ballantine, 1970.
Smith, Wayland [Victor Bayley]. *The Machine Stops*. London: Robert Hale, 1936.
Stapledon, Olaf. *Last and First Men.* London: Methuen, 1930.
——. *Last Men in London*. London: Methuen, 1932.
——. *Odd John*. London: Methuen, 1934.
Stevenson, D. E. *The Empty World*. London: Herbert Jenkins, 1936.
Vance, Jack. *The Dying Earth.* New York: Hillman, 1950.
——. *The Eyes of the Overworld*. New York: Ace, 1966.
Vivian, E. Charles. *Star Dust*. London: Hutchinson, 1925.
Wells. H. G. *The Island of Doctor Moreau*. London: Heinemann, 1896.
——. *The Time Machine: an Invention*. London: Heinemann, 1895.
——. *The War of the Worlds*. London: Heinemann, 1898.
——. *When the Sleeper Wakes*. London: Harper, 1899.
——. *The Wonderful Visit*. London: J. M. Dent, 1895.
White, T. H. *Gone to Ground*. London: Collins, 1935.
Wyndham, John [John Beynon Harris]. *The Kraken Wakes*. London: Michael Joseph, 1953.

SECONDARY SOURCES

Barbour, Douglas. *Worlds out of Words: The SF Novels of Samuel R. Delany*. Frome, Somerset: Bran's Head, 1979.
Broderick, Damien. "The Multiplicity of Worlds, of Others." *Foundation* 55, Summer 1992, 66-81 & *Reading by Starlight; Postmodern Science Fiction*, London: Routledge, 1995.
Clarke, I. F. *Voices Prophesying War, 1763-1984*. Oxford: OUP, 1966; rev. as *Voices Prophesying War: Future Wars 1763-3749*. Oxford: OUP, 1992.
Clute, John, with Peter Nicholls. *The Encyclopedia of Science Fiction*. Second Edition. London: Orbit, 1993.
Gordon, Joan. *Joe Haldeman.* Mercer Island, WA: Starmont, 1980.
McDougall, William. *Janus, or the Conquest of War.* London: Kegan Paul, Trench & Trübner, 1925.
McEvoy, Seth. *Samuel R. Delany*. New York: Ungar, 1983.
MacFarlane, J. E. Clare. "Sydney Fowler Wright: Founder of the Empire Poetry League" Address given to the Institute of Jamaica on 3/12/58 (unpublished; text available on sfw.org).

Moskowitz, Sam. "S. Fowler Wright: SF's Devil's Disciple" *Amazing* February 1965; reprinted as "Better the World Below than the World Above" in *Strange Horizons*, New York: Scribner's, 1976.

Sallis, James, ed. *Ash of Stars: On the Writing of Samuel R. Delany.* Jackson: University Press of Mississippi, 1996

Slusser, George. *The Delany Intersection.* San Bernardino, CA: Borgo Press, 1977.

Tucker, Jeffrey Allen. *A Sense of Wonder: Samuel R. Delany, Race, Identity, and Difference.* Middletown, CT: Wesleyan University Press, 2004.

Weedman, Jane. *Samuel R. Delany.* Mercer Island, WA: Starmont House, 1982.

Weinkauf, Mary S. *Sermons in Science Fiction: The Novels of S. Fowler Wright.* San Bernardino, CA: Borgo Press, 1994.

INDEX

Ackerman, Forrest J. 83
Address Unknown 27
Adventure of the Blue Room, The 81
Adventure of Wyndham Smith, The 71, 80-82, 88
Adventures of King Pausole, The 144
A.E. 18
After London; or, Wild England 27, 34, 44, 46
After Silence 111, 114
After the Rain 48
Alice in Wonderland 143
Allen, Grant 13, 26
All my Sins Remembered 130
"All the Angels Live in Atlanta" 107
Amazon Planet 100
"Ambiguity" 102
Amphibians, The 18, 20-25, 28, 38, 46, 51-53, 55
Analog 93, 96, 132
Anderson, Poul 100
Angel Comes to Brooklyn, An 106
"Angel of Death, The" 157
Apollinaire, Guillaume 144
"Appeal" 57-58
"Apprentice, The" 147
Arabian Nightmare, The 138-140, 145
Arabian Nights: A Companion, The 139
"Arabic Beast Fable, The" 139
A'rak, The 158-159
Arkham House 82
Arnell, Charles John 16-17
Arresting Delia 66, 88
Artifex; or, The Future of Craftsmanship 35
Ashbarry, Nellie 14, 36
Asimov, Isaac 105, 118
Atlantis: Three Tales 121
"Automata" 49, 59

"Autopsy, The" 157
Avon Fantasy Reader, The 82
"Aye, and Gomorrah" 119
Babel-17 117-119
Baker, Frank 47
Ballad of Beta-2, The 117
Ballad of Elaine, The 19
Ballard. J. G. 48
Bates, H. E. 18
Bayley, Victor 47
Bear, Greg 96
Beeding, Francis 64
Bell, Neil 26, 47, 64
Bell Street Murders, The 53-54, 66
Benford, Gregory 96-97, 102, 104
Bennett, Alfred Gordon 18
Bennett, Arnold 32
Beresford, John Davys 9, 13, 44, 48
"Better Choice, The" 88
Beyond the Rim 62-63
Birds, The 47
Black Cocktail 110, 112
"Black Dust" 152
Blaschke, Jayme Lynn 123
"Bonding to Genji" 99
Bones of the Moon 108-111, 114
Books of Today 79, 81
Bova, Ben 132-133
Bowen John 48
"Brain" 58
Bridge of Lost Desire, The 120-123
Brightness Reef 102-104
Brin, David 91-105
Bristol Evening Times 42
British Barbarians, The 26
Brittain, Vera 43
Brunner, John 98, 133
"Bubbles" 102
Burroughs, Edgar Rice 32-33
Butler, Samuel 23-24
Buying Time 135
Callinicus; a Defence of Chemical Warfare 35
Campbell, John W. Jr. 104
"Careperson, The" 148
Caret Magazine 107
Carroll, Jonathan 106-114

Carroll, Sidney 106
Chesterton, G. K. 14, 18
Chicago Evening Post 45
Child Across the Sky, A 109-111, 113
Childe, Wilfred Rowland 18
"Choice, The" 27, 49, 61, 71, 90
Christian Science Monitor 45
Churchill, Winston 15, 34-35
Cimarron Review 106
"Coexistence" 94
Collapse of Homo Sapiens, The 35
Collier, John 46
Color out of Time, The 156-157, 159
"Color out of Space, The" 156
"Come Then, Mortal, We Will Seek Her Soul" 155
Coming, The 136
Common Enemy, A 48
Conklin, Groff 82, 88
Connington, J. J. 34
Costner, Kevin 95
"Counterpoint" 131
Crowley, Aleister 143
Crumey, Andrew 138
Crystal Age, A 27
"Crystal Spheres, The" 96
"Cyclops" 95
Daily Express 9
Daily Mail 73
Daily Mirror 45
Dalton, Moray 18
Dane, Clemence 44
Dante Alighieri 12, 17, 22-23
Darkness and Dawn 32
Dark Reflections 124-125
Dark Sister 147-149, 151
Datlow, Ellen 157
David 68-69
Davies, Howell 48
Davies, W. H. 18
Dawn 37-40, 42, 44, 54, 56, 84, 88
"Dead Love You, The" 112
Dealing in Futures 134
De Camp, L. Sprague 95
"Decay of Lying, The" 159
Delany, Samuel R. 115-122
"Delivery" 157

Deluge 18-19, 28-51, 53, 67-70, 73, 82, 88-89
Denwood, J. M. 50
Derleth, August 82
Desmond, Shaw 35
"Detritus Affected" 99
"Devil His Due, The" 131
"Devil's Disciple, The" 89
Dhalgren 119-120
Dick Tracy vs. Crime Inc. 70
Dispossessed, The 120
Divine Comedy, The 12, 17
"Dogma of Otherness, The" 102
Doré, Gustave 22
Dos Passos, John 98, 133
Doyle, Arthur Conan 48
Draught of Eternity 32
Dream; or, The Simian Maid 46, 55-56, 67-68, 72, 83-85
Dreamside 146-147
Drowned World, The 48
"Dr. Pak's Preschool" 99
Dumas, Alexandre 12, 82
Dying Earth, The 153
Earth 98-100, 102
Einstein Intersection, The 117-119
Elfwin 50, 81
Elmer Gantry 32
Empire Poetry League, The 17-20, 31
Empire Star 117, 121
Empty World, The 47
Encyclopedia of Science Fiction, The 133
"End Game" 131
England, George Allan 32-33
Erewhon 23-24
Eve 44, 49
Eve and Britannia 49
"Ever-Reddening Glow, An" 104
Exquisite Corpse 141-142, 144
"Extra, The" 157
Eyes of the Overworld, The 153
Fall of the Towers, The 117
Famous Fantastic Mysteries 82
Fantastic 131
Farrington, Geoffrey 138
"Fat Face" 156-157
"Fishing of the Demon Sea, The" 155, 159
Flight from Nevèrÿon 120-121

Forester, C. S. 64
Forever Peace 128, 132, 136-137
Forever War, The 128, 131-133, 136-137
For God and Spain 88
"Fortitude" 104
"For White Hill" 136
Foundation trilogy, The 105, 118
Four Days War 74-76
"Fourth Vocation of George Gustav, The" 96
Fowler, Gertrude 12
Fowler Wright, Gilbert 42, 48, 68
Fowler Wright, Sydney 9-90
Freud, Sigmund 30-31, 63, 86
"Friend's Best Man" 112-114
"From the Sanskrit" 17
From the Teeth of Angels 111-112
Full Circle 46
Galland, Antoine 139
"Game of Time and Pain, The" 121-122
"Gap-sickness" 148
Gay Hunter 46
"Genji" 99
"Giving Plague, The" 99
Gloag, John 13, 35, 47
Glory Season 99-101
"Goddess in Glass, The" 155, 158
Golding, William 56
Gone to Ground 47
Graham, P. Anderson 35
"Graves" 136
Graves, Robert 129
Gray, Pat 138
Great Divorce, The 62
Great Fog and Other Weird Tales, The 48
Greenberg, Martin H. 99
Green Mansions 53
Griffith, George 13
Guerre du feu, La 56
Gull, Cyril Ranger 13
Gunpowder God 95
Hacker, Marilyn 115-116, 118
Haldane, J. B. S. 35
Haldeman, Jack C. II 127, 130
Haldeman, Joe W. 127-137
Hale, Robert 47, 74, 77
Hamilton, Cicely 35, 44

Hancock, Truda 14, 19, 73, 81
"Hand me Downs" 107
Hanging of Constance Hillier, The 50
Harmsworth, Alfred 73
Hatry, Charles Clarence 78
Heard, Gerald 13, 48
Hearst, William Randolph 32
Heart of the Comet 96-97
Heaven's Reach 102, 102
Heidelberg Cylinder, The 113-114
Heinlein, Robert A. 131
Hemingway Hoax, The 128, 135-136
"Hero" 127-128
Hidden Tribe, The 68, 77-78
Hobbes, Thomas 43
Hodgson, William Hope 9, 13
Hoffmann, E. T. A, 141
Hogg 124
"Horror on the #33, The" 157
Houghton, Claude 26
House of Lost Dreams 148, 150
"House of the Rising Sun, The" 148
Hrdy, Sarah 98
Hudson, W. H. 27, 53
Hustler, The 106
Hyne, C. J. Cutcliffe 13
I'll Blackmail the World 64
"Images" 134-135
"Incident at the Monastery of Alcobaca, An" 145
Indigo 150-151
In Dreams 147
Inferno, The 19, 23
Infinite Dreams 128, 133
Infinite Summer, An 48
Infinity's Shore 102-104
Inheritors, The 56
Inquirer, The 31
Inquisitive Angel 87-88
Interview with the Vampire 138
Inverness Courier 44
In Yana, the Touch of Undying 156-157
"I of Newton" 130
Iron Magazine 107
Irwin, Robert 138-145
Isaac Asimov's SF Adventure Magazine 130
I, Said the Fly 157

Island of Captain Sparrow, The 37, 46, 49, 51-53, 56, 62, 77, 82, 88
Island of Doctor Moreau, The 52-53
It Makes a Nice Change 47
Ivanhoe 10
Jameson, Storm 44-46
Jane, Fred T. 13
"Jane Fonda Room, The" 112
Janus; or, The Conquest of War 35
Jefferies, Richard 27, 34
Jensen, Johannes V. 56
Jewels of Aptor, The 116
Jewish Record 45
John o'London's Weekly 44
Johnsen, Suzanne 146
Jones, Llewellyn 45
Joyce, Graham 146-152
"Just a Hint" 93
"Justice" 57
Justice and The Rat: Two Famous Stories 81
Kahn, James 133
Kendall, May 18
King Against Anne Bickerton, The 50
King of the Rocket Men 70
Kissing the Beehive 113-114
Knights of Malta, The 68-69
Kraken Wakes, The 48
Lamb, William 45
Land of Laughs, The 107-109
Last and First Men 44, 47
Last Days of Pompeii, The 82
Last Men in London 26
"Last Rising Sun" 147
Lawrence. D. H. 86
Left Hand of Darkness, The 100
Le Guin, Ursula K. 99-100, 120
Leningrad Nights 151-152
Le Queux, William 73
Lest Darkness Fall 95
Lewis, C. S. 62
Lewis, Sinclair 32
Liberty 102
"Life of My Crime, The" 112
Life of Sir Walter Scott, The 67
Light Out of Darkness 78
Limits of Vision, The 140-142
Locus 128-129

London, Jack 32, 94
London Calling 44
London Mercury, The 44
Long Habit of Living, The 135
Long Journey, The 56
"Loom of Thessaly, The" 93
Lord of Life, The 47, 64
Lord's Right in Languedoc 66, 68
Louÿs, Pierre 17, 144
Lovecraft. H. P. 156
"Lungfish" 96
Lytton, Lord 82
MacDougall, William 35
MacFarlane. J. E. Clare 20
Machine Stops, The 47
Mad Man 124
Madsen, David 138
Magazine of Fantasy & Science Fiction, The 157
Magick in Theory and Practice 143
Malory, Thomas 16
Marguerite de Valois 82
Marriage of Sticks, The 113
"Martian Reception" 87
Marvell, Andre 48
Matthewman, Sidney 17, 18
"Mazeltov Revolution, The" 130
McAuley, Paul J. 147
Megiddo's Ridge 74, 76-77
Merton Press 17-19
Metcalfe, John 18
Middle East in the Middle Ages, The 138
Miles 26, 47
Mille-et-Une Nuits, Les 139
Mindbridge 133
"Mind of His Own, A" 128, 133
Mines of Behemoth, The 158-159
Mitchell, J. Leslie 46-47, 56
Momma Durtt 157
Moonchild 143
Moorcock, Michael 118
Moore, Lt.-Col. Sir Thomas 78
"More Than the Sum of His Parts" 136
Morte d'Arthur 16, 19, 79
Moskowitz, Sam 18, 46, 89-90
Motion of Light in Water, The 115
"Mountain Kills People, The" 148

Mr. Cannyharme 159
"Mr. Fiddlehead" 112-113
Murasaki 99
Mysteries of Algiers, The 141
Nash's Pall Mall Magazine 34
Neveryóna 120-122
"New Accelerator, The" 94
New Faces 106
New Gods Lead, The 47, 50, 57-62, 64, 69, 79, 81-82
Newman, Kim 147-148
Newman, Paul 106
"New Meme, The" 102
New Pleasure, The 47
New Worlds 118
Nifft the Lean 155-156
Night and Horses and the Desert 139
Night Gallery 130
1968 128
99% 47
Nordenholt's Million 34
"Notes on Prosody" 17
Nova 117-119
Odd John 26
One Sane Man, The 64
"Only War We've Got, The" 130
Ordeal of Barata 80
"Original Sin" 79-81, 88
Otherness 101-102
"Outbreak from Earth" 87
"Out of Phase" 129
Outside the Dog Museum 110-111, 113
Panic Hand, The 112
Panische Hand, Die 112
"Paris Conquers All" 104
Parsifal 118
"Party at Brenda's House, The" 107
"Passages" 134
Peacemaker, The 64
"Pearls of the Vampire Queen, The" 155
"Pendulum" 47
People of the Ruins, The 35, 40, 44
Perseus 115
"Persistence of False Memory, The" 145
Phallos 124
Pheneas Speaks 48
Phillpotts, Eden 26

"Piecework" 99
Piercy, Marge 1000
Piper, H. Beam 95
Plunderers, The 157
"P.N. 40" 58-59
"P.N. 40—and Love" 49
Poetry 16-18
Poetry and the Play 18, 20, 31
Police and Public 19, 49
Poltergeist 133
"Polyphemus" 157
"Postgraduate" 112
"Postman, The" 94-95
Postman, The 95-96
Potter, Mary Gay 127
Potocki, Jan 139
Power 38, 63-66, 68-69
"Power Complex" 129
Powys, John Cowper 14
Powys, T. F. 14, 61
Practice Effect, The 95
Prayer-Cushions of the Flesh 144-145
Prelude in Prague 73-75
Priest, Christopher 48
"Privacy" 99
"Privacy is History—Get Over It" 102
Promethean, The 115
"Proof" 58
Purgatorio 88
Purple Cloud, The 34
"Quarter Past You, A" 112
Quest for Simbilis, A 153-155
Ragnarok 35
"Rat, The" 49, 57, 60
Ratcliffe, Dorothy Una 18
"Reading My Father's Story" 106
Red Book 49
Red Ike 50
Requiem 147-149
Return to Nevèrÿon 121
Revenants, The 138
Reynolds, Mack 100
Rice, Anne 138
Riding of Lancelot, The 19
River of Time, The 93-94, 96
Roanoake Review 107

Rosny, J. H., the Elder 56
Rousseau, Jean-Jacques 15, 85
Rousseau, Victor 32
"Rule" 60
Sacred Edifice 47
"Sadness of Detail, The" 112
Saragossa Manuscript, The 139
Sassoon, Siegfried 129
Satan Wants Me 142-144
Saul's Death & Other Poems 136
Saurus 26
Scarlet Plague, The 32
Scenes from the Morte d'Arthur 16, 18
Schreiner, Beverley 106
"Science—Destroyer of Life" 45
Science Fiction Adventures in Mutation 88
"Science versus Magic" 102
Scott, Sir Walter 12, 67-69
Screaming Lake, The 68, 77-78
"Seasons" 130
Second Deluge, The 32
"Secret of Life, The" 99
Secret of the Screen, The 54, 66-68, 70
"Senses Three and Six" 96
Serapions-Brüder, Der 141
Serviss, Garrett P. 32
Seven Thousand in Israel 19, 54
Seventh Bowl, The 26
Seymour, Ian Allen 17
"Shadow and the Flash, The" 94
"Shadows" 115
"Shall We Commit Suicide" 34
Shanghai Orchid 69
Shanks, Edward 35, 44
Shea, Michael 153-160
"Shhhh" 92
Shiel, M. P. 13, 14, 34
"Shining Thing, The" 106
Siege of Malta, The 81
Sillman, June 106
Silverberg, Robert 99
"Singing Underwater" 145
Sixth Omni Book of Science Fiction, The 157
"Skip" 107
Sleeping in Flame 109-110
"Slit, The" 47

Smith, Clark Ashton 153-154
Smith, Edward E. 104
Smith, Geoffrey 138
Smith, Wayland 47
Smoking Poppy 151-152
Some Songs of Bilitis 19
Song of Arthur, The 67
Song of Solomon, The 19
Song of Songs and Other Poems, The 18-19, 68
"Songs from Balochistan" 17, 19
Songs of Bilitis 17
Son of David 69
SOS Tidal Wave 70
Southwold, Stephen 47
Spiders' War 24, 46, 73, 83-87
Splendid Curse, The 68, 73-74
Splendor and Misery of Bodies, of Cities, The 121
"Stage of Memory, A" 96
Stand on Zanzibar 98
Stapledon, Olaf 18, 26, 35, 44, 47, 89
Star Dust 64
"Star Pit, The" 117
"Starschool" 130
Starship Troopers 131
Stars in my Pocket Like Grains of Sand 121-123
Startide Rising 94-95, 97-98, 103
Star Trek 92, 133
Star Wars 92
Stevenson, D. E. 47
Stevenson, Robert Louis 69
Stormwatcher, The 150-152
"Story of the Stone Age, A" 56
Strange Horizons 18
"Suicide Club, The" 69
Sunday Dispatch 73
Sunday Express 32, 48
Sundiver 91-93
Swan Press 17, 18
"Tale of Dragons and Dreamers, The" 121
"Tale of Fog and Granite, The" 122
"Tale of Gorgik, The" 121-122
"Tale of Old Venn, The" 121
"Tale of Plagues and Carnivals, The" 121
"Tale of Potters and Dragons, The" 121
"Tale of Rumor and Desire, The" 121
"Tale of Signs and Cities, The" 121

"Tale of Small Sarg, The" 121-122
Tales of Nevèrÿon 120-121
Taylor, Helen 138
"Tangled Web, A" 130
"Tank Farm Dynamo" 96
"Temperature of Gehenna Sue, The" 81
Theodore Savage 35, 40, 44
There is no Darkness 130
They Fly at Çiron 124
"This Night" 57
This Was Ivor Trent 26
"Thor Meets Captain America" 96
"Those Eyes" 102
"Threat of Aristocracy, The" 102
Three Go Back 46, 56
Three Men Make a World 48
Three Witnesses 69
Throne of Saturn, The 9, 58, 82-83
Thurston, E. Temple 18
"Tides of Kithrup, The" 93-94
Tides of Lust, The 124
Time & Tide 43
"Time Considered as a Helix of Semi-Precious Stones" 119
Time Machine, The 16, 23
"Time Piece" 127
Times, The 9
"To Howard Hughes: A Modest Proposal" 133
"To Fit the Crime" 130
Tom's A-Cold 46
Tool of the Trade 135
Tooth Fairy, The 147, 149
"Toujours Voir" 96
Transatlantic Review, The 107
Transparent Society, The 102
"Tricentennial" 132
Triton 119-121
Trouble on Triton 119
"26 Days on Earth" 131
"Uh-Oh City" 112
"Uncle Tuggs" 157
Under the Brutchstone 50
Uplift War, The 97-98, 103
Valois, Ninette de 18
Vance, Jack 153-154
Vengeance of Gwa 67, 71-73, 79, 81, 85
Verne, Jules 105

Virgin Planet 100
"Vision of Judgment, A" 62
Vivian, E. Charles 64
Voice of our Shadow 108
Voices on the Wind 19
Voltaire 144-145
Wagner, Richard 118
"Waiting for the Zaddik" 145
"Warm Space, The" 96
War of 1938, The 73
War of the Worlds, The 43, 105
War Year 127
"We Are Very Happy Here" 131
Web, The: Spiderbite 149-150
Weird Tales 49
Wells, H. G. 13, 16, 23, 26-27, 43, 44, 45, 49, 52, 56, 61-62, 94, 104
"What Continues…and What Fails" 99, 102
"What to Say to a UFO" 102
Wheatley, Dennis 143
White, T. H. 47
Who Else But She? 70
Who Murdered Reynard? 54
"Whose Millennium?" 102
Wilde, Oscar 159-160
Williamson, Jack 104
Windling, Terri 157
Wired 102
Witchfinder, The 79, 81-82
With Cause Enough 87
Woman on the Edge of Time 100
Wonderful Visit, The 26
Wood, S. Andrew 64
Wooden Sea, The 113-114
World Below, The 22, 25-27, 37-38, 47, 49, 52, 56, 81-82, 88-89
World Ends, The 45-46
World of Women, A 44
Worlds 133-134
Worlds Apart 134-135
Worlds Enough and Time 134-136
Wright, Stephen 12
Wright, Victor 32
Wyndham, John 48
Year's Best Fantasy, The 157
"You Can Never Go Back" 132
Zangwill, Israel 18
"Zero Sum Elections and the Electoral College" 102

ABOUT THE AUTHOR

BRIAN STABLEFORD was born in Yorkshire in 1948. He taught at the University of Reading for several years, but is now a full-time writer. He has written many science fiction and fantasy novels, including *The Empire of Fear*, *The Werewolves of London*, *Year Zero*, *The Curse of the Coral Bride*, *The Stones of Camelot* and *Prelude to Eternity*. Collections of his short stories include a long series of *Tales of the Biotech Revolution*, and such idiosyncratic items as *Sheena and Other Gothic Tales* and The *Innnsmouth Heritage and Other Sequels*. He has written numerous nonfiction books, including *Scientific Romance in Britain, 1890-1950*, *Glorious Perversity: The Decline and Fall of Literary Decadence*, *Science Fact and Science Fiction: An Encyclopedia* and *The Devil's Party: A Brief History of Satanic Abuse*. He has contributed hundreds of biographical and critical entries to reference books, including both editions of *The Encyclopedia of Science Fiction* and several editions of the library guide, *Anatomy of Wonder*. He has also translated numerous novels from the French language, including several by the feuilletonist Paul Féval and numerous classics of French scientific romance by such writers as Albert Robida, Maurice Renard, and J. H. Rosny the Elder.